THE RUTHLESS
Guide to
BDSM

Ordered by
MISTRESS KAZ B
AND LADY RAMPAGE

Dedication

Lady Olivia Rampage: This book is dedicated to my partner and my favourite slave, Smoke Slave, my house would be filthy without you cleaning the entirety of it with a toothbrush. Thank you Kaz for being so brilliant at life.

Acknowledgments

Kaz: I'd like to express my thanks to my harem of loyal subbies who have been a great support. To JB - my wisest sub and confidant, LB - an inspirational man who never fails to make me laugh, SissyboiNatalie, one of the sweetest and most loyal subs thats helped with so many things, HumanTeller - who I have travelled with extensively and put the worlds to rights with in many a seaside cafe or restaurant, and so many more. I love you all!

A huge thanks to Lady Olivia Rampage for a wonderful experience writing this book with her. This has been my first book collaboration and it's been an exhilarating and hilarious journey, which has brought out the best in me and left me feeling inspired after every single chat.

Thank you to Gadfly press for publishing our book and providing invaluable feedback.

Thanks to all the dommes that have been part of my life and do the right thing, even when no ones watching. Thanks to everyone who helped us create this fantastic book by writing their kink stories and thanks to you - the reader, who we hope will enjoy reading this as much as we enjoyed writing it.

Spelling Differences: UK v US

This book was written in British English; hence US readers may notice some spelling differences from American English: e.g. color = colour, meter = metre and jewelry = jewellery.

Contents

Meet the Mistresses

Lady Rampage

My specialities and favourite sessions include CBT, humiliation and pain play as I am always known to be the first Mistress to get my riding crop out and start welting up my slaves cock and balls! My dungeon is leafy Hampshire, where I have an iron cage built under my bed to lock my naughty slaves in. It's even been known for me to keep a slave locked in the cage below as I sleep between layers of satin sheets. On occasion, my boyfriend will visit and my slave will be bound and gagged. Well, I'm on the receiving end of a good rogering! In the corner of my dungeon, aside front the St Andrews Cross is my human toilet seat, where slaves' faces regularly appear to receive my golden shower and brown nuggets! My favourite type of sub or slave would be the respectable but naughty submissive client who is like a petulant child. With over 14 years in the BDSM industry, I thought it was about time I shared some of my experiences which are documented in this book. Unfortunately, I have to remain anonymous for professional and personal reasons and also to add a little mystique to the book!

Mistress Kaz B

Hello darlings, I'm Miss Kaz B, a pro-domme from Wiltshire, my base where I punish naughty boys bottoms and dress them up in pretty lingerie and instruct them to put on a sexy catwalk show for me or give me sultry lap dance whilst they lunge around, slipping and sliding in heels.

My first foray into the realms of kink was in my teens with

my childhood sweetheart but it wasn't until a long time later that I considered it as a profession. I was working in broadcasting and modelling for many years and it wasn't until I started broadcasting webcam shows that all my kinky talents rose to the surface. I swifty escalated from making men hit their balls with a slipper on webcam, to dominating them myself in real time sessions. I've always had a bit of a kinky side but dominating men allows my imagination to run riot! I have a real passion for roleplay, mind-fucking and manipulation scenarios whereby my subs will do anything to please me and my favourite role to play is a supervillain or secret agent.

Due to the lack of community based books out there we hope this book will not only give you an insight into the BDSM world, but also a glance into the psyche of all the wonderful kinksters that make up our dynamic little community and we are confident that there will be plenty of laughs along the way as well!

Chapter 1
BDSM

BDSM = Bondage and sadomasochism

BDSM could be said to be an artform which incorporates bondage, domination and submission, sadomasochism and discipline. Elements of this can include pain and sensation play, slave training, restriction with rope, chains or other paraphernalia and it's a total power exchange, based on consent.

BDSM lovers will enjoy different facets of the kink and for a whole host of different reasons. Some may enjoy painful sensations or submitting to another in a space safe. For others, it may be a more emotional experience. When we focus our energies on an outlet time and time again, whether it be kink or something else, it can often be a return to a feeling of safety. That might sound like a contradiction to someone outside of the kink world and I hear them say, "How can something feel safe by feeling whipped?"

BDSM should always be centred around consent and these acts take place in a controlled and safe environment using safe words. Being whipped could be a physical or emotional release for the submissive when they have developed a trusting connection with their domme. Their safe space isn't necessarily a beautiful landscape or a desolate beach, it can be so many things. Familiarity can also be safe. There's a common belief that public schoolboys that were whipped at school have a penchant for going under the whip. Well there is a reason for that. It's familiar to them but also they are now experiencing it out of choice. That inner child who was forced to endure something heinous at the hands of a sadistic teacher has now embraced their kink and turned it into a safe fantasy where they will be nurtured and receive aftercare.

This is not the case for everyone who enjoys BDSM. Others simply enjoy a full range of experience and take delight in experiencing the flip side in life, whatever emotion that evokes within them and whether it be vulnerability, safety, degradation, being needed or desired.

We aim with this book to give assistance if you are considering entering the BDSM world or wanting some new fresh ideas for your play time. Or you can just enjoy the journey of our highs, lows and musings.

Before we indulge your curious mind into our word of debauchery, we will start with the important topic which is consent.

Consent between two adults is of the utmost necessity before every session between a Mistress and sub. I would personally advise a consent form but in a personal setting a safe word also works alongside a list of likes and dislikes. Find out your play partners interests! Not every sub is into pegging or electrics so communication and consent is key.

Every chapter in this book covers personal experiences from Mistress Kaz B and Lady R that can help you on your BDSM journey. If you are new to this, we hope you will read on with an open mind.

Lady R: My safe word is RED because as you can imagine the sub always pants no, no, no in his game of submissive space.

"You filthy little maggot fuck boy! I think you deserve another ten lashes on that sweaty little arse of yours."

"No, no, no, mistress, honestly, I'm a good little maggot."

After three lashes, I really pelted him on the fourth.

"Red!"

Immediately, I stopped.

When the sub calls the safe word it is in my line of care to stop the session and give him a point of respect, meaning we do not violate boundaries into uncomfortable activity that is no longer consensual or can be dangerous. Before every first meeting, my sub will send a list of the perfect session ideas, from which I create scenarios and envisage how far I can go. I'll ascertain their pain threshold by practising with a paddle or whip on the chunkiest arse flesh before the full session.

Right now, I'm getting an influx of slave training, which I will touch on later in the book. The typical slave training session involves a light whipping to start followed by them cleaning my apartment while I put my feet up (sometimes using the subject as my personal footstool) – a great gig right?

Mistress Kaz B: Every BDSM journey is different. Each Mistress will have her unique style. For some, that might be a love of sadistic pain play, others may have a cruel, teasing style and some may enjoy more sensual play or strictness and humiliation. While there may be some overlaps in styles, one thing that we all have in common is that all great domme/sub relationships are built on consent, good communication and trust.

Equipment you can use in the home:

Lady R: You don't have to head over to the first website selling professional gear to start having fun if your partner or subject is into light whipping. I would go into your kitchen drawer and pull out a spatula, wooden spoon or something to that effect. I am almost sure that you can build an entire kit from household items or heading down to the local hardware store. Think bondage for example. For years of my sessioning career, I would purchase tie down straps from the popular hardware stores, pay under £10 for two and attach them to my iron casters under the bed. I would buy two mediocre but durable handcuffs and hey presto you have yourself bed restraints.

Kaz B: I started out just like Lady R, improvising with household items. It's worth signing up to newsletters to your favourite sex shops and keeping an eye out for discounts and having an Amazon wish list to encourage your subs to buy you pieces too.

Subspace

Lady R: Subspace is for me a heightened special place the submissive partner enters when he/she reaches a natural chemical high and/or causes a change in the mental/emotional balance of the brain chemistry and potentially state of mind. I have had many slaves/subs enter subspace in our session. I find it is best achieved when total trust is built between his/her Dominant and a bond is obtained prior to the session. If I hypothetically started barking at my Subby before he entered the door, demanded him on all fours and told him to take it like a man, I probably would have scared A LOT of people off from ever wanting to see a Dominatrix again. The art of domination and leading your sub effectively and gently in subspace involves more than just actions. I find a whisper in the ear telling them what you "might" do with them frightens them into an excitable panic which more often than not leads them into subspace. Try asking your vanilla partner to do something for you with a light whisper, I bet it gets the job done. There is a reason you purchased this book and I bet it isn't because you are not interested in trying some of the topics. One of my favourite examples of how easy it is to send that little subby into the space abyss is with Smoke Slave whose fetish I will tell you about later in the book.

My most memorable experience with a slave entering into subspace involves breath play and a PVC vacuum bed. I was hiring out dungeon space in the southwest where it had every piece of equipment at your disposal including cast iron cages, a human toilet seat and a fucking machine which is a massive dildo attached to a long rod and machine that when turned on mimics the fucking motion and you can turn the speed from a slow fucking to a hard, fast fuck!

My slave who had booked the session on that particular day was an experienced sub and had been to the premises before and knew what equipment he enjoyed. Today he wanted to try the vacuum bed and breath play. So to start the session, I told him to immediately undress, get on all fours and proceed to lick my leather 6-inch stilettos clean while I gave him a few slaps of my paddle on his rump arse cheeks. When my shoes were suitably cleaned, I ordered him over to the bed, dripped oil all over his body to lather him up and told him to lie flat inside the baggy PVC bed covers. I inserted the breathing tube into his mouth and encased him in the bedding. One swift flick of the switch and the device was humming away, sucking and pulling the material tighter over his physique and sucking all of the air out of the vacuum bed until he could not move his little finger. With the PVC cocooning his entire body, he could not see anything, nor hear, smell or speak and I was in total control of his breathing through the tube. I plonked my bum on his chest so he could feel the weight of my body on him and placed my thumb over the air pipe to block it... After counting 3,2,1 I removed my thumb so that he could gasp for breath. A minute or two later, I repeated the teasing of breath. After watching his chest rise and fall with each breath, I saw he was panting. I knew he was getting excited and aroused and entering subspace. I kept him in the bag repeating the teasing of breath and sitting on his body for another half an hour before I decided to release him.

Once out of the bag, I instructed him back to all fours on the floor and lubed up his arsehole, ready for the fucking machine to give him his special reward for being such a good boy in the vacuum bed. The 7-inch dildo at a slow speed entered him and when it was at a comfortable pace I turned it up to a good hard fuck. The slave was loving it, groaning and panting with ecstasy with each thrust from the machine. It didn't take long before the poor little subby had to explode his white mess all over the floor, screaming with pleasure. While he was cleaning up and getting himself ready to go, he explained that during both the body-bag experience and the hard fuck his mind had gone "elsewhere." He felt like he had an out of body experience which he later discovered was subspace. Let's just say this was my first experience of witnessing one of my slaves entering subspace, but it most definitely was not the last.

Kaz B: Sissy Nalia has been visiting me for years to get dolled up and be my personal source of entertainment. We have a fantastic bond and her love of being humiliated brings me so much delight when she's prancing around in a tutu and performing pirouettes as I pump out Swan Lake on the loud speaker. Nalia looks like someone who has played rugby for many years and has the hairiest of legs, so it's always astounding watching how gracefully she carries herself when I order her to do so. Especially considering that a number of my sissies are lumbering, knock-kneed, hunched, and perform their moves in heels like clowns walking fiery tightropes, above a sea of ravenous crocodiles, while being pelted with dog poo.

Aside from ballet and making tea for me in her frilly dresses, in the last year Nalia discovered subspace and there were a couple of things that led to this. Firstly, we began experimenting with a rubber poppers mask that covered Nalia's face. I controlled the flow of poppers into her airways via a pump to allow her that heady state of bliss, while alternately whispering words of degradation into her ear, then punishing her nipples which were pinched with clover clamps. Then I'd murmur to her:

"Nalia, you will obey my every word, I am your Goddess and I command you to play with your tits and jiggle them for me. Entertain me and tell me how slutty you are for me or I will yank the chain on your clamps harder and make you squeal."

Of course, Nalia adores the nipple punishment, so with her, it's not so much a threat but she is my star pupil and never disobeys.

"Yes, Mistress, I will bounce my slutty titties for you and show you what a good little bitch I am. I will always do anything you say."

In these moments, I can see her eyes glaze over slightly as she starts to slowly drift away into that heightened state of euphoria, a look of utter bliss resting upon her face. This was just the beginning of her journey into subspace but I didn't want her floating round at the edge of the planet, I wanted to send her far into space, at the final frontier where no man has been before without his mind being completely altered forever.

So I probed at her, delved deep into her mind and pulled out all her most innermost and secret fantasies. It transpired that Nalia had a secret fantasy of being a bukkake Queen, and so like a dark fairy of fantasy, I decided to weave my magic and take her on a deeper journey into her subconscious and into subspace. I didn't reveal my intentions to Nalia but at points in the session, I would lower my tone and whisper erotic delights to keep her in my thrall, encapsulated in a world of dreamy fantasy.

In the last segment of the session, I stripped her naked and lead her by her pink diamante leash into the shower. There I had lined up a row of big rubber dildos which I had stuck to the wall and told her it would bring me great delight if she sucked them slow and sensually while gazing into my eyes. I barely finished my sentence before her lips softly wrapped around the first dildo, her piercing blue eyes locking firmly onto mine.

"You must not break away from my gaze, Nalia."

She affirmed with a nod, moaning softly and she sucked each dildo, never breaking contact with my eyes once.

"I want you to start touching yourself for me now, Nalia."

Her hand was instantly upon her erect cock, our eyes locked into a slow, erotic dance and I saw that familiar look as they began to glaze over, as her lusty, submissive desires ignited like a fireball.

"Today, sissy, you will be my bukkake Queen and like a good girl, you will please all the boys for me. Only then will you be allowed your happy ending."

She weaved her way from one phallic toy to another with expertise, me reminding her now and again that she had to keep them all equally satisfied as it would be good practise for when

I got her the real thing. I could tell Nalia was becoming more aroused although not in a frenzied fashion, more of a gentle, dizzying fall into utter, boundless pleasure. It was time to pull out the big guns. I whipped out a bottle of lube, purposefully selecting one that looked nice and creamy, then started to squirt them onto the dildos, which I flicked towards her, resulting in the cream splattering her face, mouth and body.

"You are my bukkake Princess now, lap it eagerly, then luxuriate in rapture as every single stream, squirt and hot, steamy jet splashes down on your face."

She pulsed with every squirt, her body and mind invaded and controlled by me, her Mistress.

I squirted more directly onto my sissies face and followed this up with some long strings of saliva from my lips, dribbled directly onto her checks. Her eyes were like rippling lakes of icy fire, which softened and melted away and I knew in that moment she had smashed through the erotic version of the Van Allen Belt and into deep space. My sissy was both with me but yet floating far away in another galaxy and operating on a differently level as I ushered my final words.

"You have pleased my big boys well. I want to watch you explode for me hard now."

The explosion that followed reminded me of two asteroids colliding, a colossal vibration of trembling limbs and shuddering, then several thuds in a row as she plastered herself with her magic juice.

Allowing her just a moment to recover, I instructed her to lick up her mess. She complied happily, a state of bliss which she basked in for several moments.

Finally, I was the one to break the spell:

"I can't wait to see you do the real thing soon but for now, shower for me, sticky girl."

We both chuckled, taking merriment from such an intense and hypnotic session and the easy banter we have. It's not always easy to take a slave into subspace but it is so worth the journey.

So what is sub drop?

Kaz B: During a session of intense play, a sub's fight or flight response is activated causing the release of endorphins, oxytocin, dopamine and other chemicals to flood his or her system. This sensation has been described at times to be similar to morphine in the way it can cause the subs pain tolerance to increase and gives the slave a high.

What goes up must come down!

A day or so later, the sub can experience the drop as his body has been depleted of many essential chemicals. This is especially common I have discovered in professional domme-sub relationships, especially when the sub feels separated from his Mistress and from the BDSM lifestyle. The sub may experience lethargy, fatigue and a low mood. This is extremely common and subs may start to doubt the lifestyle and feel shame and disgust towards themselves and their kinks.

As far as I know there is no cure for sub drop, but there are a few things you can do to help your mind and body cope and rebalance more quickly.

I may be a domme with a slightly sadistic streak but I also realise that my subs are human beings with feelings. I always offer a hug at the end of a session as I believe hugs are healing for the mind, body and soul.

Here are a few suggestions to help combat the dreaded drop!

Food

You'll need to feed your body with plenty of vitamins including B vitamins. Don't forget fresh vegetables, lean protein, eggs and whole grains. Resist the urge to cheer yourself up with sugary snacks as it will only exacerbate your condition.

Visiting your domme can cause your dopamine levels to spike, in fact, even just thinking about the visit can induce spikes, so you'll want to include dopamine rich foods into your diet. I'm not a nutritionist and each person will need a tailored approach but I have read extensively about diet and advise you research what works for you.

Herbs

Support your system with feel-good herbs such as ginseng (an adaptogen that helps nourish the body, combat fatigue and counter stress) turmeric, ginkgo biloba, and magnesium which helps balance dopamine and will help towards alleviating a low mood and help you to sleep more deeply. These herbs will help to elevate your happy chemicals and boost your mood.

If you feel anxious or agitated I recommend L-Theanine – an extract also found in green tea that will help you feel calm and focused.

Sunshine and Exercise

Sunshine provides valuable vitamin D to the body and also boosts serotonin levels in the brain, but it's not always possible to get plenty of sunshine if you live somewhere cold like Britain. However, even just getting out in the fresh air and going for a walk can help. Exercise is a great way to boost your mood and rebalance your body whether you are pounding it out in the gym or taking a stroll in the park.

Be Mindful

Say to yourself '*I am feeling this way because I am having a sub drop. It is temporary and it will pass.*' Be aware of small changes in your mood and notice what triggers them. Keep a journal or diary if it helps as this can be highly therapeutic in itself.

Surround yourself with likeminded people.

Not many kinksters will have friends who share the same life-styles, however it is a lot easier to make likeminded friends than you think. Consider attending a 'munch' which are events and meetups for those who follow the BDSM lifestyle. You can find a wide array of groups on sites such as Fetlife. There are events all over the country every month for kinksters and fetishists such as the London fetish fair or the Birmingham Bizarre Bazaar that always holds an after party after market day and shopping. Kinkster tend to be extremely welcoming, open and friendly to everyone from any walk of life. Don't feel embarrassed or as if you won't be wanted. These groups are open to everyone and you will be made to feel welcome.

Most importantly, remember that without the lows you wouldn't enjoy the highs as much. If money was no object and you could visit a dom every day, not only would you be thoroughly sore, but after a while you would cease to get the same high and would seek more and more extreme practices. The reward is so much greater when it's a treat, not an everyday practice.

Chapter 2
Chastity

Chastity harks back to the 14th century and was allegedly used as a method of ensuring purity and prohibiting maidens from engaging in penetrative sex. The earliest drawings of a chastity belt go back to 1405, although some modern day historians and writers suggest that the chastity belt was a metaphorical symbol of chastity, rather than something that was implemented widely.

Nowadays, you are far more likely to see chastity cages for male genitalia and there are multiple reasons for this. Some may wish to practise semen retention, the art of preserving ejaculation to focus the mind and the cage removes the temptation to masturbate. For others, it's an act of submission in refraining from sex or touching themselves and some subs view it merely as a kink that will enhance their play after a period of having their genitalia locked up. Social media has made chastity play more popular and as a result trends have developed in the kink community such as Locktober - which involves locking the penis in a plastic or metal cage for the whole of October. There is also NOvember which translates as - no masturbation for the month of November. Chastity lovers are not bound by these months and may opt to enter chastity at any point in the calendar but the months of October and November have become particularly popular and having a community of subs all experiencing the same thing, may make the experience more enjoyable and durable for the slave who feels as if he is in the same boat as others, with the same restrictions and goals.

Miss Kaz B: Note: During sissy play the pronouns she/her are used. Not all sissies are trans by any means. Most sissies, at least in my own experience tend to be straight bi-curious men, from all social backgrounds and races who merely enjoy the component of reverse power play. Most of my sissies tend to be white or Asian, however.

I have also sessioned with trans women who use she/her pronouns but the difference is because they identify as female, rather than wanting to experience cross-dressing.

Locking a sub into chastity is one of the most exquisite ways a slave can show his devotion to me. To make the commitment to abstain from any kind of self-pleasure and discipline his mind, proves his dedication and loyalty to me. This is usually an agreement which is made once I have built a good rapport with the sub and mutual trust has developed. If subs enter into chastity for a longer duration, weeks rather than days I instruct them to keep a journal for me so I can enjoy the journey with them, the challenge, the trials and tribulations and the fascinating way in which it can send their minds into overdrive and they start to become more submissive by the day.

Many of my subs have agreed to take part in Locktober and Locktember - which means they will be locked into chastity for the months of October or December for a whole month. They must send me the key, which I wear around my neck on a silver chain. I often take photographs of myself wearing the chain or short video clips teasing them that they still have a while to go before their big release, that they must behave and please me well if they wish to earn their way out. This drives my subs wild and allows them to reach new heights of ecstasy from the build-up and the constant thoughts of being utterly helpless about their situation.

I wouldn't advise subs to run out and buy any old cage if they are committing to a longer sentence in chastity. You don't want it to rub or cause too much friction as this can develop sores. Plastic can sweat and doesn't tend to be my preference for extended use.

I much prefer the metal cage, which a sub should ensure fits him well before lock-in. Many of the metal cages are more hygienic as there are spaces between the bars so a sub may keep his usual standard of hygiene. I have had subbies tell me they had bought the wrong cage in the past. One slave was enjoying a brisk swim in his local pool when his cage came loose and sank to the bottom of its watery grave!

Another slave wore a pale pink, rubber cage to work. Unfortunately, he didn't realise how ill-fitting it was as he hadn't managed to come and check with me first. He was admonishing his secretary about a late report when he felt a strange motion and his cage slipped off, snaked its way down his leg and rolled out in front of his secretary. Neither knew where to look! The right size cage is paramount, especially if your crown jewels are particularly on the large or small side. Too big and it can come loose, too tight and it will chafe. I also like the Vice range as they come in 3 sizes, various colours and have a range of attachments to tailor to your size! Basically it is Lego for your meat and two veg!

The classic worry of a chastity slave losing his or her key is common, but what happens when this becomes real and the key is nowhere to be found?

This only ever happened once in my experience. My sissy Steph usually brought her key with her, so I hadn't looked for mine. That was quite a build up to this and the evening started with me telling my pet sissy that she would need to take a nice hard spanking, followed by the cane for me, then I sent her off to change. When she returned she was wearing a beautiful baby pink, satin dress with white frills on the sleeves, collar and hem. Underneath her many pink chiffon frills, was a candy pink chastity cage She was wearing a brand called The Vice, one of the strongest, most durable cages that exist!

She looked so cute, that it almost persuaded me to go a little more gently on her. Of course, *almost* is the operative word in this sentence, and just as quickly I changed my mind and decided to give her the works.

With my sissy bent over, ruffles surrounding her pale bottom, I delivered some stinging slaps until her cheeks were pink. Every now and then, she would squeak 'Ow' which had me giggling and spanking her harder. The pale white flesh of her bottom is pleasurable to spank as it shows up every slap and swipe. I could see a blend of soft, dusky pinks and darker, more angry streaks of crimson red. When I fetched the cane, Steph was visibly trembling by this point. Her buttocks were akin to a delicious, wobbling strawberry trifle, waiting to be plunged into and attacked with my canes. The first cane was a traditional schoolmaster cane with a curved tip. One always feels extremely old school when brandishing one of these and it makes such a wonderful whooshing sound as it slices through the air and THWACKS down hard onto a meaty rump. Just six swipes of the cane were enough to coax some wonderful red welts to bubble across my sissies flesh. I ran my finger across them and felt that the skin had raised and felt plump and swollen.

I then used a leather-wrapped cane on sissy's posterior. It's a much longer cane and thinner for a more intense sting. Three of these had sissy yelping!

Whilst my sissy is an absolute pro in strap-on play and chastity, she was a virgin to the cane and I could see that she was reaching her limit.

I always save the best for last, so I drew out the dressage crop. An extremely thin, black whip which has a tailed end that savagely bites into the flesh on impact, taking some of the top skin cells with it! On the first stroke, sissy uttered a cry and shuddered. "Oh my goodness that one is more intense!"

I smiled, knowing her words to be true and gently told her, "just two more, be brave now my good girl."

My sissy braced herself and I thrashed the whip across the backside once more. The fronds at the end of the whip grabbed hold of her flesh as they flicked past, causing an angry rash to arise where she had been struck.

I could tell she was dreading the final stroke and I lingered, allowing her to take a deep breath. This time I swung the crop higher and harder. The last stroke should always count and leave a small memento behind on the slave's bottom.

We both inspected her bottom and were mutually satisfied to see a beautiful lattice of pink blobs and spatterings and red welts. For a short moment, I contemplated playing a game of hangman on the criss-crosses on her bottom, but I was eager to push her limits in other ways, so stored the thought away for another day.

The session went swimmingly and it was time for my sissy to finally experience the electrics. For this I would need to remove her chastity cage, only when I popped in the key to unlock her, it was not the right key. It looked like the right key, felt like the right key, but the right key it was not. I opened my pink unicorn box and took out my key collection. Alas, it seemed that none of them would fit.

I had teased Steph many times about this in the past and pretended to misplace the key, so she assumed I was joking and playing a prank on her. Only when she saw my expression did she realise that this was a serious matter, and I saw a panic flash in her eyes.

In the past when we had sessioned, I remembered that Steph's cage had been yanked off with a rope by another domme. I suggested we oil her up with baby oil and try sliding her little dobbin out of the cage. I applied baby oil liberally to the cage and soon Steph was extremely slippery, as were my fingers but the cage was still holding on fast.

"Perhaps if I squeeze my balls through," Steph suggested. I nodded in agreement and the cage moved ever so slightly, then refused to budge another millimetre! Her ball was stuck in the wrong position in the cage and was quickly starting to swell.

Steph was now pink in the face, looking flustered and her breathing became more ragged as the panic rose in her. I couldn't help but giggle! My sissy was panicking and pulling at the cage, the way a claustrophobic might bang on the lift doors during a power failure. It was futile. The cage was stuck and it was not to be shifted. After giggling to myself for a moment, I could see that sissy was becoming a little distressed and I concluded that I would need to put her out of her misery soon.

"In the American movies, they always manage to pick the locks," I mused, "let me try this safety pin.

I inserted the pin into the lock and wriggled and twisted it to no avail. I tried this with various safety pins, with the same result.

Pondering for a moment, I decided that I wasn't using the right tool for the job. I sifted through my make-up bag and pulled out a hairpin.

"Don't worry, I've seen this in loads of spy movies," I soothed, with conviction.

Over the years, the likes of Bruce Willis, Jason Statham and friends have taught me that every   secret agent or person bound by handcuffs, merely needs a humble hairpin to resolve the situation!

It was mostly bravado on my account, blended with a mix of grim determination to solve the issue. I was curious and eager to put it to the test. I twisted the hairpin into an L shape as I have seen the Hollywood stars do, then tentatively I inserted it into the lock. I twisted left and right and nothing happened. I rotated the pin, I jiggled and made some impressive hand movements that were designed to say, "Don't worry, I have done this before!"

I could almost feel the heat radiating from her and I could sense she was holding her breath, hoping that her Mistress would find a way.

Steph was no closer to being free of her cage, but I was not giving up! I pushed the pin towards the top of the lock and swivelled it and then to my surprise – CLICK – it opened!

"It's unlocked!" I sang happily, as if I knew it would work all along.

"Really, are you sure Mistress?" Steph gasped, thinking I was teasing her again. Her eyes shone with fear and hope, longing for my words to be true.

I pulled the pin out of the lock and removed it from her cage.

I don't think I have ever seen such a relieved sissy! With oily, shaking hands, she removed the rest of the device from her now swollen clit and balls! I stood back with a sense of satisfaction and with a wink, declared, "I can now add 'master locksmith' and 'cage breaker' to my CV!"

Steph chuckled heartily, happy to be freed from the torment and the vice-like grip of the cage's eager jaws. It was a moment of triumph and we were both delighted.

Of course, shortly afterwards when I assembled the electric cock loops on sissy's nethers and started to turn up the voltage, I could sense that she was suddenly wishing that she were back in the safe confines of her chastity cage.

"Perhaps next time my dear sissy, we will have to sentence you to a longer spell in chastity," I taunted. She agreed happily, excitement dancing in her eyes.

There is so much fun to be had with chastity but here are a few does and don'ts:

1. Do test your cage out first for fit and comfort. Ensure you can easily wash yourself

2. Do play around with short stints in the cage if you are new to this, before engaging in longer term play.

3. Do understand that you will be tempted to unlock at times but the sense of satisfaction you will get from abstinence and pleasing your keyholder will far outweigh any temporary dopamine hit. Long term satisfaction beats instant gratification.

4. Have a backup key somewhere in case of an emergency, but is not so easily accessible you are tempted to cheat and unlock.

5. Don't send the key to anyone you haven't researched thoroughly. Ensure your keyholder has experience of chastity and understands the implications.

6. Do wear loose fitting trousers and be mindful of certain activities such as jogging or swimming while you are locked.

7. Avoid using too much lotion, your cage may slip off, causing unnecessary embarrassment.

8. Don't text your domme constantly. You want the key back at some time, right? So don't annoy her.

9. Do have a celebration planned for your release to incentivise your chastity sentence.

10. Do expect some disturbed sleep at times. Men can experience erections during sleep and this may cause you to wake throughout the night, until you are used to it.

11. Do have fun with it! Plan some activities either on your own or with your domme that do not include any kind of self-pleasure.

Lady R: Over my 9 years of experience as a Mistress, I have had many of my subs request me to be their trusted keyholder. Trust is the most important role in this position and one that must NOT be abused although I did from time to time joke with my subs that if they didn't behave I would simply swallow the key in front of them, forever leaving them and their manhood in my possession. As Kaz has kindly explained the logistics of chastity at the start of this chapter I will continue into a story of one of my most memorable sessions.

Slave T was an extremely loyal slave who always kept to his regular appointments. Usually his kink was spanking with some light pegging but on this particular day he wanted to go home extremely frustrated. As he entered my playroom and perched sheepishly on the ottoman at the end of my bed, I wondered what he was going to cheekily suggest.

"Mistress, I wanted to maybe try something new today that I have seen online?"

I presented a long pause before my response which was simply: "Continue, slave"

"Well Mistress, usually after our session you let me go home satisfied but today I would like you to do all of the things you usually do with me but to attach this chastity cage to my cock and to wind me up throughout the session and for me to the leave today with my new toy attached, but to keep the key in your possession until I return."

To create tension after his brave request and to show him who was in control, I simply replied, "Clothes off and kneel."

After removing all of his clothing, he then proceeded to pull this pink, plastic cock cage out of his rucksack with the lock attached and placed it next to my whips, which I had prepared for the day's session. He dropped to his knees and knelt before me. Without hesitation and no dialogue, I slapped on my black plastic gloves, picked up the pink cage and placed it around his slightly semi-erect cock and secured the lock.

The session could now begin.

"Bend over the bed and prepare yourself for 10 of my finest for being so cheeky at the start of the session."

Slave T did just that as I made my way to my whip collection, to choose which one might be suitable for today's punishment.

"I think I will go with Sandra today (Sandra is the nickname for my electric blue horse crop) as she does like to cause a sharp sting for that cheeky tongue of yours."

Slave T looked up at me with a slight smirk of excitement before quickly hiding his look of guilt and enjoyment as I made my way to his meaty ass.

"Let's get your bottom warmed up and count them as we go."

His body jolted after every swift slap of the crop, with his faint voice counting the 10 strikes I had decided to impose, leaving fresh red stripes across his pale skin, a reminder for days of our session.

After punishment I always like to follow with a gentle tease to keep the mystery and excite the senses during sessions, so I picked up my pinwheel and gently started to roll the device over his ankles, slowly make my way up to his knee and applying a bit more pressure reaching the top of his inner thigh, causing a static tingling sensation, almost guaranteed to give him a solid erection. This of course, would stop at his mind as his cock was trapped in chastity. I could tell Slave T was rather frustrated at this point, so I continued my cruel campaign of teasing with my vibrating wand, placing it full speed on the tip of the cage sending vibrations through his manhood which cannot become fully erect.

This continued throughout the session with Slave T gushing with excitement with every stroke of the crop, or teasing touch of my nails running over his bottom or thighs.

After an hour, I decided he should return home until our next meeting with regular updates of his frustration. Not 2 hours after he left was he begging to return, but I assured him that if he waits a little longer it will be worth the wait.

A week later he returned for his release and I could tell just from his smile that it had been a groundbreaking experience for him. He had spent the week day and night thinking naughty thoughts but not being able to act on them. The ultimate punishment and control! As I undid the lock and opened the cage, his cock without hesitation sprung to action throbbing.

"Now you can have your treat for being a good boy for the week."

I picked up the multi-speed, vibrating wand and in the lowest vibration mode, I placed it on the tip of this bell-end. His body jerked for all of 5 seconds before he released his spunk all over my playroom floor.

"Now there is a good boy."

Slave T now returns regularly for monthly lockups and I still like to wind him up that I have misplaced the key.

Conversations between Lady Rampage and Miss Kaz:

R: What is the longest you have held someone in chastity for?

K: The longest in one go was about a month and I had a slave keep a daily journal for me. I watched his frustration increase day by day as his kinky thoughts spun off into unique directions and he craved all manner of filth…that he was not permitted to enjoy! How about you?

R: The longest has been 1 week. It drove him mad and I had constant updates of his sexual frustration, which I found amusing. I always worry that keeping them in chastity for too long will do more harm than good. What would you say is the maximum time?

K: I wouldn't instruct more than one month in highly restrictive cages per unlock, even if it's an hour or so to air the meat and two veg, as I believe that's unhealthy in terms of mindset and the physical aspects. Although. I'm aware of slaves and Mistresses that enjoy longer play. Have you found that subs thought processes get more bizarre after being caged for some time?

R: Yes! I find that their fetishes and fantasies get more extreme. They agree to try things they wouldn't normally consider during a session. My slave T would buy more extreme toys for the session whilst in chastity. One day while under lock and key he turned up with a leather body bag so he could be wrapped up in it and locked in.

K: How did you feel about that!

R: To see him wriggling around in a leather body back, sweating his bollocks off in the height of summer, with electrics attached to his genitals - I can't lie, I loved it and found it hilarious. What about yourself Kaz?

THE RUTHLESS GUIDE TO BDSM

K: So one slave used to love pegging and sucking a strap-on but half way through his stint in chastity he was even starting to consider forced bi and would send me monologues about how he was craving more perverse desires and imaging himself on his knees, sucking a real dick for me. Would you say that chastity is good discipline for a sub or does it make them ultimately naughtier?

R: It's a mix of both. There is mental and physical discipline present but the day dreams become more extreme.

K: I agree, some may crave kinkier scenarios, but may not necessarily act on them.

Chapter 3
Pegging

Pegging is a sexual act in which one partner wears a strap-on dildo or vibrator for anal penetration with another other person. Pegging refers to the male receiving anal, usually from a woman, although technically, a man can peg another man with a strap-on. It's an act that has become more popular in recent years with the taboo around men enjoying anal play becoming less of a factor. Mainstream film may have had an impact on this along with the increase of pegging becoming more prevalent in femdom porn.

Let's face it, most men probably aren't likely to tell their mates down the pub that they enjoy a good pegging but they are more inclined to admit it to their significant others or their dommes.

Why do so many guys like pegging now?

The male prostate is located in the anus and this being stimulated can create a harder erection as well as feelings of desire, which may even lead to orgasm. Sometimes a different type of orgasm can take place which involves the prostate being 'milked.' This can often result in the prostate being stimulated to leak seminal fluid and can lead to an earth-shaking orgasm.

As the prostate is internal and is relatively inaccessible. With the use of fingers or a dildo the area is much easier to reach and many men find that pegging gives that stimulation that they desire.

Kaz B: I first experienced pegging back in 2005. My then boyfriend Jorge and I were asked to make a video with a difference for a Dutch film company and they suggested pegging was extremely popular. Jorge lapped the idea up and was keen to try. We bought a small strap-on from a toy retailer, the sort of equipment I would laugh at now, but we were both beginners and it was ideal. Jorge had some experience already with using toys on himself so it didn't take long to figure out how to lube it well and slip it inside him and the viewers went wild for it! Fast forward to 2014, pegging was becoming increasingly popular and by 2015 at least half of my subs were keen to experience the joys of pegging at least once to find out what all the fuss was about.

Since I've been to pegging parties where there are multiple Mistresses and subs, we play party games and the lucky subbies get to be pegged in all manner of gloriously kinky positions.

Pegging was always seen as a taboo and I have no doubt the countless dommes that broadcast pegging videos and preach about the merits of pegging have helped to tip the balance. Other than chastity, it's one of the most prominent ways a slave can submit to his Mistress and involves a lot of trust.

There are different reasons why men enjoy being pegged, for some it's the taboo. For others they want to indulge in that feeling of being vulnerable and helpless. The prostate or Male G Spot is also inside the rectum, and there is no way to access it with insertions from a finger or toy. It can add a whole new dimension to orgasms and bring new excitement to the bedroom.

A few pointers - whether playing with a Mistress or partner discuss what size toys will be used and use a good lube. I'd suggest using condoms on your toys where possible for hygiene reasons. You'll also need a good quality toy cleaner. Isopropyl alcohol in a spray bottle is my personal preference. You will need to take an enema first. You can buy douche bottles from all good sex shops filled with lukewarm water and insert the pipe into the rectum, then empty over the loo. You will need to do this several times and abstain from eating for at least 5 hours beforehand. While sometimes there may be a little residue on the toy, you don't want to be squirting all over the place as this can turn the experience from something fun into something less pleasant. I have witnessed on countless occasions where slaves have failed to douche properly. I have even sent slaves to the bathroom to clean up, or there will be no pegging time. This is something I am extremely strict on - hygiene. I have seen slaves on set have accidents. I remember one time a domme friend of mine was pegging her sub with a particularly large toy and well......it reminded me of when you visit the zoo and the elephant has to drop the kids off!

Another time which was absolutely hilarious was when I visited Sexhibition in Manchester. My friend H and I got chatting to a rather lovely man that requested a pegging session. He brought a bottle and we enjoyed a nice Pinot grigio - he'd been drinking rum most of the day I believe. We bent him over and inserted the strap-on...I heard a strange rumble and my spidey senses kicked in and I sidestepped 2 feet away, pulling the strap-on out. What hit the wall was absolute carnage. Slave was instructed to disinfect the area until it was immaculate. After the initial shock, we had a bloody good laugh about it... so I cannot stress enough - if anal play is on your list, douche, douche then douche some more!

Lady R: Like every chapter in this book I have the burning desire to write about each subject in as much physical detail so You the reader almost feel as if you're in the room with me at this present moment. Imagine you have a man bent over on all fours in-front of you, totally naked with his chocolate starfish smiling directly back at you ready for the taking of sexual pleasure at its finest. Pegging is definitely an art that needs perfecting and preparation before the performance. Lube and a gloved finger wiggle always helps to loosen the anal sphincter.

I remember a client coming to me for this service for his first time. He had recently divorced and wanted to try pegging, almost like a celebration of his recent separation.

We will call him Doctor Sub, no need to guess what his actual profession was.

Doctor sub arrived at my premises immaculately clean and fully prepared, which is sometimes rare for a first timer. He had brought with him a small dildo with the strap-on belt that was to his preferred size and after a long discussion on his expectations of how the session would go we got started.

Undressed and on all fours I could tell Doctor sub was ready for his fucking. I started to tease his inner thigh with my feather as he started flinching with excitement. Standing back I pulled the strap-on off the bedroom side and pulled it over my legs and up to my crouch ready for action. After lubing my finger and loosening his hole in a gentle circular motion I pulled out as I knew he was now waiting for my little pink cock to slide into him. Grabbing my new cock I placed it near his hole and asked if he was ready. "Yes Mistress" he squealed with excitement. I slowly entered him, easing the dildo inside and starting with a slow thrusting motion.

Doctor Sub was definitely enjoying his first fucking as he couldn't stop panting with excitement. As I picked up speed sliding in and out of his anus I instructed him to start playing with his already hard shaft to which he obviously obliged. After 5 minutes of a good fucking I could tell Doctor sub was desperate to cum. "Keep playing with that cock Subby and I might let you cum today".

"Please Mistress I beg of you, please let me cum." He cried.

I could tell he was struggling to hold himself so after another minute or so and a few light spanks on his pert ass I let him release himself all over the towel on the bed. He screamed as he came like a wild animal. He must have needed it!

Needless to say he came back many times after that memorable first time.

But not all sessions go as pleasant as Doctors Subs. Some get really messy quite quickly, especially if the sub isn't prepared. The most disgusting session I have had the unfortunate experience participating in is not for the faint hearted.

The sub in question was experienced in playtime and should have known better.

This day in particular Subby had chosen to have the duo session with myself and Mistress Lacey, We decided to start the session with some foot worship, so with Subby lying on the floor me and Mistress Lacey draped our toes all over his naked form, rubbing them in his face, mouth and all over this cock and balls. As his member started to rise with pure excitement I quickly slapped it back down with the strike of my whip. "Now now Subby, we don't want you getting too excited before your fucking do we?" I exclaimed before Mistress Lacey chimed in with, "Bend over the bed and let Lady R give you what you came here for."

I have never seen Subby move so quickly, as he jumped off the floor and onto the edge of the bed on all fours with his ass clearly displayed ready for entry.

Now this Sub was experienced in strap-on play and can take cocks on the large side so without hesitation I picked one of my bigger sizes which is a good 9 inches of solid shaft and equally large in girth.

After a quick finger fucking with lube to warm him up I stuck the girthy cock in his ass and started thrusting hard into him. He was enjoying the cock so much that he even reached around and grabbed my leg to thrust it even deeper into his anus.

I moved my pelvis as fast and deep as I could manage but I could tell he still wanted more, so after zero deliberation I decided to get the bigger size involved.

Pulling the cock out of his ass I instantly regretted it, all over my favourite dildos were subby's insides. MY COCK WAS COVERED IN SHIT!

I instantly grabbed a plastic bin liner from the side to stop the dripping shit from hitting my immaculate cream carpets. Mistress Lacey could see the sheer horror written all over my face and jumped up to see the carnage and immediately sent Subby to the shower to clean up his stinking mess.

After his return from the shower he stood dripping water everywhere having failed to dry himself properly, the Sub had zero shame in what chaos he had caused in today's session and implied that he wanted the pegging to continue. If that wasn't rude enough, I reminded him that his allotted time was now over and that under no circumstances was I to continue such a session with someone who had spilled their dinner all over my floor.

After 20 minutes of faffing about he reluctantly left. My precious dildos stunk to high heaven and the room smelt like a sewer. It took me over a week to get the stench off my toys even with bleach and a whole can of air freshener for my playroom.

Note to subs and slaves reading this... PLEASE COME PREPARED!

This next segment is a series of WhatsApp chats between Rampage and Kaz - read on for the raw, graphic details and what we chat about off the record!

K: So, Rampage, I was reading your last chapter and roared out loud with laughter! Is this a common occurrence for you with subs and was this the worst incident you experienced, or has there been anything that's happened in a session that's topped this?

R: I would definitely put it up there in the top ten Kaz, but it is by no means the worst thing that's happened! The sub being an experienced slave should have known better and cleaned himself and prepared before the session. 9 times out of ten there's a small nugget at the end of a dildo, so even if a sub had prepared this sometimes happens, which isn't their fault. There have been sessions involving toilet play which becomes much more graphic, involving shit, piss and vomit as mentioned later in Chapter 23, if the reader has the stomach for this - don't say I didn't warn you though!

K: Wow, I'm not going to lie, that story is shocking! The worst thing I saw was when a slave came for a spanking and I pulled down his pants to see the biggest dirt log stuck between his cheeks....so with that in mind, have you had any dirty slaves turn up, what happened and did they get punished?

R: The biggest log? Disgusting. I would definitely send them straight for a clean-up, hygiene is so important in sessions as I believe it is not my job to play mummy and clean them up! Unless it's an adult baby of course. Have you ever had any disputes with a slave about their cleanliness?

K: I send most of my subs to the website first and tell them to acquaint themselves with my rules, and usually they have no problems in either following instruction or heading to the shower after a disapproving look. However, there have been a couple of stubborn filth mongers but I find a wet wipe and a big splash of Tabasco sauce makes a great disinfect for their rancid penises and also works as a good deterrent for future bad behaviour!

Chapter 4
Sissification

Forced feminization, or sissification, refers generally to the feminization of a person who identifies as male. The term was originally used in the context of BDSM to refer to the forced feminization of a male-identifying submissive. As with any activity, each party has to give their enthusiastic consent and have the right to withdraw the consent at any time, for any reason.

The official term autogynephilia refers to a male who fetishes womanhood and imagines themself to be female. In a mild sense, this can include dressing and acting as they perceive a female to be, or this paraphilia can include the male to even imagine themselves lactating, menstruating or having female organs.

Kaz B: When sissy-curious subs approach me, I email them back and ask - "Have you always dreamed of being glamorous and feminine but don't know where to start? Or perhaps you long for a full transformation and long to be a true sissy slut?"

Over the years, all manner of deviant slaves have undergone a sissy transformation and paraded around for me, relishing in their absolute fabulousness as a newly Christened crossdressing sissy. I tell them how to achieve the perfect inner and outer goddess and say they won't even be able to recognise themselves in the mirror if they follow my instructions.

Here's a little guide I wrote for my sissies in training.

1: Depilation.

If you want to be feminine, you need to remove all of your body hair. Your beard, any nose or ear hair with trimmers and a razor, the legs, armpits and of course the trickier bits – your man garden! You can buy a Veet cream for your man pussy, simply apply, leave on for ten minutes then rinse! Don't forget places like between your bottom cheeks either. There's nothing worse than a beautiful thong with gorilla hair poking out the sides and back!

Define your eyebrows and pluck your stray hairs, making sure to only pluck under the right side of the brow, not on top or too the left, though you can sculpt these with an eyebrow razor. If you can't do these yourself, get them shaped in a salon. Whilst some think the Scouse brow is trendy (by the way it isn't, it's hideous on so many levels) the monobrow is never going to be in fashion!

2: Skincare Routine

Purchase an exfoliator – scrub your face and body all over to make your skin super smooth, then apply face and body moisturiser. There is nothing feminine about rough skin, so do this every day. Skincare can be overwhelming at the best of times so if in doubt, both Nivea and Clinique do a good range for men. All you need is cleanser, exfoliator, moisturiser and body lotion. Exfoliate once per week and cleanse and moisturise every morning and night.

3: Make up time!

This is a tricky one as most men know nothing about makeup. Your options are either watch tutorials on YouTube on how to apply makeup and research beauty products online, or if you are not quite confident to do it yourself you could always visit a Mistress who specialises in feminisation and cross dressing. Simply search your area and see who's local, ie type into your browser feminisation and local town.

With makeup, less is more. Apply a little at a time. Choose

heavy eyes or lips not both at the same time. Try to contrast eye shadows to your eye colour. For example, most colours go with green eyes (except blue) but try not to use the same colour on your lids as your eyes. You want to create contrast and lift and define.

4:Lingerie

Every Princess loves beautiful lingerie. (Hint hint!) Forget cheap Primark bras and undies. Treat yourself to some decent underwear and measure your bra size. You can google how to do this online. All you need is a tape measure. Your lingerie should match and be of good quality. Stockings and suspenders always make any lingerie set dazzle!

Colour wise, if you can't decide, play it safe with black. Go for textures that feel good to you. For some this will be satin or silk and for others lace. If you want to create the illusion of a bust go for a bust enhancing padded plunge bra or Wonderbra.

5: Cross Dressing

Many of my Sissies tell me that the hardest thing about cross dressing is getting time to themselves to indulge their fetish. It is often difficult for them to get any privacy at home. The more costly option is to book a hotel and order your desired items online. The cheaper option is to find a Mistress who will not only give you a private place to dress, but will also assist with clothes and make up and advise on looks. A good Mistress is likely to have a range of makeup and clothes for you to dress in and will help you indulge and enjoy your fetish in the best possible way.

If you want to buy your own outfits, think how you want to feel whilst you are wearing them. Do you want to feel feminine or sexy or trashy or cute? What look would suit these moods? A tight mini skirt and fishnets would be trashy for example. A long tight dress elegant, a more flowing dress feminine and a pleated mini and a v neck top would look cute! Once you know how you want to feel it will make selecting outfits much easier.

6: Posture/Movement/Voice

What's the difference between a woman and a guy apart from the obvious? It's the way women stand, move and speak. Elevate yourself and pull your shoulders back. When you walk, put one foot in front of the other and try to move with poise, but don't overdo it - I'm forever saying, "You aren't walking a bloody tightrope!"

Britain's Top Models is a good show to watch to emulate the way some of Britain's most beautiful women walk. Now for that gruff man voice – soften it! No need to squeak in a high pitch tone (unless you are going for ridiculous) just speak more softly, flutter your lashes, just a tad, practise a coy look and smile and be demure! Of course, these are all stereotypical aspects of womanhood but it *is* fantasy roleplay!

7: Sitting

Women don't sit with their legs spread wide. They hold them together or cross them. Practise your sitting posture and your walk. If feminisation is your lifestyle rather than just a sexual kick you'll want to practise the little things that really define you as feminine. Slow down your eating and drinking. Cut your food into tiny morsels and always use a knife and fork, unless it's a pizza, which makes you look haughty. Just remember, ladies don't gobble dear, Sip your wine, don't glug, hold your glass daintily and remember your manners. Yes, if you want to be a woman for the session you will have to endure all the things us women have endured too! With me, you are either all in or not at all!

Think about limits and how far you are comfortable to take the fantasy. For you, simply cross dressing may be enough to sate your needs. Or you may want to indulge in more extreme play. Again, think about how you want to feel. Do you long to feel degraded and humiliated? Or perhaps you want to feel soft and vulnerable?

Many of my sissies enjoy slut training and they enjoy sessions where I *'brainwash'* them. This involves activities such as me instructing them on how to fellate a dildo, or get pegged. Brainwashing in the sense of a fantasy role play involves me encouraging my sub and teasing them that this is how they should always be. That their current self is their fake self and that their true self is the inner slut inside who is dying to be released! I encourage them to release their inner slut by vocalising their needs and repeating mantras such as *"I love your strap-on Mistress. I am a sissy bitch."* **I must reiterate once more, this is all done with consent and in a safe space. My subs are free to use their safeword or even simply take a breather during a session.**

Some sissies' idea of this type of role play is steeped in misogyny. They may have watched too much porn and think women are sluts, or in some cases they want to experience the most extreme end of the scale. If I sense the former, I am sure to give them a session that makes them feel thoroughly degraded and throw in some mocking comments along the way. Usually, over time, their views on women start to become more balanced.

In more extreme cases, I will tell my sissies they should only be allowed to ejaculate whilst they are being penetrated and that every time they ejaculate they must think of my strap-on.

Some of my sissies enjoy this as a lifestyle and not just as a fetish and so I will tell them to wear lingerie under their everyday clothes. I even had a sissy wear a butt plug to work every   day for a week as part of his training to show his commitment to his transformation. It's harmless fun and something that will remain a secret between my sub and me. He gets to enjoy the feeling of wearing women's clothing, knowing that it will go no further than the two of us.

The final stage

Not every sissy wishes to reach this level. They might even enjoy the fantasy but not want to actually go through with it. The final stage involves a bi experience whereby they perform sex acts on or with another guy. It's quite a big decision to make so think it over carefully. If you have done so and are fully comfortable with the idea, your Mistress may suggest you interact with another sub. Make sure that you have met your Mistress at least once prior to this so you know her personality and feel comfortable. A safe environment with a Mistress you trust is paramount.

One of my subs in preparation for this ate his own seminal fluids for a week to be certain he could handle the next step. I reminded him that the Atkins diet can be greatly beneficial for the body and mind and a little extra protein in the diet wouldn't do him any harm.

One word of caution would be never to practise bareback sex. Anal sex is particularly risky and your life and health are more important than a cheap thrill that lasts ten minutes…I'm being generous there, five minutes in some cases!

Kaz B: A good number of gentlemen that visit me are eager to undergo Sissy Slut Training and be transformed into girly super sluts. It's a safe way for men to express their vulnerable sides and embrace their femininity and embark on a voyage of self-disco .

One lad we'll call Sadie, visited me wishing to undergo the complete Barbie transformation and was keen to go for a 'Trashy school girl' look.

Deciding on a beautiful purple eyeshadow, I smoothed it on to his lids and added a smoky effect. My fingers worked their magic, lining his eyes with black kohl, filling his brows with a dark brown and adding lashings of black mascara, which transformed his face completely. It was almost like a pretty girl was staring back at me, he just needed contouring with a few clever flicks of blusher brush. Oohing and aahing, I explained what I was doing throughout the process. His hands trembled and there was a giveaway twitch at the side of his face as he smiled. The final touch was adding a big dollop of gloss to his lips and then fitting a brown wig on his head which I then put into low pigtails on each side.

It was time to dress my dolly and so I handed him a bra and

THE RUTHLESS GUIDE TO BDSM

pads to wear, along with a black thong and suspender belt and I helped him dress into his stockings. A blue school tie, grey skirt and some black heels later and voila – he was ready! I was surprised at how much he looked like a naughty schoolgirl. There was a sort of doll-like look to his face too and the make-up suited him perfectly.

Grabbing his hand, I led him to the mirror encouraging him to twirl around and then bend over so he could admire my work from all angles. He was delighted and gave a girlish laugh which suited the look perfectly! He looked every inch a St Trinian – a very naughty one too, might I say!

Ordering my naughty St Trinian to dance for me, she wiggled and grinded admiring her new look in the mirror.

"What sissy name would you like?" I purred.

"Just Bitch boy!"

"Bitch boy it is then!"

Some girls grow up playing with Barbies but grow out of it. Then you get the ones like me who never really grow out of it properly but instead expand their playtime into making little Barbies out of men instead. It's a much more amusing game having a real human toy to dress up and play with!

Lady R: Now my experience with Sissification is pretty slim as most of my clients were more on the crossdressing side than sissy's (please look at chapter 17 for details on the difference). My clients mainly wanted to play dress up for the occasion rather than the more aged sissy. If you picture a man with a full beard and unkempt eyebrows in unflattering lingerie, you may be slightly close on the mark. I used to find it rather entertaining when a new client would come to dress up, a little on the plump size with a beer belly and ask to squeeze into my size 8 lingerie.

I used to have a client that loved skimpy knickers and stockings but was a bit sensitive over the size of his gut. He wanted to borrow one of my corsets, so I took pity on him and found a corset with the longest adjustable strings. I couldn't help but laugh at the pickle he got into, tangling it round his waist and penis! This was what I expected as most crossdressers and sissies can't dress themselves! They attempt to put their heads through a sleeve hole, put everything on backwards or upside down and you should see them try to put on a pair of stockings! For the love of God - why is it so complicated to roll the stocking up and delicately pop your toes in, then the heel, then roll up the leg. Nope - sissies will often stand on one leg and try to hop into the stocking, nearly falling over backwards in the process! If they do manage on the second or third attempt they will no doubt shove a big hairy, hobbit foot straight into the nylon and a long, crooked yellow toenail will snag it straight up. They will then yank up the stockings so they ladder all the way up. They fail to pull the stockings to the thigh, so they will constantly hang around their knees, wrinkled during the session. I did my best to intervene but sometimes I just gave up out of sheer exasperation!

Anyway, I had to assist him but after getting him untangled, the corset would not go around his one pack. I suggested he ordered a corset in his size, which he did. Actually he ordered three, then became addicted to buying corsets and even started to wear them under his shirt to work. Over time, his posture improved significantly. As for the belly, well, that's another story!

Chapter 5
Roleplays

No doubt you've heard the term roleplay, most likely you have engaged in it yourself. It can take many guises and forms and incorporate dressing up in cosplay as characters or in roles of authority. Role play is popular because shedding the trappings of our lives and stepping into someone else's shoes can add an extra layer of fantasy to any kink play and even help us forget our inhibitions. Everyone should try a roleplay at least once. The worst case scenario is that you may keel over laughing and then at least you've got a good laugh out of it, or you never know you may have the time of your life and find it is the perfect outlet to release life's pressures and unleash your inner Goddess/naughty sub!

Kaz B: I'm a big fan of role play, although it's not something I'd advise a novice to try when meeting a mistress or master the first time. An introductory session is a starting point to get to know one another a little, discover what one's sub is looking to explore on their journey. My reasons are this, during a roleplay a sub might be less inclined to use their safeword and role plays can often melt away some inhibitions as the sub and Mistress get into character. A roleplay is much more enjoyable when there has been an opportunity to build some rapport and understanding. There's a greater sense of ease and less second guessing.

Some of the most popular role plays I have come across vary from the traditional Head Mistress, or the bad cop through to angry wives, blackmailing neighbours and the ever popular bitchy boss scenario where the sub must "do as I say if you want to keep your job." Of course, they don't have a job with you, so they don't have to do anything they do not wish to but many people love to play out these scenarios and love the idea of being 'forced' to carry out some kinks from their list.

Kink is not about sex. It's a mindset and the psychology behind it is complex. There are so many reasons why an individual desires experimenting with a kink. It can be as simple as curiosity. One sub told me he was a bit of an arsehole at work and wanted to be humiliated to see how it feels. Perhaps his HR department had given him something to think about, who knows, but he told me later it helped him understand his employees more. For others, they may be aroused by humiliation, pain or fetish, whereas for others, it can come from a place of wanting to experience different emotional ranges. This can include but is not limited to, vulnerability, feeling sexy or ashamed or simply under the power of another person. For some it can even be comforting. Now you might be thinking, how can being dominated be comforting. I'll give you some examples - a guy with a foot fetish may love feet because it takes him back to when he met his first love or a time he felt safe, or in the case of adult babies, it reminds them of a time when they had no responsibilities or cares in the world and all their needs were meant. They are soothed by an ADBL session where they can suspend reality for a short time and go to their safeplace before they go back to managing a company of 250 staff. I shit you not! We'll talk more about adult babies later!

Lady R: I do not know any Mistress who doesn't enjoy the art of roleplay. I have tried every roleplay you can think of from the typical and more popular headmistress scenario to the more unique handmade requests. I don't believe you need anything other than a vivid imagination combined with a bag of creative flair to perform the perfect roleplay session. I always found myself to be quite the confident actress so perhaps it came naturally to me. One of my most memorable sessions was with a lovely handsome and young slave called Slave Pip.

It was Slave Pips first experience with a mistress and I could tell from the email I had received that he was already shaking with nerves. His request was a bit out of the ordinary, he wanted me to be a wicked witch who captured him and kept him in the broom cupboard naked for a long period of time with regular punishment intervals. His likes list included whipping, anal play, pegging, CBT and electrics, which I was to incorporate into the scenario and In my mind I had created a Hansel and Gretel role play to end with me pegging him over my bed.

Before his arrival I got into my witches costume which involved a short sexy black dress with stockings, suspenders, a long black cloak that I had purchased in Camden market and a long brunette wig. I had chosen to do my makeup dark and gothic with bright red lips. Last but not least was my pointy black hat. Outfit on and already in character I sent Slave Pip a simple text inviting him into my lair.

I opened my apartment door to a well-dressed and groomed nervous slave who I immediately led straight into my playroom pulling him by his hands and ordered to strip, before placing a blindfold over his eyes and tying his wrists behind his back with my leather cuffs.

"I have tricked you in my lair Pip and now I am going to keep you hostage and punish you until the cauldron has boiled"

"What are you going to do with me Mistress, are you going to eat me?" asked a shaken Pip.

"Be quiet Pip and bend over the bed" I barked before letting out my best cackle.

"I better get that rump of yours warmed up before I lock you away in the broom cupboard."

I pushed Pip onto the bed, picked up my crop and spanked his cheeks with 5 whips, each one leaving a bright red mark as proof of my punishment. I then led him over to the cupboard and attached the cuffs to a pipe inside to secure him and ordered him to stand straight and silent before my return.

I gave it a good 5 minutes to let him sweat before my return to which I came back with my violent wand aka my magic wand and with him still standing in position with his hands behind his back I started to zap his cock and balls. Watching him squeal like a pig in heat with each zap gave me so much pleasure that I couldn't help but let out another loud cackle before I lubed up a small 3 inch butt plug and inserted it into his rectum. I could tell Pip was loving the role play as his cock was standing stiff for the occasion, so I started to tease his inner thigh with my long, black witch-like nails while zapping his penis one final time before leaving him in the cold darkness with nothing but silence and visions of our last encounter for another 5 minutes to torture him with his own thoughts.

This continued for another 40 minutes with each of my returns bringing an electric shock or whips with the crop combined with cackles and promises to put him in the cauldron when I've finished with him. Then on my final return I undid the cuffs from the pipe and demanded:

"Before I eat you I'm going to give you one last hard fuck."

I forced him face first over my bed and pulled my strap-on over my thighs, lubed up and inserted my 6 inch cock into his tight hole.

With every thrust he moaned with pleasure as his cock was also rubbing on the towel between him and the bed. I could tell it wouldn't be long before he came from the humping motion alone so I undid his cuffs and instructed him to reach for his member and tug until he squirted. That took all of a minute and I let out one final cackle as I spanked his cheeks hard as he came.

I certainly felt like the wicked witch after this appointment as Slave Pip exclaimed that it was one of the most thrilling experiences he had encountered. He returned many times after and each scenario was just as unique. Thank you Slave Pip.

Chapter 6
Butt Plugs and Douching

Before engaging in anal play you'll want to douche or take an 'enema' for the most pleasurable and hygienic experience. Before we take a look at buttplugs, let's talk douching!

Douching is always good practice if you intend to partake in any form of anal play. It avoids embarrassing moments and if you are well douched, it will ensure that your Mistress doesn't run from the room screaming should you leak something less than enticing from your rear end. I'm being facetious of course. Most Pro dommes are used to seeing biological accidents, but the following steps will make the experience more enjoyable for both of you.

I have had various experiences with slaves that have not possessed a good standard of hygiene and let me tell you – it is not much fun!

There have been occasions when subs have failed to douche and it would be an understatement to say that they were not my favourite experience, although memorable and in hindsight - amusing. One slave once pooed himself seconds after I slid the strap-on in. Another slave managed to fire some anal debris onto a wall. On neither occasion was I impressed and the temptation to make them clean it up with their tongues was overwhelming. Instead I had them clean the wall with disinfectant. We are all biological beings and sometimes nature just takes its course and can't be helped!

If you wish to impress your Mistress and arrive cleaned out, this is how you do it and the only recipe you will need to keep your bottom as clean as a whistle.

Firstly you need to purchase a douche. You can find these in every sex store as well as on sites such as Ebay and Amazon and you can pick them up for as little as £5.

Then you need to put some time aside to prepare. You will need:

1 Douche
Access to warm water
Some lubricant
A Toilet.

Directions: Fill the douche with warm water. Cold water will cause cramps. Hot water can burn you – so get the temperature right and spray a little onto the back of your hand from the tube to test it.

Now you want to slide some lube onto the tip and insert it into your bottom. I suggest you are naked on the lower half for this, otherwise you may trip with your trousers around your ankles and have an accident. If you are a cross dresser, the same goes for heels. Pop them off to avoid it all going horribly wrong!

When the tube is in, squirt the water into your bottom until the douche is empty and carefully pull the tube out. The water will stay in and you don't need to give your bottom extra clenching.

Massage your tummy, walk around the bathroom if you care to, just ensure the warm water is moving around inside you. After a couple of minutes sit back onto the toilet and evacuate all that water and the debris that follows it.

Now, you will want to repeat this at least 3 or 4 times to ensure you are squeaky clean. You'll want a nice hot shower afterwards.

When To Douche

Ideally you should douche 30 minutes to 1 hour before the session. Do not eat anything now until after you have enjoyed your anal play or strap-on session. Ideally, you should fast for 6 hours beforehand, put that pie down Percy! If you eat, this ruins all your hard work so resist being a little piggy and don't let anything other than a big dildo pass your lips!

How Often Can I Douche?

You can douche every time you indulge in strap-on fun. If this happens to be everyday you can take a probiotic supplement or eat live natural yoghurt to ensure you don't flush away all your healthy gut bacteria.

Is It Good For You To Douche?

If you have an odd day of constipation, douching can be helpful, although you should not rely on this if you have a long time problem. You should address your diet and ensure you consume plenty of fibre and vegetables.

You can also make up a douche with slightly cooled (but not cold) green tea which is believed to have anti-cancer properties. It is also a known thermogenic so may speed up your metabolism as well as giving you a lovely cleansed feeling and extra energy. Again, I must repeat, this is not medical advice, please do your own research before trying anything anyone but a doctor has told you.

What Should I Not Put In My Bottom?

You should not insert anything large without practising with smaller items first. You should not insert any food produce, any-thing that does not have a base and could get stuck or anything sugary. These are all bad for your back entrance. Sugar breeds bacteria and may even lead to a yeast infection which will be irritating and difficult to shift without medication.

Oh No I've Ran Out Of Lube! What To Do!

A simple oil such as baby oil or vegetable oil will act as a temporary replacement. Always ensure not to cross contaminate and make sure you handle products in a hygienic manner. Ie if you are using vegetable oil from the kitchen, pour a little into a cup and take the cup into the bathroom with you, don't take the bottle in with you then put it back in the cupboard. The bathroom harbours an absolute minefield of bacteria! Also thoroughly scrub your hands afterwards. Good grief, let's master basic hygiene at least!

Great! Now you are all clean, fresh and ready for anal fun. Enjoy!

Get Plugged in

You've probably heard of a buttplug before and they come in all shapes and sizes with the most common style being a teardrop shape and slightly tapered off at the tip. They can come in a range of materials from silicon through to metal.

Why do people use buttplugs?

Buttplugs are popular with those who enjoy anal stimulation. They can be used as part of foreplay or sex to stimulate the senses or to help open up the rectum for anal sex or pegging.

What are some common myths about butt plugs?

A buttplug may get lost inside

This isn't technically true. If you use a small egg shaped plug on a wire and the wire snaps, you may encounter some issues. The general tear drop or T bar shaped buttplugs have a built in base to prevent the plug travelling up too deep. This base also makes for easy removal. Just don't use a plug that is too small, this is when problems are more likely to be encountered.

It will be painful

There's no reason a buttplug should be painful. If it hurts, the right technique is not being used. The plug should always be clean and plenty of lube applied before entry. Beginners should start with smaller plugs before advancing to larger plugs (but not so tiny it disappears up inside). It sounds obvious but it's astounding how over ambitious some can be when it comes to these things.

Straight men can't use buttplugs

Anyone can use a buttplug regardless of their sexual orientation. Many subs have said to me, "I'm curious about trying a butt plug but I'm worried it will make me gay."

I always ask them these two questions -

"Are you attracted to men?"

"No."

"If a woman puts a butt plug in you, will you start being attracted to men?"

"No."

There we go then, wearing a butt plug will not change your sexual preference.

I think what they mean is that using buttplugs have been stigmatised because they have formerly been associated with gay men who use them to warm up the anal passage. I shouldn't have to state it in this day and age that there is nothing wrong at all with being homosexual, however I do understand why some men might be reticent to voice their desires after being conditioned all their lives to think a certain way. It's a defence mechanism and deeply programmed into their psyche. Butt plugs are becoming more popular with straight men but there still is some stigma attached. Let's look at it purely from an anatomical side. The prostate or G spot is located inside the male rectum and it's near impossible to access without entry of the rectum of some kind, though using powerful wands may be able to give a small amount of stimulation. A buttplug or small toy is able to stimulate that magic spot, increasing pleasure and sometimes leading to more powerful orgasms. Now rub a massager against the base to inten-sify the sensations two-fold!

Buttplugs can cause anal incontinence

This is an urban myth. We've all heard those awful stories about men using buttplugs who now have to wear them every day, so they don't mess up their pants. Sensible anal play should not lead to any long lasting damage. I would always caution against using large toys you are not experienced with unless you have thoroughly relaxed the area first….and take it slowly! If rushed, this could cause some anal fissures (tears in the skin) and would be unpleasant. However, regularly using buttplugs is highly unlikely to lead to anal incontinence.

With regards to how long you can wear butt plugs safely, there are mixed opinions. I would suggest that you begin with short durations to begin with and ensure that your anal play doesn't interfere with regular bowel movements. I've had subs ask about wearing buttplugs overnight and to me it seems a bit pointless. Personally, I would say remove your plug in the evening and sterilise it.

Following the above advice will help ease your introduction to anal somewhat, although do bear in mind, none of this is medical advice.

Kaz B: Over the years I've borne witness to many novice submissives experimenting with anal play and observed their playtime via webcam. Some have used tiny buttplugs, others have experimented with huge sets of beads as long as their arm! Here are a few moments that stand out for me.

I skyped with a sub from New Zealand a few times who wore a buttplug that could be operated from an app. We agreed that he would give me access to the app and he would keep the plug in that evening. I would set it off vibrating at random intervals so he would never know when it was coming. He told me the thrill of not being in control of it was intense.

On another occasion, I sent a sub to the shop while he wore a vibrating plug. It was completely silent and no one had a clue but he knew it was there, so felt as if he was doing something naughty. If this falls under public play it's a much safer form as it's not involving people who haven't given their consent and no one needs to be aware of the situation.

The following story is not for the faint hearted, so if you are squeamish then skip this next passage - no pun intended! I cammed regularly with a lawyer called Cyril who had a penchant for large plugs, beads and humiliation. So picture this, I'm watching Cyril's webcam. He's naked on all fours wearing a buttplug and sucking a 10 inch dildo, bobbing his head up and down like a happy labrador chewing on a bone.

"Mistress, I want to please you, can I use my beads and eat my shit for you," he asked me.

"You may Slave."

Cyril popped the plug out and began to insert a long length of fat, black beads into his anus. I was doubtful whether they would fit initially but he sucked them up like a hoover, each bead disappearing with an imaginary 'pop' sound in my head each time. The slave was really getting into it and 12 inches must have disappeared before he began to retrieve them. The beads slid out, one by one, and the slave held them up in front of the camera. They were thoroughly coated in, let's say - his chocolatey chunks. At this point, most slaves lose their bravado, bottle out of making their grand claims a reality and tend to switch off the camera. He did not. Slave slid the beads into his mouth, chunks and all and started to chew. It wasn't until he flashed me a toothy, brown grin I fully grasped what he had just done. Just when I thought I'd seen it all, I was reminded that someone, somewhere out there will always find a new way to make me realise that I hadn't.

I would never kink shame someone for what they are into but I hoped he used a good mouthwash to keep those pearly whites bacteria-free!

Lady R: Over my career, I have had many interesting experiences with butt plugs but one of the most amusing stories that springs to mind actually took place outside of the dungeon, with an ex-partner of mine. Let's call him Steve for the books sake.

Steve had come home from work on a Friday evening and suggested after a few too many drinks, that he would like to try using my glow in the dark, anal beads. I had actually purchased them for one of my clients but as Steve was so insistent on trying my new toy how on earth could I refuse? The beads start small in size and grow to just 3 inches in girth, offering a gentle introduction to anal and come in a light green, smooth PVC, firm, yet flexible.

So, after some heavy lubing, I placed one by one the little green beads into his ass. He liked the instant feeling and after the last bead was in place we agreed that later that evening and after our friends had left we would engage in some sexual activities with the new toy. As the night wore on and the drinks kept flowing, the thought of the beads must have slipped our intoxicated minds as we both passed out in bed. The next day we both woke in a haze and started our daily routine, without a second thought about the previous night's agreement. It wasn't until the following day (Sunday) we remembered, when Steve came bursting into the bathroom, while I was on the toilet mid piss and he jumped bum first onto the sink to pull the forgotten beads out of his rectum. Let's just say the beads were no longer green. Lesson to anyone wishing to try plugs or beads at home, Do NOT engage in this activity half-cut.

My advice when trying butt plugs or beads for the first time is start small. My smallest plug is no bigger than my index finger and a majority of my clients would be eased into the session with this one, leading up to the much larger options. It can be one of the most enjoyable experiences for both men and women when done correctly, just don't be greedy!

Chapter 7
Electric play

Electric play is the process of running an electric current through sensitive tissue areas on the body where there is an excess of nerve bundles to create a pleasure sensation, or perhaps even a painful sensation if pain is your game. Always make sure to purchase approved equipment from licensed sex shops rather than 'having a dabble at home.' This is not the kind of play you want to get wrong!

There are so many types of electro play available from violet wands with a range of different shaped glass bulbs to give inter-changeable effects through to electric buttplugs, chastity cages and pads that can be placed on the body. If you are new to electro play, take it slow to start with and experiment with what works for you.

If you are using main powered electrics, always check first if your play partner has any existing heart conditions or a defibrillator.

Electro play can be a wonderfully titillating form of experi-mentation and can add a little extra zing to your bedroom play!

Kaz B: Some of my subs yearn for the tingle of electric current running through their flesh, zapping, pulses and spreading waves of pleasure and pain through their nipples, testicles or genitals. So why has electric play become just as popular as spanking now? There are a few reasons for this.

1. Clever marketing. Most of the big brands use words

like 'Electro-stimulation' which is exactly what their products do, they stimulate the body and senses and depending on the practitioner and device used, the level desired can vary from mild to extreme. Many of these gadgets can be the bridge between pain and pleasure which can be kept at one end of the scale or the subject can happily slide back and forth into a state of electrified oblivion. With toys given names such as the Electro Vagina Masturbator or Tension Lover Digital Electro Sex Unit, what's not to like? If gadgets were called the electro-shocker of doom for example, this might be off putting to a novice but the use of sensual and seductive words that are used instead, conjure up visions of sexual utopia.

2. With electrics you can dabble with all kinds of sensations and pain play safe in the knowledge that not a single mark will be left on your body. So if you haven't slept with your wife for 15 years and want to keep your penchant for electro play a secret, there will be no tell-tale marks.

3. From a personal viewpoint, I have introduced new subs to electrics and touted their merits in blogs. This is because I find them a safe and effective part of domination and for those seeking to experience something new, it's going to tick those boxes. I have experienced electrics myself years ago with a partner. I did this when I was learning how to master the arts of femdom as I felt it would give me a greater understanding of what my slaves would experience. Of course, with them being male (mostly) their experience will always be different to what I experienced, but it gave me a much broader idea of the kinds of sensation involved and the levels of intensity.

One of my slaves is an absolute pain freak - and I use that as a term of endearment! He is an elderly gentleman and is married, therefore he isn't able to have any marks on his body. He is retired and loves the odd game of badminton and an even greater love of being dominated by a powerful female and being subjected to some intense pain play, but with no marks of course! Over a number of years Jeffrey came to me for nipple torture, electrified cock rings on his penis or balls or an electric butt plug inserted into his rectum. Over time, subby's tolerance built up so we went from experimenting with not just one E-stim box, but two, then a much more intense device called the pebble. Occasionally I would bring the violet wand out to tease his sensitive spots as the rings and clamps whipped him into a beautiful frenzy of exquisite pain. During this journey we experimented with nipple clamps and weights, pinwheels (which are like mini pizza cutters with tiny spikes on them) and bastinado - taking alight cane to the soles of the feet as they do not mark with moderate to heavy caning or whipping. His mainstay will always be electrics because once that powerbox is in my hands, he never knows what to expect. He feels blissfully out of his comfort zone, while being in a safe space with his limits respected.

Lady R: I got a call from slave Tony. He wanted electric play while tied up. Excellent! I can use my kit of violet wands! When he gets here, I make him kiss my gorgeous feet and order him into the bedroom. The bed has already been prepped with rope. I ordered him to strip to reveal his pathetic cock while I shouted abuse at him. His face went so red... loved it! I basically pushed him down and I tied his ankles and wrists. He was securely tied and unable to escape. I get my kit out. My lovely violet wands to torture him with. He's watching me as I rub the wand up his leg, causing him some discomfort with the electric pulses then near his balls. I smile at him and cover his eyes with my hand. I start to rub the wand over his cock and balls. He squirms and squirms ha-ha! And slowly moving my way up his tummy and to his nipples. Oooooo he's moaning. So I slap him and laugh. I play with his nipples with the electricity sensation. I order him to stick out his tongue, he begs me no, absolutely begs but I slap him and spit in his face. This is enough for him to stick his tongue out. So I zap the tip of it. Haha! He groaned like a bitch. I zap it again and again three more times before I go back down to his cock. And start pulling the foreskin back and zapping its head! He squirmed even more. He was a good slave and WILL be back for more.

I have also had a less than glamorous experience in electric play which is rather shocking (no pun intended) Slave Jeff was a regular visitor of mine and came for a usual session of humiliation, CBT, anal and electric play. On this occasion he had requested a duo session with me and Miss Marissa.

As we started the session with Slave Jeff on the floor, he begged to be spit-roasted - deep! Marissa slid her strap-on up over her thighs and I stepped into my beautiful pink strap-on, while he trembled on the floor. Jeff opened his mouth wide, for his cock surprise and latched onto the dildo, sucking on it like it was the first meal of the day! I spread his wobbling cheeks wide as he gasped and groaned, eager for more. His hole greedily sucked my 4 inch dildo in deep, I could barely see the rim. At this point I thought, 'he's not getting enough CBT', so I picked up the violet wand and started zapping his hairy balls, while he jerked around in pleasure and pain, whilst still hungrily sucking on Marissa's massive member. The base of the strap-on disappeared up his anus, so I wrongly assumed we wouldn't be seeing it for some time. MASSIVE MISTAKE! As I proceeded to zap his cock and balls with the wand, I decided it was time to turn up the electrical current to give him even more of a shocking experience. Before I could react, my worst fears came true when his arsehole opened up like the Mersey tunnel and the small pink dildo shot out onto my lap, with nuggets of excrements closely following and covering my black, silk dress. At this point I had to pause the session to clean up. The slave was incredibly embarrassed so we decided to continue the session but avoiding the ass play.

K: Some of your sessions sound like biohazard zones! Do you have a special kit for clean-up jobs for slaves you know are going to spray their juices around?

R: I usually like to have a target area ie. a towel in place in the danger zone areas but obviously sometimes things get out of control and that can't be helped, so wet wipes are a saviour! If it's something like food play you need to put something like tarpaulin down as that shit can get messy!

K: Wow - sounds like a bong party I once stumbled into many years ago by accident! So on that note, have you had a sub turn up out of it, whether high or under the influence of alcohol and how did you deal with it?

R: If a sub turned up under the influence of any drug or drink, I would refuse to see them. Play time could turn nasty in these situations, so I take my safety into account as well as the fact they can't consent to more extreme play. I don't think they should play if they are not in control of their actions or themselves.

Have you had any bad experiences with any subs relating to drink or violence?

K: Many years ago when I lived in Birmingham there was a sub that had come a few times prior and he'd had a few drinks but other than being a bit cheeky, verbally I hasten to add, he'd never been a problem. Then one night, he arrived and whipped out a massive bag of drugs and sniffed it all up. I was taken aback but he seemed in control so foolishly I didn't ask that he left the premises. Then after a couple of hours the drink magnified whatever he had sniffed up and he started to act in a bizarre way. His eyes were like saucers as he shuffled around the room rambling incoherently and started to make the most vile requests. He asked me to turn up at his house and drug his wife by putting powder into her drink and try to persuade her to take part in some of his sick fantasies. I was admonishing him and telling how out of order this was and that he needed to leave. He proceeded in his drugged up, waffling fashion to try and 'convince' me whilst I pointed towards the door and instructed he pop on his shoes and kindly fuck off, or I was calling the police. He seemed to think I was asking him if he wanted a cup of tea as took no notice. Rather than create a conflict and whip out my implements of terror, I had my other safety slave come up from downstairs who ordered him to leave. He tried to reason with him, and the two of us ushered him into his shoes, coat, pushed him out the door and booked him a cab.

The even more disturbing thing was when he then tried to 'arrange' a kidnap of myself by calling a mutual friend - who obviously phoned me straight away, concerned. His idiotic plan was for the friend to knock the door and he could rush in and push me into his car. Luckily, I found out about his agenda but had he even tried, he would have left with his kneecaps fractured. I might be petite but I have a strong survival instinct and I'll happily do anything to defend myself, including using anything and everything to deter a degenerate from criminal behaviour.

R: What the fuck! Never have I heard such a disturbing story. I'm so glad that we are raising the not so glamorous subjects in this book. To all the slaves reading this… A sober slave is the only slave in my opinion!

Chapter 8
Outdoor play

Outdoor play is exactly what it says on the tin - it's a form of play outdoors. The fresh air on your face while experimenting with your sub can add a whole new dimension to your play. Needless to say, for your privacy and for the consideration of others, it's always best to choose a quiet location that is not frequented by cyclists or dog walkers. Ensure that you haven't chosen an area near a school or church and have a large coat ready for your sub to cover up quickly if needs be.

Kinky fun should always be safe, sane and consensual.

Kaz B: I'm not one to indulge in outdoor play unless it's private land and not overlooked by the public or passers-by. For me this comes down to consent. A domme session can involve your sub either being in a state of nudity or wearing heavy fetish costumes or accessories. A passer-by is not part of your agreed, consensual kink and so this rules out public spaces that are overlooked for me. It's shocking the number of subs that have asked to do public play where they might be seen. They received a resounding no and a telling off from me. Of course I'm happy to use a private garden that's not overlooked, such as the discrete dungeon I occasionally visit in Berkshire, or if the sub has his own private land, but upsetting vanilla folk is not worth the risk otherwise.

Assuming the private space has been found, outdoor can be exhilarating, being with nature and feeling the sunshine (or more often than not in Britain- the wind in your face!)

Where outdoor play is possible, my favourite pastime has been to dress the slave up as a dog, with a dog mask and walk him on a leash on all fours.

Years ago I lived in a house that backed onto secluded fields and I also had an outhouse in the garden. My sub wanted to feel what it was like to be tied up and left somewhere, so I took him into the outhouse, had him strip off for me, then I bound his wrists and tethered them to a rafter in the ceiling. "I may be back in ten minutes, half an hour, or maybe sometime tomorrow," I teased as I tied off the rope. Then I sauntered out and back to the house where I got on with some emails. Half an hour later I returned (it wasn't the warmest of days and I do have a care of duty to keep my subs safe). He said the half an hour had felt more like two hours, but he found it exciting not knowing when I would return. He had struggled against the rope but due to the type of knot I used, it only tightened as he wriggled against it, creating more tension. In this moment he felt powerless and under my control entirely - his ultimate fantasy.

Lady R: What else can be more naughty and erotic than the thought of getting caught while fulfilling your ultimate fantasy outside. I had one slave in particular called Slave Dave who loved the thrill and enjoyed testing his boundaries. Slave Dave was always up for an outdoor session and this time in particular, it was in the middle of a cold winter. We met at my place before he jumped in my car and we headed out to the countryside. As soon as we arrived at the wooded area I placed a blindfold over his face and bound his hands together so he felt incredibly powerless. I then led him on a short walk towards the lake and found a suitable tree to tie him face first into. Hands bound round the tree I undid his trousers, dropping them to the floor and exposing his white flesh to the forest. I had brought a couple of implements with me including my trusted horse crop and immediately gave him 3 swift whips across his bare cheeks. As Dave squealed with excitement with his semi hard cock rubbing against the tree bark, I then told him to start humping the tree purely for my entertainment.

"I think you are getting a bit too excited now Dave, don't you?"

To which he let out a slight groan followed by a whimpering, "yes, Mistress".

"I will hand you ten more of my finest before you face the real punishment."

His body was convulsing violently between hits as the fresh crisp winter breeze hit his red sore ass cheeks. Only then, I decided it was time to face his final punishment. I untied him from the tree and ordered him to remove all remaining clothes apart from the blindfold before placing a dog collar round his neck and attaching it to a lead. Without any dialogue I led him over towards the icy lake and about a foot from the water I stopped before ordering him to continue. He let out a frightful shriek as the freezing water touched him bare feet and he realised his fate. I then ordered him to remove the blindfold and continue to walk into the lake until he reached above his hips. With each step I could tell the Slave was well and truly suffering between the panting and whimpers, after he had reached the required point, I then ordered him to do 10 star jumps for my pure amusement.

"Beg me to come out of the water then slave and I might let you have a reward."

I have never heard him shout "please Mistress" repetitively with so much passion before.

As I ordered him back out of the lake, I could tell he was slightly suffering but also enjoyed the experience. I picked up the lead and led him back to the tree for his reward, which was him playing with himself and finishing over the tree.

I think that day we took ice bathing to a new level.

Another fun way to have fun outdoors is in the summer in stinging nettle season. There is nothing more thrilling and painful than slapping a fresh bunch of stingers over a slave's ass, cock and balls. JUST MAKE SURE YOU WEAR GLOVES!

Chapter 9
Adult babies

Adult baby fun isn't always a sexual kink. Many adult babies love the feeling of returning to a time when life was much simpler, much in the same way your cat may be most relaxed when it reverts back to kittenhood and sits on your lap needing its paws back and forth. For some, dressing in a nappy and romper and being spoon fed is like slipping into a fantasy world of safety where their basic needs are catered for and they feel protected.

Kaz B: We touched briefly on this subject earlier and adult baby play or ADBL is often misunderstood due to the word 'baby' in the title. Someone into this tends to derive comfort from wearing a nappy - or diaper if you are American, maybe a Babygro and being fed milk or juice from a bottle. In my experience, I have not seen a sexual element to it and it's probably one of the most innocent fetishes I've encountered. I've had clients ask to call me Mummy, and as the play is not sexual, I'm happy to partake in the roleplay and provide the comfort they seek. I am by no means a specialist in this area and do not have my own nursery, but I have worked alongside specialists and have engaged in many role plays of this variety. A photographer I worked with many years ago ran a fan site and he would tell me how some of the subscribers loved diapers or some would prefer the plastic pants that go over the top. Some of the fans enjoyed dummy sucking and bottle feeding or playing with stickle bricks and stuffed teddies, it was all about a return to that place as safety they once remembered.

One thing that I do get asked to do a lot is dress the adult baby in a nappy and Babygro, being sure to pop talc on him first and then wrap him up in a blanket with a teddy and 'read a bedtime story.' The AB's will bring children's books about dragons or dinosaurs or talking animals and ask me to read to them, so putting on my softest voice, I read aloud the adventures within the pages and show them the pictures while they point to them and suck their thumb. Some might think an adult male wearing a diaper and sucking his thumb is preposterous, but if it's safe, consensual and makes someone feel comforted, who is anyone to judge this?

I used to regularly phone chat with an AB who would request bedtime stories before he went to sleep. I'd dig one of my favourite Oscar Wild tales for children and read it to him and he'd sleepily sigh, "thank you mummy" and fall asleep. One night, I said good night and hung up and 5 minutes later he called back, "Mummy, I heard a noise outside! I'm scared!" A strict Mummy came out that night and told him he was naughty and to go back to bed, although I did reassure him that it was windy outside and it was most likely a shed door banging or something blowing over he could hear.

Some might suspect that AB's might have lacked maternal love in their lives and are making up for a lost childhood but to the contrary, they are often seeking to re-experience that maternal love they experienced in youth, which made them feel happy and at peace. I often wonder if some of the hardest men in the world, who keep their feelings repressed, would benefit from showing their vulnerabilities a little more in a safe, trusted space. We all need to feel loved and cared for, whatever our sex. There is no such thing as too much kindness.

Interestingly, the segment from an ABDL fetishist in Story 19 of the kinkster stories (later in this book) contrasts with mine, so do have a look at that if ABDL is a kink that interests you.

Lady R: Before writing this chapter I had a discussion with my partner about Adult Baby Minding as he asked if it repulsed me now that I have children and have changed many dirty nappies, to which I replied "No". I still find the psychology behind such an act fascinating. When you go to the toilet and you wipe after a poo and some excrement might get on your hand by accident it makes you feel dirty and you have to wash your hands immediately? When you have skid marks in your fresh white boxers surely you change them immediately?

Now the gentlemen I see would get off on dirty hands and underwear, in fact they would definitely have a wank over the thought of soiled pants. Now the appointment I'm going to relive with you today The slave couldn't relieve himself while his nappy was soiled as I also put him in chastity during our session as Slave Baby B had an Adult baby minding fetish with a unique twist, Let me explain:

Baby B arranged his usual appointment on a Tuesday afternoon precisely at 3pm. When he arrived in his smart casual clothes you would not foresee what extreme kink was hiding in the black rucksack he had clutching his back. As he entered my playroom we began talking about the session he had in mind for the day. He wanted his usual mummy and baby play but he wanted to add laxatives, chastity and blackmail into the agenda.

We started the session with Baby B undressing and lying on the bed with his legs and bum in the air ready for his nappy to be popped on. As I placed the huge, thick white nappy in front of his bottom he started wiggling like a baby would making cooing noises.

"Stay still for mummy Baby B, we don't want a leaky nappy now do we?" I soothed as I frantically scampered around him to fix the nappy in place.

Baby B just giggled as he knew what difficulties he was causing acting up.

After the nappy was finally in place we then went on to a cuddle where Baby B jumped on my lap and cuddled me tight as a baby would. Now this part was what I consider quite innocent but what's to come might be considered more sinister.

I disappeared to the bathroom and came back with a glass of

water and the laxatives. The game Baby B wanted to play now entailed me choosing a random and unknown to him number of laxatives out of the pack and to force feed them to him, put him in chastity which required a code to release and send him home to soil himself while messaging me begging for the code over the next 12 hours. He wanted to soil himself but not only that he wanted to be in great pain while doing so.

So out of the pack of 12 laxatives I choose 6. I enter my playroom hiding the pills and ram them into his mouth and force him to drink the water and swallow. Step one complete. I then grab a black bin liner and place it over his nappy to avoid leakage through the night and secure that in pace with Gaffer tape, followed by the chastity. Now this chastity isn't like a penis shape one that we discussed in the chastity chapter this one in particular goes over your thighs and secures round your waist and the lock is coded with 4 numbers which of course I set without Baby B seeing the code.

Baby B then dressed in his "normal clothes" to go home, now I'm not going to lie, you could see the bulge of his nappy bursting over his jeans. Not as discreet as one may think but nevertheless he headed home to wait for his shitty fate.

At around 11pm that evening I received the first message from him describing the stomach cramps he was enduring to which I responded with a simple text. Stop moaning.

At midnight, the shit storm arrived and he started the begging messages for the code. Of course we had briefed about this happening and him begging before the morning and I was "under no circumstances" allowed to release him of his painful ordeal. He still hadn't used his safeword and this seemed like the perfect opportunity to slip between my satin sheets and head off to dreamland and enjoy the pure indulgence of my comfy bed while the slave suffered all night.

I woke up to a string of messages getting increasingly desperate for the code.

These were some of the messages he sent me.

"Oh no it's coming!"

"I'm in agony!"

"Please, you're such a cruel Mistress!"

"Arrgh the shit is leaking out and coming down my leg!"

"It's gone all over my wife's side of the bed and is flowing down! She'll divorce me if I don't clean up before she gets back!"

The texts were increasingly graphic and I can only be grateful for the fact he didn't follow up with photos!

After my morning coffee, I decided it was time to release him of his agony which was a simple - 1234! Surely, you'd think most desperate people would have tried this. The only thing that might stop them would be if there was a mechanism that would chop their dick off if they got it wrong. However, it was a simple device and he could have relieved himself of his agony at any point, which is laughable.

His wife was due home the following evening, so luckily for him he managed to get himself cleaned up and burn the evidence before she arrived.

Afterwards, he text me various times to re-book but our diaries never coincided. I wondered if he found someone else crazy enough to relive the experience.

Chapter 10
Discipline

Kaz B: Discipline is such a broad term but defines punishing your slave in some way for failing to meet your standards. It can also refer to using correctional behaviour to rid one's sub of unwanted habits, such as being demanding, touching or any other unacceptable behaviour.

When should discipline be used?

This is the Mistresses choice, but I would advise during moments the sub is not paying attention, failing to carry out a task to the best of his or her ability or displaying negative behaviour.

What methods are used for discipline?

There are multiple methods that can be used. Here are a few:

Physical punishment - which could be from impact play using a paddle, whip or preferred implements or device, a stress position such as holding a squat or a series of hard exercises such as star jumps.

Humiliation and dehumanising - for a length of time the sub is not allowed to speak, must stand in the naughty corner with his hands on his head or only drink from a dog bowl on the floor, for example.

Ignoring - speaks for itself, leave your sub to his or her own devices and refuse interaction, then allow them a chance to apologise, ensuring they know why they are apologising, what they did wrong and how they will take steps to avoid negative behaviours in future.

I speak of these all in a consensual domme/sub dynamic. Do not use these on your significant other unless you are in a consensual BDSM relationship. It will just make you a horrible person and you'll probably end up dying alone.

Many of these methods can often be pleasurable for a sub that's into pain play or humiliation so if it's a punishment you are administering, obviously you will choose a kink that they do not like (such as a stress position) rather than something that thrills them. Otherwise you're simply rewarding bad behaviour.

Discipline sessions go hand in hand with training and can be used in a positive way to elicit the best response from the sub. For example, the sub may love foot worship but part of their training and discipline requires certain practices to ensure they have deserved this treat. It could be as simple as crawling along the floor on a leash at your heel patiently or include elements of BDSM to teach the sub patience and appreciation for receiving his kink.

There's not been many occasions where I have had to severely discipline a sub physically. I'm fond of the phrase - you can catch more flies with honey than vinegar and it's usually the case. We are talking punishments here and not standard kink play.

There was an occasion once when I stood over a slave on the floor to dominate him and he quickly reached up my skirt to try and touch my knickers. My reflexes were on form and didn't disappoint. A lovely bamboo cane swiftly struck across the back of his knuckles ensured a swift apology and that this intolerable behaviour was never repeated.

Generally it's cheeky comments that I need to rectify - requesting to touch off limit areas of my body or general back-chat. If close to hand, the tip of a riding crop thwacked against a delicate nipple or the tip of his penis works wonders. If I'm feeling more devilish, sometimes I'll pretend to let it slide until they've forgotten about it, then I'll bring out the big guns! By guns, Obviously I don't mean firearms, but it will be one of my wonderful kink gadgets that will have their eyes popping wide as they regret them and their big mouth! Depending on the sub and situation, it could be an electric prod, a multi-pinwheel or in more extreme scenarios - the ball crusher! This is two clear Perspex rectangles with a hall in the middle for the cock and balls and attached by 4 cogs, one in each corner. Once his crown jewels are popped through, the screws are twisted, tightening the two layers of Perspex to achieve a 'crushing' effect. Some subs have a huge kink for this and I call it pancaking, when you tighten the device and the balls start to resemble a little pancake. Once the screws are loosened and the pressure released, the testicles bounce back to their usual shape. Unless the sub has balls like Donkey Kong this shouldn't cause damage, although it might make them think a little about their loose tongue and how to use it more wisely in future.

Lady R: One of my first appointments as a baby-dom was a discipline session. I didn't have a clue how to be the bossy queen I was going to manifest into and it certainly did not come naturally to my friendly nature to begin with. I would hype myself up outside the playroom door by thinking of angry thoughts, such as my cheating ex-boyfriend before I entered and began to inflict my strict torture to the slave. I always used to love the phrase, "fake it till you make it!" and certainly put that into practice on several occasions.

In my experience most discipline sessions start with role play, the most popular that springs to mind is headmistress and naughty school boy. The scenario would start with myself dressed in a tight, white shirt with a latex, pencil skirt and heels, and the sub/slave dressed in a short sleeved shirt with shorts, striped tie and a peaked cap. I would set up my desk in the playroom with a cane lying perfectly across the edge and any paddles I might use for the session.

I would have the slave waiting in my makeshift "headmistress's office" for a good 5 minutes after the session was due to start, to cause fear and anticipation of what was to come!

I enter the room after hyping myself up behind the closed

door and position myself behind the desk with the slave standing in front of it.

"So why have you been sent to my office today Timothy?"

To which Timothy meekly replied, "I got caught looking up the older girls skirts" (this honestly was the most common response)

"Good gosh Timothy, have you not learnt from the last time you were in this office? This is vile and disgusting and therefore you must be punished! Now bend over my desk while you receive 10 of my best"

The Slave would always be aroused by the time I had pulled his shorts around his ankles and revealed his hairy, sweat dripping, flabby ass. I would always prefer to start with the paddle for the warm up, so after the 10 slaps I would proceed to ask him if he was going to look up any of the other girls skirts, to which 9 times out of ten they would say they would not again but that was never the end of the punishment. I would hand the slave a pen and paper and instruct them to write lines. 100 of them!

I WILL NOT LOOK UP GIRLS SKIRTS MISTRESS.

After their hands were exhausted by the lines, I would get them to lay them flat on the desk, pull my cane high and give them a further 10 across the knuckles. I would sometimes get seriously cheeky clients who would answer back and talk when not spoken too. Of course, these little fuckers got more punishment, so after another 10 canings across each ass cheek leaving a bright red stripe with each swipe, I would remove their socks and start caning the soles of each foot, which I heard is one of the most painful areas to cane due to its sensitivity. Most slaves would pant and jolt with each swipe of the cane hitting their cold flesh. Roleplays are different from an average session. There is almost a dance between the Mistress and slave whereby the slave starts to show signs of struggling with his torment. Without asking, the mistress must determine if he has reached his limit. I would often frown and in a strict voice say, have you learned your lesson now. Their response would give me an answer. For example, they might say "yeah." Which would lead to another ten strikes of the cane but if they said, "yes Mistress," and followed this up with an apology, I knew that they had received enough punishment. After me and the slave had finished our game of cat and mouse and I thought they had enough, I would usually get the naughty school boy to pick up his socks and wank his cock into it until he came. If they were particularly naughty, I would make them wear the squelching sock home.

I would always feel after the appointment that I had let out all my pent up anger from the week including the amount of time wasters and crappy excuses I had heard over the phone.

I almost saw it as anger management therapy, so for that reason I do believe it may be considered a nice release for both parties. Slave gets his discipline and I get to show off my latex pencil skirt.

Chapter 11
Gynoid fetish

Kaz B: A gynoid refers to a female android and there is a sub-sect of submissives who enjoy roleplaying within the realms of gynoid fantasy.

What aspects of the gynoid kink appeal to submissives?

Each sub has their own personal take on gynoid play. It can simply act as if one is a robot, speaking in a monotone that would suggest one is a form of artificial intelligence, making robotic movements or delving deeper into role plays that involve the gynoid being part of an organisation, often with corruption and transhumanism at the helm. It's one of the more unusual kinks and one that I love to role play with subs personally.

One of my favourite experiences was opening wrapping a sub torso with wrap tape, putting him into a large cardboard box with bubble wrap (to protect his casing and circuitry) and 'sealing it' while ensuring there were air holes. I then 'find' the box freshly delivered to my factory and unwrap my slave. Usually I am an evil scientist, a half human, half borg hybrid. I then subject my subject to a series of rigorous scientific tests to ensure his casing and controls are fully functional and his software is up to date and that his protocol is compliant. I test his airways, cavities and cyber skin using a range of 'tests' such as face-sitting, probes, flashlights in his receptacles and orifices, including the mouth and testing his waterproof skin with watersports. I love to ad-lib, so after the gynoid passes the test I often *recruit* them as one of my drones in an evil bid to take over the planet with my army of advanced AI bots. I'm not going to tell you all of my secret intelligence but let's just say one evil mastermind of a plan is AI mosquitos which come out of the gynoid who is activated for the assignment when he is in the designated area and ready for the cyber wars to begin!

If you enjoy this topic, you'll love the Human tellers story on this later in the book.

Chapter 12
FLR verses femdom

FLR means - female lead relationship. This means that the female makes a lot of decisions in the relationship and may control some of the finances. Sometimes BDSM may be an element in the relationship, but it's not compulsory. An FLR may centre around BDSM, but sometimes it can be more to do with the dynamic of power in the relationship and how that is split between their partner, with the female being the dominant force. This harks back to matriarchal cultures where the woman is in charge. So as not to get too far off topic, some good examples of these can be found online.

On the flipside - femdom is female domination which is centred around BDSM and kink. Depending on the domme/sub dynamic the sub may get some say and get to choose some of the play experience, although in some relationships, this may be less prevalent. Some Mistresses would say a sub having input is him trying to 'top from the bottom.' It really does depend on the dynamic and what sort of domme you are.

Kaz B: Some dommes, like myself, enjoy reading subs likes and creating a play session while incorporating some of them. For some dommes this is a strict no no and it's all on the Mistresses terms. For me, variety is the spice of life and I love the fact they are always guessing what I may or may not include from their list.

Femdom, I love a series of play sessions. FLR I'm not 100% sure on in my personal life. A relationship is about discussion and agreement and yes, there are certain aspects I could certainly enjoy such as the man doing the cooking, cleaning and tending to my needs, running me baths, there are certain aspects of traditional relationships I enjoy too. For one, dominating someone around the clock, every single day would turn something I enjoy into a chore. I'd find myself telling them to use their initiative and growing tired of making all of the decisions... I prefer to keep these things for my play time with my subs. Is it possible that too much of a good thing can be bad? I'm not sure I want to find out.

Chapter 13
Puppy play

Human puppy play is when an individual takes on the characteristics of a dog or puppy. This can include but is not limited to wearing hoods that resemble a dogs head, running round on all fours, displaying dog like behaviour such as barking, begging, chasing their tail, or playing fetch. Often the pups will have a *handler*, a person who instructs the pup and trains them. Pups are expected to be obedient and carry out their handlers instructions, although as we know, all pups in life can sometimes get a little bit over excited and not listen to instructions!

Kaz B: Human puppy play emerged onto the leather/gay scene initially and was a much smaller community than it was today. Nowadays, there is less association with LGBTQIA groups but pups can be any sexual orientation. Human pups are predominantly male although I have met one female pup who visits fetish events where she can dress, and roam…or crawl freely and express her inner puppy. Although I have yet to see a human pup event, I am informed that the pups play with one another, run around, play tug-a-war & interact on a non-sexual level. Sometimes they may gently pull at a play partner's clothes, mimicking a dog and the play partner may do this back or growl to chase them off whimpering. If the pup has a handler, he or she will keep an eye out for any issues or bad behaviour and will keep their pup under control.

For some reason puppy play is a kink that I've been asked

for many times in domme sessions and I would say 99% of the time it's not even covertly sexual, in fact it's a safe way to experiment with submission and training if whips and chains seem overwhelming. I employ similar training methods during a pup session as I would with my regular subs, although I tend to use a slightly more upbeat, and animated voice, especially for good behaviour. Pup play isn't just about degradation, although that can be part of it. It's also about letting your inner animal run wild, behaving in a way you normally wouldn't and allowing yourself to run awash with a sense of freedom that only animals can have. We are a nation of dog lovers. They are associated with loyalty, devotion and a sense of joy. There's nothing like the feeling of a dog running up to you in the park, its tail wagging in greeting, and part of pup play is that feeling of playfulness and fun.

The average human pup could be naked like a regular slave, or they might wish to dress in accessories or clothing that enhances the role play such as hoods, harnesses, paw-like gloves or collars and leashes.

Three requirements I have of my pups are - that they always wag their tail for their Mistress in greeting or if I am instructing them. This consists of them waggling their bottom excitedly from side to side and sometimes panting. I require that they sit up into the beg position if offered a tasty treat such as a sweet (luckily humans have a broader diet than dogs) and they should listen carefully to all of my instructions and carry them out to the best of their ability.

My most memorable session was with two human pups. Both subs were open minded, enjoyed humiliation play and were keen to please their Mistress by following my instructions. I had the pups sit side by side and taught them various commands - sit, roll over, beg, bark and fetch. The pups followed my instruction exactly and did a great job of following my commands which varied between a slew and a fast pace. Next they were encouraged to sniff each other's bottoms , as dogs do. I didn't even try to keep a straight face for this. Humiliation play does amuse me and I make no secret of this and I cracked up watching two subs carry out my request. "I love your wicked giggler," one of the subs grinned, appreciating how entertained I was by the session.

This was all too easy for them so I threw in some challenges in a competition to see who the best dog was. They would complete an obstacle course each, picking up dog toys and popping them into their baskets, crawl through and round hoops (not dissimilar from Crufts) and then return to me, roll over, play did and then return to the sitting position, while proffering a paw. Those subs did not disappoint! Watching them in their haste to win was hilariously brilliant and I clapped and shouted words of encouragement to the two. This egged them on and they stepped up their game, eager for their prize. They bumped into one another, tried to push the others balls and toys out of the way to slow their opponent down and use some downright dirty tactics.

They performed so well it was hard to pick a winner based on style, technique and innovation. I rewarded them both with a sweet then said the one who could make me laugh the loudest would win the bulk of the sweets. One of the slaves chased his tail, cocked his leg and pretended to pee, sniffed the other pup's bottom then pretended to play dead as a result. The other pup dragged his butt along the floor as dogs do when they have an itchy butt (they were dressed so I didn't mind) and then he hopped onto the other pups leg and dry humped it (this kind of contact was formerly agreed before the session began, as it always should be). I was roaring at both! Who would win the pissing, butt sniffer who passed out? Or the dirty leg humper with the itchy butt? There was no way I could choose between the two performances and so the treats were shared out to two happy human pups.

My example of a pup session is in places unique to the style I encourage, although many human pup styles may vary from this and there is no right or wrong way to be a human pup. If you are keen to try I would suggest you leave your inhibitions at the door, keep an open mind and don't take it too seriously. Human pup play should be a fun activity that allows for behaviour which is at times carefree, and other times an exercise in discipline.

Lady R: Who doesn't love a cute fluffy obedient puppy to play with?

Well it depends if the puppy is mischievous and untrained. I particularly enjoy a long session with a naughty sub puppy who is in desperate need of training. For the new clients I always instruct that they bring a new collar and lead to the appointment for me to officially own them but before which I always make sure they are up for the challenge by getting them to perform a few simple tasks like sit, roll over and bark. Simple right? Well that all depends on whether your sub secretly wants to be trained or enjoys playing up just to get a punishment.

You can have so much fun in the session with tasks such as walking (crawling) on the lead, playing fetch (with dildos of course) or of course feeding time. Which can involve all kinds of food or drink some of my favourites are:

Soft food like trifle or custard

Actual dog/cat food

My pee or spit

Or my personal favourite punishment if they are really naughty, their own cock juice.

One of my puppy slaves would want to be in character from the second he arrived, so from the moment I opened the door he would crouch down on all fours and start crawling into my living room ready for my next instructions which would usually be the standard commands followed by some light petting with my spanking paddle on his bottom, but this slave also had a rather unique fetish which I was happy to assist with. Puppy toilet training. So after his usual puppy play and feed time I would let him out in my back garden to run (crawl) around before he would cock his leg on one of my bushes and take a pee or squat down and take a poo on my lawn. Luckily, my house is not overlooked and yes I did make him scoop it up with a poop bag after the appointment. There is nothing quite like the sight of a fully grown man crawling round the back garden on all fours and taking a massive shit.

Punishment involved in puppy play should only be applied if that is what the sub is interested in as not all puppies want the sadistic twist, some just want to play all cute and fluffy, so like with all sessions make sure your subject comes to you with a list of their likes and dislikes and a brief description of how the envision the session to go to avoid any disappointment.

Chapter 14
Whipping

Whipping is popular in the BDSM community. Because pain releases certain endorphins, many people use painful sex toys like whips to intensify sexual pleasure. There are a vast variety of whips available on today's market including floggers, crops, paddles and the historical favourite cat o' nine tails.

Kaz B: By no means would I describe myself as a sadist, yet there is something so satisfying about holding a beautiful, handcrafted leather flogger in your hand, feeling the weight of it as you swing it through the air. The sub's anticipation builds and you see a muscle quiver in their buttock as they brace, awaiting the impact. As the whip lashes down on the flesh, delivering a delicious sting, they may flinch, yelp or even moan softly, and yet they crave more.

It's a great feeling of mutual trust, when your sub hands over their power, submits and trusts you to deliver the stinging blows to a level you feel they are capable of.

Some Mistresses are sadistic and will push hard, others may go lightly. Unless I am with an absolute pain junkie, I'll often opt for the Goldilocks zone of whipping, not too soft, not too hard, it's just right! How do you know it's just right though? Elementary my dear Watson! Elementary meaning - testing the waters and building up the intensity, until the slave starts to show signs of stress or surges of adrenaline. Some subs might play up and be overly dramatic, so I always assess from their baseline and how they react to a series of tests to assess their pain threshold, or in this case - whipability!

A spanking bench is my preferred place to bend a slave over. I have one at home. It's a bespoke piece, hand made by creative fingers, a soft pink leather covering the top. It's sturdy with adjustable legs, so I can lower the sub or level them up if I'm wearing particularly high heeled boots. Underneath is a beautiful row of LED fairy lights to add a touch of charming glamour.

Once they are laid across the bench, their arms falling down in front, I may strap them done and deliver a series of strikes with my flogger. If engaging in heavier impact play, I always warm up the buttocks with a hand spanking, trailing long fingernails across the flesh of their rump. I like to take my time. It's not a race for me, it's a leisurely stroll, with a keen sprint at the end to keep them on their toes!

The bizarre thing is as a Mistress you can see trends changing over the years. When I started, impact play usually went hand in hand with latex wearing slaves in gimp masks and ball gags, or sometimes a Headmistress role play in which they would face punishment for acting like an unruly pupil. Nowadays, many men who call themselves sissies enjoy impact play, in fact it's become popular amongst men of all ages.

Quite possibly the most unusual whipping session I've participated in was with another domme many years ago. We sessioned from an exquisite dungeon space in the countryside where there was nothing but rolling meadows for miles. Inside the old stone dungeon, it was warm and cosy. It felt so homely with the gentle roar of the fire in the hearth, its golden flames flickering upwards. I can still picture the blue gingham tablecloth over an old oak table. Apart from the array of equipment it resembled a country cottage and I could picture pots of assorted James and steaming mugs of tea. An unusual setting for what was about to take place.

The sub, we'll call him Matthew, had several kinks which he enjoyed to an extreme level. To start we stripped him bare and then attached around 60 or more pegs to his cock and balls. There were no gaps of flesh left unpegged. A warm bowl of wax was poured across each single peg and he was left waiting with his hands on his head until the wax set rock solid.

This in itself might be an extreme concept for some of my subs but Matthew was a self-confessed masochist. With our help, he stepped into a tight, shining black, rubber catsuit, which zipped up all the way to the neck. He was ready. Now we would whip his crotch until the pegs started to loosen.

Peg games are not to be confused with pegging which is strap-on sex on a man. It's hilarious how many guys have asked for pegging by mistake and then turned white when I pull out a strap-on! Mind you, some of them said in for a penny in for a pound - no pun intended!

If you have never witnessed peg games, you might not realise that if a peg is struck by force and does not come off, the plastic can slip apart a centimetre or so and pinches the skin. Now add to this the fact that the pegs would not slip right off easily, there would be a lot of pinching going on.

First he was thoroughly whipped with the latex suit on and while he felt the impact, the suit did fairly well to hold the pegs in place. His fate became worse when the suit was removed. The wax had set hard, so harder strikes were needed and still some of the pegs simply shifted around, pinching and biting and his dangly bits. As more pegs pinged off, our array of whips and crops sought to find bare expanses of flash which had him grimacing, teeth clench tight, eyes screwed up. Still, the slave did not use his safe word. A few full pelt strikes were needed to remove the pegs and this took some time. Slave seemed to reel between agony and ecstasy, not complaining once, thanking us for our perseverance. The endorphins had kicked in and he was experiencing a surge of adrenaline throughout his system. His knees were bent and the muscles in his legs shook, yet he straightened himself up after each blow.

Eventually, all the pegs were scattered on the hard, stone floor along with chunks of pink candle wax. Slaves nethers were lobster red with splatterings of blue that circled across his skin.

That day the cosy cottage had become our chamber of torture, two grinning Mistresses dishing out hearty servings of punishment to a slave full of gratitude.

Lady R: So for this chapter, I thought I would give 2 different examples of my experience with using the whip for pain and pleasure.

One of my favourite clients who came in for just a whipping service was known as the Punish Train Guy on my phone, due to the fact that he loved talking about trains as he was a keen trainspotter and all he wanted was whipping for the hour appointment. It was like I was playing a game of tennis with the constant whipping action.

PTG would bring a selection of around 12 paddles and whips, most were made with hard brown leather with a vintage look and some would have sharp pointy spikes on the end. It's quite rare and refreshing for a client to bring his own equipment as although I am fully equipped, some slaves have been visiting mistresses for such a long time that they built their own collection, which saves us ladies playing the guessing game of what the client likes and can handle. Now PTG was by far one of the most extreme customers when it came to whipping.

His objective was to be whipped on the bottom only and as hard as I could swing my arms, hence the reference to a game of tennis. When he arrived he would lay all of his paddles and whips out on the bed from small to large and pull his trousers and pants off ready for his punishment. There would be no warm up for PTG, just straight to the beating! The only condition was that if he started bleeding, I had to stop immediately, so I would simply pick up the smallest paddle and give ten of my finest. This was unlike most whipping appointments which are combined with roleplay or punishment. For example, the conversation was natural and matter of fact and how you would talk to a friend who had popped around for a coffee, exchanging pleasantries, while I reached my arm back as far as it would go and put my full force behind it as the whip lashed down. After every 15 - 20 lashes with one whip, I would change the implement to the next bigger size. All the while he was talking about the latest trainspotting escapades he'd been on and more often than not, he requested that a camera would be trained on his arse no pun intended. This was so he could enjoy the content at a later date of the red stripes and welts suddenly appearing across his cheeks.

When it came to impact play, PTG always wanted the session to be extreme. He loved to be left with welts and bruising and not to be able to sit down properly for days. This was a fond reminder of the session for him for a few days afterwards. The slave never once touched his penis during the session, so I can only imagine that when he went home a full on masturbatory session ensued while watching the content back.

If ever the session dragged on, after the hour was up then I would select a thinner implement to strike him with which would cause a graze on his buttocks. I knew this would be the point he'd want to finish the session until next time, because the only condition was that he didn't want to bleed profusely as he had a mild phobia of blood. If a spot of blood did appear, he would nip to the bathroom for 5 minutes to tend to it before getting dressed and leaving, acting embarrassed as he did so. Now this was really a one off appointment as normally the client would want roleplay or other activities involved in the session and to have someone who purely wants to come in and be whipped within an inch of their life while talking about bloody trains is unheard of…

The second session that really sticks out is - let's just say - a bit more eccentric, and which also covers every other activity in the book, which brings me to my client Toby.

Toby was by far the most extreme client I ever met. Literally anything goes in the appointment. He would bring his own leather body bag, which you will find more details about in the bondage and restriction section of the book. He would want everything including pegging, electrics, nipple clamping, CBT and best of all to be left alone in his body bag unable to see or speak for hours on end. Now, let's get back to the whipping! Toby was one of my first clients and he helped me build up my kit, which as a new starting domme was   handy! He bought me my first ever crop and I would whip each part of his body with it, paying particular attention to his arse, cock and balls. He built up a tolerance to the riding crop quickly and soon he bought a selection of canes and a leather bullwhip so he could experience greater levels of pain play.

The sheer level of pain that Toby could endure was not what other slaves would generally ask for. He would book 6 hour sessions on average and he wanted in his words, "to not be able to sit down" until our next meeting. I would always start the session off with slightly lighter spanks and strokes but build up to full blown whacks with all my effort, he would wince with his eyes and body gesticulation but wouldn't be able to make a sound with the ball gag firmly placed in his gob. Basically Toby was an extreme and experienced sub with a high pain threshold.

Never would I advise anyone reading this book and curious to experiment with an implement to go full force with pain, neither would I advise anyone to use a ball gag as its important to communicate during your playtime especially if it is your first time you NEED to be able to know the consent of your sub is approved and enjoyed.

Aim for the chunky/flabby/meaty bits on the bottom, start with a paddle or just your hand and between strikes ask the sub if it is OK.

Happy Playtime!

Chapter 15
Fisting

Fisting refers to the act of slowly inserting a fist into the rectum. Gloves should be worn for hygiene purposes, plenty of lube administered and a slow process should ensue, then begins with one finger, then two, gently filling the area and testing its capacity to discover whether a full insertion of the fist is possible. If not, it should never be forced as this can cause anal fissures.

Kaz B: Fisting isn't top of my list of kinks, I prefer implements but I've had various experiences of performing this on submissives. . The first person I fisted was a porn star and it was her party piece. We were on the set of a popular tv station and she grabbed my wrist and pulled it inside herself. As I wasn't expecting this, I had no gloves on and if I'm honest the experience of having an entire bare mitt in someone's vijaya did cause me to quietly heave. It was not a pleasant feeling and akin to shoving your paws into a nest of violent slugs, all squeezing around your hand and jostling. There's also the added side effect that your hand looks like a jelly fish has committed suicide and bashed itself to death on your hand.

On another occasion she pushed my foot inside, so if inserting a fist is called fisting, is inserting a foot called footing? Can you say in any saucy conversation, "Oh yes I gave her a good footing!" "What, you gave her a bunk up?" "No, a footing, ya know? Oh never mind!"

There's quite a difference however between fisting a woman and a man. If the thought of withdrawing your mitts from a lady's secret garden without a glove leaves you feeling queasy, then you will most definitely want some nice strong latex gloves for a rectum, it can get a little gruesome, even if they have had an enema beforehand.

The most unusual experience I've encountered with regards to fisting is double fisting a slave with a dominatrix called Miss Bailey. The sub was a diehard fisting fanatic, so much his slave name was a tribute to his fetish. Obviously, I can't give that away unless he is still on the circuit but for example, his name could be something like Ringo - to say, 'go in my ring'.

Miss Bailey was first to don the gloves and slide a couple of slender digits. There's quite an art to double fisting and you not only have to navigate and analyse the space/time continuum of his back package but you must also navigate your way around each other's hand. After taking it in turns to slide in digits from opposing hands to each other, we formed a prayer symbol between our two hands. There was nothing symbolic in this, it's merely the best position to slide two hands in. Once the 8 digits are inside, you can work them in symbiosis to warm up and stretch the area until it is ready for a deeper probe. Next the thumbs pop in and this is where it starts to become a little more tricky, you need to curl your fingers to form a fist shape. It helps to butterfly the fingers a little, fluttering them around until there is enough room to curl them. Finally, after much wriggling of our fingers and getting stuck against each other's digits, we managed to form a fist, much to the joy of our sub who finally got to tick this off his kink list, having been wanting to try this for a long time.

Fisting is the strangest sensation, especially when their muscles contract. You can feel them closing tightly around your hand and you wonder for a fleeting second if your fingers will be crushed. Also the temperature around your hand soars and all you can dream of is ice water. I think all these irrational fears of crushing and heat exhaustion is probably why it's not at the top of my list, plus there's always the fear that if the sub follows through, it will be all over your gloves!

Lady R: My first experience with the art of fisting was one of extreme measures. I had never done the act before and perhaps I was in over my head when a gentleman called for an appointment insisting he required my hand shoved up his ass and asking if I had done it before. I had in fact only ever placed 3 fingers max in someone's sphincter prior to this appointment, so I was definitely a novice. But due to the lack of clients that week being the school holidays I told a little white (brown) lie and thought to myself how hard can it really be to fist someone?

Slave T promptly arrived ready for his session with a bag of goodies which included a massive tube of lube, disposable blue polythene gauntlets (to the shoulder gloves) and a large tub of lard. As he sat on the end of the bed shuffling we discussed how the performance would proceed and his safe word which was of course "red" if he could not take anymore.

Now I have to mention before we begin that I do not have petite hands. I have been told over the years I have hands like shovels and make some men look smaller than usual if they are not aroused.

Slave T undressed and got onto all fours on the end of my bed while I pulled the gloves up to my armpits, lathered my fingers in lube and made my way towards his chocolate starfish.

One finger inserted with absolute ease I didn't muck around and jumped straight to 3 digits working his anus round in a circular motion to open him up before i inserted my pinkie inside, now at this point it felt if the lube was drying up and he wanted to be filled more so Slave T insisted that I bring the lard into the mix, So i pulled my fingers out carefully and opened the jar of lard that you would under normal circumstances expect to find beside the oven Christmas day to lather the turkey, and smothered my fingers and knuckles in the product before positioning my fingers into a pointing position and this time tucking my thumb in nestling them together, and inserted middle finger first my entire hand into his anus stopping shy of my wrist. Slave T didn't even flinch so I could tell this wasn't his first rodeo.

Now while inside I formed into the fist position and slowly started to pull and push rocking the fucking motion with my arm while adding more lube and lard outside to get in a little deeper each time.

With a nice fucking rhythm in play I assumed this was a successful fisting session until slave T insisted I go deeper.

"Can you go to your elbow, Mistress?" he barked abruptly.

Shocked at the thought of going much deeper, I replied "I can slave but is that safe?".

"Yes Miss, I have had other Mistresses put their entire arm inside of me, in fact I would like you to try that today."

Taken aback by how demanding Slave T was during a dom/sub session and also a little curious at the same time, I thought why not in for a penny and all that jazz.

I lathered my entire arm in copious amounts of lard and lube and proceeded to slowly push my arm into his hole. With each extra inch of me inside of him I could feel what I can only assume is flaps of skin passing my hand as I'm navigating through his ass and diving deep into his stomach. By this point I'm only half way until my elbow but it feels so alien and intrusive but Slave T is absolutely loving this!

I started to feel queasy the closer I got to my elbow retching at each centimetre of my body disappearing into his asshole, passing more and more flaps of skin believing I must be passing into his stomach by now. Just as I thought we had reached his limit Slave T bellowed "deeper mistress, deeper". He wanted my entire arm up his ass!

This is not the fisting session I had in mind or even mildly similar to anything I had seen on porn sites, more like delivering a cow, so I told Slave T politely that if I carried on much deeper my hand would simply pop out of his mouth, I had reached my limit and that to continue I would pull out a little more and so this act as seen on the internet, a fist going in and out of someone's asshole in a fucking motion. Slave T seemed rather disappointed that I wasn't prepared to be a veterinarian performing the calving procedure this particular day but agreed to a heavy but short fist fucking while he played with his cock. After a few minutes of my fist thrusting and his personal wank up front he let out the highest pitched cum while twitching to finish. Job done.

Lesson to anyone looking to try fisting for the first time, do your research before trying the act and make sure you and the fister have good communication prior.

Chapter 16
Slave Training and discipline anecdotes

Submissives need to be disciplined at times for various reasons. This could be to enforce the message that the dominant party holds the power if the sub is trying to top from the bottom, or it could be to train bad habits out of them or even to punish bad behaviour and instil the message that it is not acceptable for a submissive to behave this way. While a sub may have certain likes and limits, it is not for him to control each   aspect of the session. When playing with a kinkster, a domme might be more inclined to allow a greater number of requests to be met. A submissive however should be concerned with pleasing his Mistress and attending to her needs equally, whether this be giving a foot rub, making cups of tea or running errands and buying gifts. If the sub should forget his place and step out of line with his behaviour or comments, discipline is a necessary component of a healthy D/S relationship. The punishment should be something the sub doesn't enjoy though it should never be a hard limit. It could be a verbal or physical punishment or something mundane such as writing lines, which will bring the sub no pleasure to do.

Kaz B: My Slave had been a very, very naughty little chappie. I told him to bring a list of reasons why he should be punished. If I didn't think he was telling the truth, I would beat him. If I thought he was telling the truth, I'd beat him. It was pretty much a lose-lose situation for him to be honest.

He decided that honesty was in fact the best policy – good boy – and brought his list along. This is how it read:

Looking at explicit photos on the internet.

1. Wanking over explicit photos on the internet without Mistress's permission.

2. Trying to look up women's skirts on the tube.

3. Lying to Mistress last week about looking at pictures on the net.

4. Squealing like a bitch boy when the Mistress punished me last.

5. Dressing up in my flatmates knickers when she was out.

6. Being cocky and not addressing my Mistress properly last time.

7. Failing to please my Mistress

8. Being a useless specimen of the male species as pointed out by Mistress

9. Not putting in a 100% and doing my best.

Oh dear, oh dear. Little Twinkle Toes was in very, very big trouble indeed it seemed.

He arrived and I politely asked him to sit. "I think it's time you and I had a little chat." I said slowly.

"Have you brought me what I requested?"

He proffered a list with shaking hands. He always knew he was in big trouble when I was calm and focussed. He wiped a bead of perspiration from his brow with a trembling hand

"Mistress, permission to speak"

"Granted my little cupcake." I commanded, tossing a lock of hair behind my shoulder.

"I have brought you a gift, Mistress. I hope it doesn't disappoint you too much."

"Why, that is very, very gracious of you." I said, "It was very, very considerate of you to bring me a little present." I tossed aside the chocolates without looking at them.

"Now, on to more pressing matters." I pondered the list before me. Then I looked up and smiled. He seemed to exhale a breath of relief and I slapped him across the chops twice, wiping off the smile that had begun to form on his face.

"Now sit and wait. " I told him as I left the room to fetch water.

Upon my return the little bleeder was smoking. A prohibited act that I had forbidden him the privilege of.

"Looks like you left something off the list Twinkle Toes." I took the cigarette from his shaking hands and stubbed it out on the leg of his jeans. He shrieked loudly.

"Next time it will be straight onto the flesh" I warned.

"Understood Mistress!"

"Now my little ray of sunshine. Strip naked for me." He took off his clothes and I proceeded to empty a bottle of vodka over them. In fact it was water but my bitch boy did not know this.

"I'm popping these in a steel can in the kitchen. If you disappoint me in this session I will throw a match in with them and you will have to go home in one of my tiny miniskirts, a crop top and a thong. Understood?"

"No please, Mistress!' I slapped him hard across the face. "Sorry Twinkle Toes, I didn't hear you. Say that again.."

"Nothing Mistress!"

I left the room with the clothes and hung them to dry on the radiator. Then I lit a match and blew it out.

I returned to the room with the smoking match and breathed a sigh of satisfaction. He looked like he was about to soil himself. I love to mess with their minds sometimes. The silly billy was clearing envisaging his clothes roaring in a fury of flames. At least that's what his face told me.

"Don't worry Twinks, be a good little boy for me and everything will be hunky dory."

Grabbing his hair, I forced him to his knees then popped a ball gag in his mouth and tightened it. One swift push and he was on all fours.

"Twinks. I need some good quality entertainment. Today you will be putting on a little show for me."

Opening the wardrobe, I pulled out a blowout doll I had dressed in a bra, suspenders and hold ups.

"Dolly has been feeling a bit lonely lately, Twinks. I want you to make love to her and show her a good time."

He slid himself into the doll awkwardly looking very red in the face, eyes cast downwards.

He started a slow rhythm pumping the doll on the floor whilst I sat on the bed and mocked his efforts.

"She doesn't look too happy, sunshine. Surely you can do better than that. No wonder you can't get a woman! Caress her breasts, play with them. Slower, faster. Stop, now fast….and slow…."

Twinks was struggling and looked flustered, and I laughed. "Now fast!" I ordered "faster, faster!" he started grunting like he was about to explode. "STOP" I hollered.

Reluctant, he stopped, with a huff of disappointment through the gag. A whack on his backside with my bamboo cane swiftly followed.

He yelped as I shoved his face into the carpet. In that absurd position with his face on the floor and posterior in the air, I stepped into my strap-on, then pulled off his ball gag and seated myself on a comfortable cushion. I chose a fluffy one as I like to dish out my punishments whilst indulging myself in absolute comfort.

"Crawl towards me." I commanded.

He crawled on his knees, fear in his eyes.

"Open your mouth."

He opened his mouth, and I slipped my lovely little 12-inch dildo into his waiting cake hole. He started sucking greedily, so I slapped him again.

"Slowly bitch." I directed, "Now kiss it." My sub kissed it with little pecks.

"Tell my dildo that you love it and want it."

"Dildo I love you and want you." he said blandly.

"With conviction boy, with conviction" Exasperated, I whacked him in the mush with my fluffy slipper.

He grasped the dildo and eyes wide, he said "I love you so much dildo. I want you! I want you so much!"

I smiled and ruffled his hair. "Good boy. Guess what? My dildo wants you too. Face in the carpet – now!"

He buried his face, his rump high just how I liked. I spit on the strap-on and then slowly worked it into him from behind, pumping him for a moment then sweetly told him to ride back on it like a slut. He complied and started to ride it with moves to rival Demi Moore in Striptease.

"Good little Slut!" I rewarded him "Now moan like a girl." He started to moan and groan like a Porn star and quivered all over.

For the final part of his training, I told him from now on he was only ever allowed to cum whilst he had something in his arse and was moaning like a girl. Otherwise, there would be big trouble. He agreed readily at this point, and I slapped his cock slowly with my leather paddle and ordered him to ejaculate onto a towel.

He squirted hard with the strap-on deep in his arse. I retracted it and said, "Oh you dirty little dog. Looks like you have had a little accident." I grabbed his hair and pushed his head down and rubbed his face in it.

"Now eat it up and jobs a goodun." I ordered. He looked up at me with big pathetic cow eyes, whilst cowering on the floor.

"Just eat it and be done with it. I don't have time for this, you dirty little weasel"

I pushed his head down and he stuck his tongue out slurping between moaning sounds of misery. This one does like to ham it up, the little tinker!

"Right, I'm done with you for now," I said in a bored manner." You can have your clothes intact, on one condition."

"I will do whatever you say Mistress."

"Good," I said. Pop in this butt plug. Put on this thong, fishnet stockings and bra."

I left the room, retrieved his clothes, and went back in. He was wearing everything I requested. I checked he had the butt plug in and then allowed him his clothes. I gave him a final whack on the backside and dismissed him from my presence. The unworthy scoundrel slunk out of the room thoroughly humbled!

Another standard day in the life of a Mistress.

Lady R: I, like Kaz, rather enjoyed it when my slave was always a little bit cheeky in our session and tried to be brave. Slave D in particular was always trying to push my buttons but was always willing and open to trying every new creative idea that would slide into my twisted mind during a session. When Slave D first came to me for training he was not a virgin or novice, in fact he had the letter 'A' branded on his ass cheek right by his chocolate starfish from another mistress, who apparently owned him, so that in itself was proof he could take punishment like a pro.

During our sessions, I would regularly include candle wax play, electric play, impact play and humiliation. One session we even had a competition to see how many clothes pegs I could attach to his genitals.. The answer, 40! Of course, they were not removed gently with my hands but in fact whipped off with my riding crop one by one. The funny thing is - he barely reacted! Most slaves would at least out a squeal but this slave was so experienced, he barely flinched. Sometimes, he even tried to instruct me on how to do it so it hurt more and left bigger welts, which I found bizarre! With the candle wax, I would drip it slowly over his nipples and cock and one time, I made a cock mould out of wax. To do this I dripped the wax over his cock continuously, using multiple candles in different colours and allowed it to set. Then I carefully peeled it off which left me with a fun and unique penis shaped ornament for the shelf in my playroom. We joked that we could use more of these as ice cube trays to serve in drinks at sissies parties and this inspired us to create smaller trays by using his nipples as a template. Obviously I didn't tell any of the consumers that the ice cubes were modelled on my slaves tits, it was our little secret joke!

Usually we'd indulge in some electro fun and I would add electro pads to all of his most sensitive areas, sending a strong current though his flesh, increasing it quickly to gauge his reaction as I laughed at his - again non responsive face. Soon it would be on the maximum setting with multiple pads and he would finally - slightly grimace. There was nothing I could do to shock this slave! He would even bring a small wire, shoe brush for suede boots that I would scrape across his dick and balls until he bled and he would giggle! At least it was a good way to remove the wax. He'd be totally covered in wax at this point, so I'd fetch my Henry Hoover from the cupboard and hoover his body. When I hoovered his cock up, he seemed to enjoy this and would be smiling all over. One of the most enjoyable slave training sessions we did was when he asked for humiliation and we decided he would be a washing line for all of my dirty lingerie. He brought in some fishing line which I wrapped around his dick and balls, pulling it extremely tightly and tying it to the handle of the bedroom door. Using the clothes pegs, I attached these to his penis and extremely saggy ass scrotum, then hung my laundry from them. The dirty clothes were soaked and weighty, so acted as ball weights, stretching his genitals. During this punishment, he would chat away as normal, asking how my week had been and suggesting possible future pain based tasks for him to complete - the more ridiculous the better! I think this is why he was one of my favourite slaves and one of the easiest to so-called-train!

With slave training consent is always important and I was lucky that Slave D consented to all of my suggestions, including deep heat on his balls as he trusted me not to do anything that would cause actual harm. For the record, deep heat is extremely hot and while it won't cause any damage to the skin, it is fucking painful!

Chapter 17
Bondage and restriction

Bondage and restriction is the artform of tying, tethering or chaining someone's limbs so that they are unable to move and are utterly helpless. This can add to the eroticism of a play session as it's a total power exchange and the bottom in the scenario will enjoy the feeling of being completely in someone else's hands. Bondage can be mild - light silk ties binding the wrists or it can be more heavy duty and might involve restraints around the chest, stomach and thighs which limit all movement, and even bondage hoods and mitts which prevent the sub from seeing, hearing, touching or feeling. Mild bondage is popular but those fanatical about restriction often love to indulge in complete sensory deprivation involving hoods or even ball gags so all the sensations are denied, apart from whatever wonders the domme wishes to inflict on her sub, whether it be teasing the flesh with a soft feather , running an ultraviolet wand across the body which emits an electric current, or the flick of a leather whip, thrashing against their sensitive parts.

All kinds of wonderful instruments and restraints can be used from cuffs and ropes, through to body harnesses with padlocks. Safety reminder, if using padlocks, always have a spare key as a backup emergency or if using rope ties it's important to have a pair of scissors to quickly free the sub in case of emergency

During heavy bondage, a sub will not be able to use their safe word, so hand gestures are used. The dominant will ensure that the sub is able to tap three times if they need to get the dommes attention and communicate something.

Kaz B: One of my favourite forms of bondage involves sensory deprivation. I have a beautiful pink, leather hood with a plug in the centre. I place it over my subs head and once he is securely tied, I pop the plug in. I have a number of subs that enjoy an element of surprise so they enjoy the idea of me leaving the room for an unspecified time before I return an administer a series of punishments which could include a whipping with my leather flogger, a short, sharp shock or perhaps spilling hot candle wax slowly across their body, allowing it to drip closer and closer to their sensitive parts before it spills across their genitals, making them flinch in a heady mix of sweet agony and euphoria.

Charlie was a regular that loved kidnapping scenarios and during the 2 - 3 hour sensation we would do a roleplay where I had captured him and was holding him hostage until he complied with me and gave me the information I required. I often love to get into character so I may play an evil scientist or a big boss who is using heavy handed tactics. Part of the roleplay is the psychological mind games, so once my sub was in the hood, I turned all the lights out and played a soundtrack with thunder and lightning. I knew he would tune into the white noise and become disoriented fairly quickly. I left Charlie a while, then crept into the room with a feather. I used the very tip on the corner of his toe, watched his foot twitch and then I stayed still for a few moments. He wasn't sure at this point whether I'd returned or if a fly had landed on his foot. Next, I would come back with a couple of ice cubes, placing them on his nipples or in his crotch so he knew for certain that he was no longer alone. Another time, I may shout loudly, causing him to jump. I'd take out Charlie's face plug for a moment so he could hear me and in a low voice I would warn him that he was about to get punished and that the only option he had would be to give me the information I needed. Before he had time to respond, I would start a series of lashes with the flogger, starting softly, then increasing the force until he writhed, as much as he could while bound.

Charlies like list was much bigger than his limits list so I may surprise him with a cane of deep heat, applied masterfully to his balls, the heat building slowly until they tingle all over. Another time, I slipped into my latex gloves and fetched a thumb of ginger for some figging, which means inserting hot ginger into the anus. Between activities, I would open the plug and threaten him and tell him that he wouldn't get out alive without submitting to me and giving me what I needed. The threats of extreme and violent acts were all the more exciting to him as the line between fantasy and reality became confusing for him and he was not sure what was real and what was roleplay. At once I placed a cold fork either side of his toe and told him I had secateurs around his toe and would remove it. At other points, more intimate parts were threatened and during this I could visibly see his excitement combined with fear and how caught up in the roleplay he was. My job was to make him believe that I'd lost the plot and was capable of taking things further. I like to think I can play a convincing maniac and he seemed genuinely scared at points. I pretended to have all kinds of industrial toys and weapons in my hand when they were ordinary household objects but when the sub is unable to see, it's difficult for them to distinguish what is happening. For example, I have one vibrator that sounds and looks like a power drill. A quick flash of the gadget alongside psychological torment can have them completely believing every word you say. At one point, I had Charlie convinced that I had a couple of hardmen in the next room and that they wanted to come in and watch me terrorise him completely. He said, "please Mistress, don't let them fuck me," and I replied along the lines of, "would you rather I cut one of these little toesies off then?" This had him agreeing to the former, with made up men that didn't exist.

It would be near on impossible to go into a scenario like this with a new slave that had no experience of BDSM as it's possible they'd have a full on panic attack but we built up these scenarios over time as he got to know me and he became comfortable with some of my more zany improvisation. To finish the session, I might pop a masturbator toy on him, which he'd quickly ejaculate into and I'd remove his plug and pour it into his mouth. I'd say unless he gave me the code, he'd have to service every man in the room. Then he would give me the code or information I needed.

I find subs tend to desire aftercare more so after psychological play, more so even than extreme pain play, when the two are combined they are often shifting through a range of emotions and might be still shaking like a little jelly up to ten minutes after the session is ended. I tend to engage them in chat to see how they are feeling and offer them a hot or cold drink. Charlie was always excited after the sessions and would love to sit for a while and list all his favourite bits that really confused him and had him in a state of fear and ecstasy. Then we'd wind down with some casual chit chat and he'd head off. Normally I would get a text an hour or two later from him with a few more thoughts about what he loved and asking how I could ramp those bits up next time. Obviously, I always had a few tricks up my sleeve and he was never disappointed with my creativity.

I always secretly loved the idea of being a Bond villain and this is my way to play it out in a safe space, and my slaves love it too. Sometimes I've even switched accents partway in the session and pretended to be a foreign honey trapper that's been hired to punish him for his wrongdoings. It's a roleplay within a roleplay, so they think they are doing one roleplay and then it switches and I say I have information on and they will be punished. As the accent switch is so unexpected it can have the wonderful result of completely baffling the slave, and I just love surprising people!

Lady R: Let's get stuck in the chapter with my Toby stories, as mentioned in the whipping section I had a rather extreme sub who I started my domme journey with who would not be adverse to all kinds of debauchery. When Toby first came to me for an appointment, he was fresh to the scene and prior to our meeting he explained that he was looking for bondage with a little bit of light pain. He turned up with a small backpack with cheap, novelty restraints and one of the smallest, most pathetic whips I've ever seen in my life. He told me his fetish was not being able to escape! So, with his crappy restraints which was all he had to offer, I had to get creative and I selected the belt from my dressing gown, duct tape and an old bit of string from my odd job drawer and got him to lie down on the bed, splayed out in a star position while I used every piece of rope like material to fix him to the bed. I gagged his mouth with a pair of my knickers, applied duct tape to his mouth and across his eyes too. You can probably tell that at this point I wasn't yet fully equipped and because he wanted to be left alone and to try and escape, I simply put on some mundane massage music and left him to go and have a fag outside.

As I'd left, he was already wriggling and trying to pull at his restraints - with little effect. After 15 minutes, I returned to find him still struggling and trying to loosen the ties. I'd strike his penis with the whip now and again to remind him I was still present and after an hour, I'd release him and let him go on his merry way. Now, I thought I'd never see this client again. He was the most relaxed and easy-going client with the session requiring zero effort on my part, but lo and behold - three days later he booked another appointment, bringing with him more durable rope, a stronger whip and a ball gag. He requested the same scenario again, with me tying him up and him trying to escape once more but with better bondage equipment and more reinforcement. This continued over the coming weeks with Toby returning every week and bringing new toys and equipment he wanted to try out, building up from whips to high quality electrics. Soon he was curious to experiment with butt plus, which over time built up to him taking 8 inch dongs in his rectum but he always requested the same scenario where he would try to escape. There was no role play, simply him trying to escape every   session! So, imagine, this guy comes to see me, gets tied up so he can barely move let alone escape, ear plugs in so he couldn't hear me, electric pads covering every sensitive part of his body and a dildo as big as my fist rammed up his arse and that was his most comfortable place to be. Over time, his kinks became more extreme with him desiring the electrics on full, more pain from whipping and feeling totally helpless.

One day, after two years of his growing kinks, and his rucksack turning into a huge duffel bag, he arrived with a leather body bag. Now this looked like a leather sleeping bag with a two-way zip which went down vertically, with tightening buckles from top to bottom, so his body would be completely concealed from head to toe. It had a gimp mask attached at the top, with the facilities to attach a ball gag and eye mask so he was literally in a human body bag that you would expect to see carried out at a crime scene but made of thick, heavy leather. Before he jumped into his sweaty nest, I'd wire up the electrics to his body, allowing the wire to come out of the zip below. By this point, I was no longer tying him to a bed, I was tying him to a large, heavy footstool to allow more easy access to his dick and bum hole, via the two-way zip. I'd expose his arse for easy whipping and anal annihilation and with the electrics which were attached to the wire firmly in my grip to pulse the harsh electrics through his genitals. All the time, he would slightly struggle as if trying to escape but secretly put no real effort in as complete encasement was a kink that drove him wild.

On one occasion, I had a party with a couple of friends who came over for an evening of drinks and nibbles while Toby was laid out strapped to my poof, in his body bag, enduring electrics while me and my friends drank wine and used him as a footstool. Toby loved this comedic factor being added to his torture, in fact he got off on it in a huge way to the point he was booking longer sessions each time and even an overnight where he was tied up and left while I slept. I don't think I could have gone any further with Toby, except blood play which I would not do as it's a limit of mine. The next step would have been castration, which is obviously a fantasy for some subs but not something that should ever be done. So, after a long time spent with Toby serving me, I decided to release him from my ownership and advised him to seek out another domme to help him on his future quests for pain! It's sad when you have to let a sub go, especially one of your first ever appointments but when they become too addicted to play time and start requesting to see you every day it becomes an unhealthy addiction and you have to do the right thing. My advice to anyone wanting to dabble in bondage is to get some quality restraints available from the stores in the back of this book. Start with wrists and ankle restraints and if your sub is a newcomer don't tie them too tightly at first, so if they are uncertain and at the experimental stage, they can escape if they wish to. With the cuffs, I'd suggest quality over quantity and choose padded cuffs as cheap cuffs may leave marks on the slaves wrist, which might not be ideal if they have someone at home who might start asking questions.

Always check your sub regularly, are they comfortable, are the restraints too tight? With bondage trust is key so if you are the person doing it, check your sub is OK with all that is happening. If you are the one experiencing it, make sure you have that important conversation before and that you trust your play partner.

Chapter 18
Smoking

Smoking fetish refers to sexualising the act of smoking a cigarette, cigar or pipe and finding eroticism through it. Often the art of blowing smoke from the mouth or onto the sub may create feelings of arousal.

Lady R: Smoking fetish is actually quite a common request that I get asked to do regularly and usually the client wants smoke blown on their face or cigarette ash flicked on his tongue and to be used as a human ashtray, but one client in particular wanted cigarette burns on his nipples, not necessarily because he enjoyed the pain at the time but when he would return home and the burns would start to heal into scabs, the now fresh scabs would rub on his work shirts as a constant reminder of our session for days and maybe weeks until the next appointment. If your sub is into smoking fetish please check how far they are wanting to take it before you start stubbing cigarettes out on the victim's cock.

Smoke slave was one of my favourite subs. He was the ultimate sub and there was nothing that this guy wouldn't do for me. As I am a heavy smoker, someone with a smoking fetish would always make my day of sessioning particularly fun. I could puff away to my lungs delight. Sometimes, the entire lounge would be thick with smoke and his eyes would light up, every time I lit up a cigarette. Now, to start our session, I would send him to the shop prior to the meeting and get him to purchase my weekly shop, which would include; bleach, toilet rolls, food, a packet of

20 Marlboro lights and a few bottles of wine, including a bottle of Moet and that was just for the session!

The minute Smoke slave walked through the door, he would be stripped completely naked and given his costume - a tiny pinny that failed to cover his crotch and I'd give him a couple of sharp strikes with the crop, just to put him in place. I was never a disciplinarian with Smoke Slave as the session he desired - I'd describe as more of a friendship, however, as I enjoy being in control and bossing my subs around, he accepted and even enjoyed this. As he started his cleaning tasks, I would often talk on a level playing ground with him about my week. Meanwhile, he would clean my shoes with a toothbrush and some Aquafresh!

I would make sure he moved the furniture around to get to all those dusty spots and make him move from room to room, so the place would be spotless. All the while, every ten minutes when I needed a ciggie, I would light the cigarette and let it burn down until there was rough ash to flick into his mouth and onto his tongue. After every flick of my fag, he would swallow the ash, looking me directly in the eyes, whispering, "thank you Mistress." while I blow the smoke into his face.

He would then resume cleaning until I was near the end of the cigarette and he would collect enough saliva on his tongue for me to stub the cigarette out on it. He'd then eat the cigarette end to show me how grateful he was for this generous reward of mine.

Next, I'd crack open a bottle of wine and the party would really start because as soon as I've had a drink, I love to chain smoke, which excited him even more! At this point he'd finished cleaning the apartment and my foot rub would be due. Sometimes, I'd have friends visiting and they too would get in on the personal masseuse abuse. I would hand smoke slave a bottle of moisturiser which he bought at the shop prior to coming over and he would kneel at my feet, still in his pinny, lathering my foot in expensive lotion and rubbing away the hard day's graft, to which I would scream at him - "Harder! Harder," while lighting another cigarette.

After a good, solid, firm foot rub, I'd then proceed to fulfil his second fetish, which was to be completely mummified in cling film, gagged, blindfolded and sometimes just left in a dark room. This kink combined several components which combined ignore fetish with isolation and restriction. The result of this was a feeling of him being exposed and vulnerable and completely reliant on me, which left him exhilarated and sent him into sub space.

If I was feeling particularly cruel, I would remove another of his senses - hearing, and would play heavy metal music through his earphones, so he could no longer hear any outside noise or whether I was in the room or not. I'd play with the light switch and sometimes the light would be on, then he'd be plunged into darkness for a period - disoriented.

As smoking was his main fetish, I'd remove my heels and creep into the room. He would be oblivious to the fact I had entered and had two ciggies on the go. I would slowly inhale and then breathe smoke out slowly all over his face. By this point, he'd be wondering if it was real or a figment of his imagination as he would be deep in subspace.

Unlike some clients, Smoke slave would never request a happy ending. After an hour of being left in clingfilm and sweating like a pig, I'd decide it was time to set him free. He was so grateful to have his fetish fulfilled, he would collect his things and head home, until the following week when I would need more wine.

Kaz B: As a non-smoker, I have limited experience with smoking fetish, as having tried it a couple of times it made me cough like an old hag from Macbeth.

Smoking fetish is sometimes portrayed as glamorous, 1950's style film stars draped in silk chemises, flowing gowns with marabou and kitten heels, elegantly inhaling a cigarette from a long pen, done with grace and style. My experience could not be further from this. I really could not seem to take smoking fetish seriously. I tended to feel like a naughty schoolgirl having a cheeky puff behind the bike sheds when I did this and I developed a pretty odd alter-ego or character which was probably as far removed from the ultimate fantasy as you can get! So, imagine this, I'm clad in shining black latex, silk nylons and sky-high patent Pleaser stilettos. I remove a cigarette slowly, a teasing look in my eye, take the lighter, then this is where it starts to go tits up! First of all, I struggle to light the bastard, then a huge flame shoots down the entire cigarette as I inhale and I start choking, smoke pouring from my mouth in a less than seductive manner. For some reason, I am compelled to adopt a voice that lies somewhere between Catherine Tate's school girl character, Lauren Cooper and Vicky Pollard from Little Britain. I have no clue why this happened but it just seemed to trigger something in me that wanted to take the mickey out of everything. I think I even threw in a "am I bovvered!"

While the client was entertained and couldn't stop laughing, I was not convinced it was their ultimate fetish and I turned down requests for this fetish therefore because I could taste tobacco for hours afterwards and don't think I really did a great job of the sexy smoking siren!

A more successful session was when I joined Lady R, her friend Mistress Amelia And Smoke slave one time. While he rubbed her feet, she asked me to collect her cigarettes from her ashtray with a fork and mash them up. I did this and we giggled and decided to pop them into a glass of wine for Smoke slave, ensuring to both dribble a long string of saliva into the glass. We had him take a large sip and hold it in his mouth for several moments before gulping it down.

Another time, Lady R and I did a session which involved 'spittoon' fetish. Prior to the session we started spitting into a champagne flute, which we proudly showed our sub as he arrived. His eyes were twinkling and he mumbled, "I will drink all the spit you feed me." For the next two hours we would take it in turns to dribble into the flute until it was three quarters full. We made him carry out several tasks to eventually earn his slippery reward! In the meantime, we would demand he open his mouth wide and we would either dribble spit into his mouth in a teasing manner, or spit aggressively in his face. He seemed to love both styles equally and we giggled away using him as a vessel for our spit.

When it was nearly time for him to leave, we taunted him and asked if he'd been a good enough boy to have warranted his reward of our delicious saliva cocktail. We ordered him to kneel and beg. He sank to his knees, desperation in his eyes as he pleaded, his eyes imploring us. We decided that first he must gag on Lady R's strap-on, until strings of saliva ran from his mouth and into the glass below. Now the beautiful cocktail was tainted with slave spit - the ultimate humiliation and he would be required to drink every drop. Luckily, we happened to have some bright pink straws shaped like a penis. We popped one into his flute, then Lady R lit up a cigarette and flicked her entire length of ash into it. Upon instruction, the slave greedily sucked it all up, slurping loudly at the end to get the dregs. He was told to lick as much of the glass clean as he could and as he couldn't reach the bottom of the glass with his tongue, he was administered a couple of nice hard whacks on the bottom from our paddles for his failings.

He then said, "Goddesses, I have been dreaming of this all week and it was everything I could ever have wanted. How are you fixed for tomorrow?"

Needless to say, he was back the next day for more, the greedy boy!

Chapter 19
CBT

CBT stands for cock and ball torture. There are many forms of this from mild CBT such as flicking or gently slapping the cock and balls, although I would tend to call this cock and ball torment rather than torture. Implements that could be used are long fingernails, spiked pinwheels, ice, hot wax, crops, whips or a mix of sensation play. At the more extreme end, some Mistresses put out cigarettes on the end of a slave's penis. Miss Red may know more about the latter as Miss B is certainly queasy when it comes to such things.

Kaz B: CBT has become increasingly popular amongst kinky or submissive men, looking for ways to expand their kink range and reach a new high. Many that enjoy light CBT will never go beyond slaps and flicks, whereas other subs will want to reach new levels of torment, always keen to push their pain barrier higher and reach that concrete ceiling.

I like to be imaginative when it comes to CBT and will sometimes use ropes and restriction so only the tip of the penis is exposed and subjected to the terror of my implements, or I may leave it fully exposed and have my arsenal laid out on the massage table, ready to strike at any point. I have a couple of favourites in my kit, especially when playing around with sensation and a mixture of ice and deep heat can sensitise a sub rapidly without leaving marks. In fact, I have a lot of slaves that don't want marks so often I'll go to the kitchen cupboard for my supplies. Here are a few things I've used on his meat and two veg:

Tabasco sauce - his peepee will be hotter than the ring of a man living on only vindaloo in the Nevada desert.

Ginger starts at around 60.000 Scovilles but once you juice that bad boy and apply it, the heat becomes more intense! If you want to take away the heat (for real, not a brief cooling with ice) use a fat, such as butter. Part of the fun is the sensation though and your subs reaction so the ice is a great contrast.

One neat tip is that if you tie the cock and balls, everything becomes so much more sensitive! You'll want to be careful using a pinwheel on tied balls as it stretches the skin and the area can bleed more easily.

My sessions tend to start slowly, increasing the level of intensity so they go in smiling and eventually climb towards the pinnacle of sweet agony before returning to the sweet spot.

Brian loved to be blindfolded during sessions and not knowing what I would do next or which part I may target. One minute a feather could be gliding across his flesh, causing him to moan softly until my sharp stiletto pushed into his ballsack, as he emitted a loud, happy yelp of pleasure. His favourite thing was to be in as vulnerable a position as possible, so I had complete control over him. I would put a sensory deprivation hood on him so all would be dark and quiet and then I would get to work. The hood has a plug which I can open at intervals but I can always tell from body language how the sub is doing, so the plug is more of a safety ritual.

The interesting thing is, once a slave is hooded, he loses all sense of what is taking place. I might use a finger nail to rake across his balls and ask him what it was and he would guess, "a spoon? A pencil? A paperclip?" It's always fun to keep them guessing and Brian was notoriously useless at this game, or at least - wasn't paying any attention to what it might be!

I sprayed a generous layer of deep heat to Brian's John Thomas and plums and then added some tingle lube for good measure. The 5 wheeled pinwheel was perfect for his shaft while the violet wand gave an exquisite electric tingle to his balls, causing him to writhe, wriggle and moan. I always love to layer the sensations when possible and send my sub into kink overload, it has them leaving like little wobbly, confused by happy jellies. I own a couple of vices too. It's two sheets of clear Perspex with a hole for subby's pecker to slip through, then two screws are slowly tightened at the base which has the effect of flattening the subs balls. I like to call this pancaking as it looks like a little pancake inside the vice. Meanwhile his dong is free for a different kind of punishment. In Brian's case, I might now attach two electric loops which I then send a current through. Some subs may go limp during the process…e   man's erectile function is different. If this happens and shrivels up to the size of an anaemic maggot then the loops will fall off and I'll have to find new forms of punishment. Brian maintains a stiffy through, therefore the loops stay on well. Mini vibrators are always fun to keep some of the pain signals registering as pleasure and the sub can far more easily take more sensation for a longer duration if there is some kind of reward cycle where pleasure is induced, such as a Doxy massager on the tip of the penis.

Brian would always reach the most intense orgasm after our more intense CBT sessions. It's as if it brought every cell in his body alive and filled them with a new energy. He turned up one day with some low grade sandpaper and suggested that it might be an appropriate finish to him that day. I put him through his paces with my array of delight implements and for the finale, I gave him permission to bash the bishop on the proviso he did so by wrapping the sandpaper around his penis and ejaculating that way. He started off happy as a pig in shit, until I could see he was becoming a little sore. I decided to help him out by whispering in his ear that he was a filthy little wanker who would come for his mistress or he'd have to knock one off with stinging nettles next time. It did the trick and he convulsed on the bed in a spectacle comparable to the bed scene in the exorcist, writhing and practically levitating off the bed. I think he even said, "Fuuuuuuuuck meeeeeeeee!"

After recovering from his crumpled state and after ten minutes or so he managed to stand up and half limped to the bathroom for a shower. "THAT - was the best session ever he said!"

Word of advice to readers - you can find many knobbly or textured sex toys to experiment with and Brian had already experimented on himself with a low grade sandpaper. Please don't pop into B&Q and seek it out for your wank sessions as unsupervised and without the right kit and experience, it could end up quite nasty. You have been warned!

Lady R: Many men after reading this chapter will be watery eyed and cupping their genitals with sheer panic and many women will be letting out a massive cackle while reading with a mischievous grin. What woman on this planet hasn't wanted to do a running kick into their partners balls after an argument. I have had the pleasure of putting this practice into real life and the men who have endured this particular kink performed by myself have actually left the appointment with a big fat grin on their face.

The history behind this kink is mind-blowing as I can only imagine it is one of the worst pains a man can endure but nonetheless it is one of my most popular sessions. That being the case I have decided to break CBT into 3 sections, first being ballbusting, followed by CBT and finally, what we like to call pancaking - aka the ball crushing device!

Ballbusting

I am not going to kid anyone, when a client would call for an appointment that required ballbusting a smile would slide across my face followed by an immediate glint in my eye. I must be sadistic and twisted to find the act of putting on a gorgeous pair of 6 inch stilettos and running as fast as I can towards my victim to kick him as hard as I physically can in his bollocks, incredibly sexy. The feeling of total power and control is second to none, and to hear your victims whimper while your stiletto point is embedded deep into his ball sack is music to my soul. When you are performing the act of ballbusting I also like to stare at the client directly into their eyes as if I'm whispering to him, "I own you".

Maybe I have psychopathic traits or a little bit of a narcissist to enjoy such a cruel act, but these guys hunted out my details online, made the call, booked the appointment. They wanted this! In a typical session you would have the client strip naked, get on all fours and start by a light swing and kick of the leg from behind and build up to harder and more aggressive kicks. Sometimes an implement such as a leather paddle slapping across his cock and balls would suffice.

Mistress Kaz and I recently performed a fabulous duo with a ballbusting enthusiast who could really take a kick. For the entire session we had the sub switching between being stood up against my fridge door or on all fours on the kitchen floor with Kaz giving him 5 of her best followed by my biggest leg swings. He was grunting and gasping the entire session, only stopping to take a few deep breaths before begging for us to continue, finishing the session with him lying on his back with our heels on his chest wanking onto our gorgeous shoes. As soon as he came we would allow the sub to lick our shoes clean, making sure he didn't miss a drip..... What a treat!

Ballbusting can be performed with a range of implements but i would suggest trying with bare feet and obviously light slaps or kicks. Always make sure your sub is comfortable with the level before stepping it up a gear. Remember consent is paramount.

This leads me to my next favourite CBT scenario which involves electric play but purely focusing on the cock and balls. I invested in an electric sounding rod which is a stainless steel rod that slides down your urethral tract almost like a catheter but around 5mm thick and when turned on, electrocutes your cock from the inside out.

Slave T loved CBT and sounding, so was my first victim to try my new sadistic purchase. When he arrived for the appointment I didn't give away what treat lay in store for him and instead continued the session as usual by instructing him to lay on the bed, arms and legs spread while I attached the cuff restraints to his wrists and ankles to keep him securely in place. I placed a blindfold over his eyes, pulled out a large feather and started running it softly down his torso, over his penis and down each of his legs. Slave T would flinch and giggle throughout and especially with the feather floating over his cock touching his member ever so slightly making it twitch and start to get erect. As his dick started to stand to attention and get a bit too excited for my liking I grabbed my horse crop, raised it above my head and immediately brought it down hard on the tip of his bell-end. Slave T let out a huge gasp before I eased his shocking pain by gently swaying the feather over his cock, almost as if to soothe the sting. I continued teasing his cock until it was throbbing with excitement and slapping it back down for a few minutes before I pulled the electrics from my kit bag for the next fun game of the session. To start I put a rubber cock ring over him to keep him in place and attached the electric pads to his balls, turning the electric box on low to shock gently but not cause discomfort and ran the pinwheel over his shaft to create the perfect mix of gentle pleasure and pain. Now to step it up a gear and bring in the sounding rod, to begin I lube up the rod and gently slide it into the slit at the top of his penis. Slave T jumps when the cold lubed rod touches the tip, so I tickle his balls for a pleasurable comfort before I continue to slide it inside him until it reaches the end. With the rod standing firm and secure in his cock I reach over to my electric box and turn it ¼ of the way up. He jolts and lets out a moan of pleasure, so I take that as a sign that I need to turn it up to ½ way. Now his moans turned to groans as his body started to jerk and flap around like a dying fish as the intensity of the electric current running over his balls and inside of his cock caused his whole body to contract. Maybe we can now go up to ¾? Of course I did, he was now getting breathless with excitement from the ecstasy of pleasure and pain. I didn't need to hold the rod in place as he was so hard he looked like he was going to explode. With that I picked up my crop and started slapping his shaft, that was it, it was too much for Slave T that even with the rod still in place he exploded everywhere while panting with relief. This Slave loved electrics and obviously my new sounding rod a bit too much that I didn't get to use my ball crushing device on him. Until next time Slave T.

Pancaking

Ball crushers come in a range of materials but on this occasion a sheer Perspex vice was used. This resembles two sheets of Perspex that resembles a vice that tightens up but with a hole in the middle for the cock and balls to slip through. Once the genitals are through the hole, you then tighten the screws in each corner so that the two Perspex sheets close in tightly around the balls until they start to flatten. If you tighten them a great deal, the balls spread out, flatten and take on a whitish hue, a bit like a pancake - hence the term pancaking!

Kaz and I regularly treat our more extreme CBT clients to this luxury and usually this is an extremely non-erotic scenario as it literally crushes the balls flat. However, on one occasion during one of our glorious duo sessions, I was tightening the screws to maximum effect with an evil grin on my face, while Kaz whispered all kinds of threats in the slave's ear. The combination of having two mischievous dommes flipping between teasing and tormenting him must have tipped him over the edge as suddenly his cock started swinging about and spurting cum everywhere! I jumped to the side and Kaz just managed to dodge a big wad of cum, we were lucky not to get coated in his mucky man milk! Had that happened, he would have been severely punished for that, although that would have probably made him come more, the naughty little man slut!

Chapter 20
Human Furniture and Objectification

Objectification: Someone with an objectification fetish enjoys being seen, used and treated as an inanimate object. Popular examples of this include the individual desiring oneself as a footstool, ashtray, inflatable sex doll. Less common examples include scenarios such as the kinkster being used as a coat rack, ie with the dominant throwing her coat and hat over him or her, or the sub acting as a doormat for the dominant to clean her shoes on. The kinkster is then left to enjoy the feeling of being nothing more than an object to his dominant.

There are many theories on why this kink appeals to many, with the most popular idea being that it is a form of degradation. People enjoy being degraded for all kinds of reasons and it can be sexual in nature or it can serve to heal a part of themselves that needs addressing. This kink can be seen as a submissive going to their 'safe place.' Little is required emotionally or mentally from an object, it is simply there to serve its function and while a slave is in object mode, he or she is safe from the obligations and pressures of the world. It's a wonderful opportunity to switch off and fulfil basic functions without overwhelming expectations.

Lady R: Sam was your average Joe who ran his own small company in trade. He was well groomed, wore the latest fashions and smart shoes and it would be impossible to guess from looking at him that he harboured a secret fetish. I was Sam's first Mistress. When we first met he explained that he just wanted to try something new and was tired of being the boss at work and always in control, which sometimes I think is a justification for trying new kinkier things because they are not able to admit to themselves that they have a submissive or kinky side.

Sam arrived promptly and wasted no time in telling me what his kinks were. He wanted to be a human footstool. This was my first time as well and I had little experience of a fetish like this, so using my creative mind, I ordered him to undress and get on all fours in front of me in the cow yoga pose. I dressed in my red, latex, thigh-high boots, perched on the end of the bed and kicked them up onto his back and asked him if this was what he exactly had in mind.

Sam screamed, "Yes Mistress but would you be so kind as to spank me too?"

I already had my electric-blue whip ready for action and after a couple of swift spanks of the crop, I teased the end of my whip over his penis and balls just to show him that with every punishment there MIGHT be a chance of reward. Of course, Sam squealed with excitement and anticipation as the leather from my crop brushed his thighs and genitals.

Now feeling like I wanted to throw a bit of humiliation into the session just for good measure, I walked over to my fancy dress box and pulled out an all in one leopard print catsuit out and ordered him to dress in that and to regain position on all fours to continue his humble role as my personal footstool. I was always reminding him during this that he is SO lucky to be one!

As I continued the routine of footstool, spanking and teasing for a good 30 minutes while constantly taunting him about how pathetic he really was and not worthy of being anything other than a footstool - the doorbell rings and Mistress Amelia had popped over for a coffee and a catch up. Yippy for me as Mistress Amelia is a proper wind up merchant and this session is about to step up a notch!

She walked in, took one look at Sam and burst out laughing! Amelia whips off her shoes, runs over to him and gives me a naughty glare, she then proceeded to pick up the lube from the bedside table, lathered up her big toe, and without any warning shoved it up Slave Sam's arse, causing him to suddenly jerk and let out a piercing squeal. I can only imagine it felt like a dog having his temperature taken at the vets for the first time! Obviously, this was not rehearsed and being the sadistic woman that I am, I couldn't help but howl with laughter at Mistress Amelia's unruly actions.

Then Amelia says, "I've always wanted to try a human footstool, does this one speak?"

I replied, "only if I give him permission, otherwise this bitch stays silent."

While Amelia's sampling my new footstool, I go and find a table runner to put over him while I make the coffees. When I returned, Amelia had truly made herself at home and even persuaded Footstool to give her a foot massage. We continued our catch up, with Footstool staying perfectly still with the occasional whip and tickle until I'd had enough of this worthless character in my house. I ordered Slave Sam to come on our feet and lick it off before he fucked off, which he obviously obliged, without hesitation. He messaged within minutes after leaving about how much of an enjoyable and memorable experience he had and for many years he continued to visit and became one of my regular cleaners, who paid me £200 an hour to clean my flat once per week. I even got him to clean 52 pairs of my shoes with a toothbrush occasionally. Objectification and cleaning slaves are one of my favourite types of submissive. Imagine someone paying you to clean your house!

Kaz B: Sub Jimmy first visited me when I was based in the Midlands. I was still somewhat a baby domme at the time as although I had a fair bit of experience, I was still learning about all the weird and wonderful kinks that existed. A lot of the theory had come first but when you are in practise, that's when the magic happens.

He politely requested a specific outfit which consisted of; a white fitted blouse, a knee-length, satin pencil skirt with a slit in the side, tan coloured tights and black, patent, closed toe, court shoes with a square toe. I approved of his choice and obliged.

Jimmy's secret fantasy was fairly specific and he confessed that he loved the idea of being made to lie under my desk while I rested my shoes on his face, and ignored him as I answered my emails. Every now and again, I would act like I suddenly remembered he was there and would grind the toe of my shoe on his cheek and throw in a little stamp to his chops, which made him twitch in anticipation. Occasionally as a treat if he had behaved well, I would use his shlong as a place to rest my foot and of course trod heavily down on his shaft. Each time I did this, his eyes would roll back in his head in ecstasy.

After a while, I was feeling mischievous and required a little more mental stimulation, so I decided to turn him into a knicker tree. Think of college drama classes where students pretend to be a tree by raising their arms like branches in the air. In this position, Subby made the perfect tree for me to hang all my exotic lingerie on. I covered him in an array of silk, lace, satin and leather fabrics in bright pinks, sultry reds, seductive black PVC as well as nylon stockings. Then he was told he must stand there for ten minutes without flinching, or blinking, which obviously I knew he would fail at! To make it more of a challenge, I decided I would pelt him with various things, starting with rolled up balls of socks from the laundry basket and dirty tea towels from the kitchen.

Jimmy was so poor at trying not to blink, I popped a pillow-case over his head as punishment and then I popped myself down on a chair and called a friend for a natter. I could see from the enormous erection poking out from under the pillow case that Jimmy rather enjoyed this game. When I mentioned to my friend I had a sub with me, I clocked a few twitches from his dicklet. Spurred on by this, I continued to talk about him to my friend, saying things such as, "I made a knicker tree today. No it's not useful, it needs improving. I might take it down later and see if I can make something else out of it."

In my subs mind, it was as if I really viewed him as an object and nothing more. At the end of the session, I said, "I'm going to dismantle this tree, it's absolutely useless, not even a charity shop would take it!."

Jimmy said, "I guess I'm not allowed to touch myself, am I Mistress?"

"No slave, objects do not have genitals! Perhaps if you are really lucky, next time your parts may be used to make a sex doll for one of my other subs to play with!"

Surprise surprise, Jimmy booked in for this fetish a few weeks later and it was both a hilarious and exhilarating adventure.

Chapter 21
Toilet play

Toilet Play falls into two categories - Number 1 and Number 2! Number 1 is the act of giving someone a golden shower in some fashion. Number 2, as you may well guess involves playing with excrement.

Kaz B: Watersports is another kink that's become surprisingly popular. When I first started out as a domme, a happy ending would involve a sub rubbing my feet or tossing himself off while dressed as a gimp. Nowadays more slaves are keen to be peed all over either mid-session or at the end. What can I say, I get people to explore the deeper recesses of their minds, those kinky little thoughts dancing silently in the shadows waiting to be born in the real world.

My sub I named Sprinkles - after his fondness of golden showers embarked on this journey with me. He had seen it before in films but never experienced the divine feminine champagne before. The first session we tried this, I did with deliberation and lots of tease, letting out only sprinkles of my vintage upon his body. He was keen to come back the next week and try a more intense version of this. I sat him down in the shower and stood over him, at first allowing little tinkles to escape, stopping and starting the stream. I am well practised in this and find it relatively easy to stop and start, the same as I would a tap. I suppose it's all in the muscle control. I would allow a stream to spray out, then pause, only to behind again. With a short time frame, Sprinkles graduated to following jet showers and hosing down and then tasting my vintage, which he said was sweeter than Champagne. Well, if that's true they need to get rid of all those vineyards and get in touch with yours truly! However, I imagine it's quite a required taste on a scale more extreme than Marmite and most would pair their crispy baked scallops with a bottle of Bolly. Still, in le boudoir, it seems that my alternative is nearly just as popular.

I rarely struggle and water helps a lot with this. For a full on jet steam you'd need a diuretic such as strong coffee or Red Bull but I tend to avoid energy drinks on the whole. Also, you tend to lose more of the skill to control the aim, speed and the stop/start switch.

To keep things interesting I've varied my watersports sessions with Sprinkles and have used various methods. I've popped a funnel into his mouth so he has no option but to swallow, I've tinkled into a dish on the floor and then had him kneel before me on his hands and knees, begging me to taste it before I give the order and allow him to lap it up and I've even made pee ice cubes for them to suck on but his favourite reward, if he has been a good boy is simply looking up at me while I shower him with my nectar.

I have various online subs that love watersports to and to the extent they will do it to themselves to show how deeply devoted they are to me and how much they love their kink! One slave progressed from peeing into a jug and swirling his dinky in it rather quickly. I suggested a pee bath, which he agreed to readily and then he asked if he should save up a few cartons of pee for a few days for our next cam show. Giggling, I approved the idea and when the big day came he popped his plug in the bath and started to fill it with the saved up pee. This amounted to a couple of inches in the tub. He stepped in and lowered himself, slow and quivering all over. As he sat down full there was an intake of breath and his eyes shut quickly and opened again. "How is it Wormy

"Cold, Mistress, feels dirty but nice. I'll do anything for you."

Wormy was then instructed to wallow in the bath like a piggy oinking for me, which he did, rolling around like a crocodile with a gazelle in its jaws, a death roll to outperform any river bound reptile. I slowly clapped him then paused.

"Take the spare cartoon and shower your head with it."

Without a beat, Wormy took the carton and began to pour the stale, bronze coloured beverage over his hair. It ran down, his hair plastered to his face, his eyes tightly shut.

"Am I doing good, Mistress? Can I get out and play now."

"You will finish yourself in that tub Wormy. If you are to enjoy such a reward, it will come with the condition that you will enjoy it only in a pool of your own stale piss."

Wormy agreed and began to batter his appendage eagerly, only pausing occasionally to smack himself in the balls at my request which sent me into a fit of wicked giggles. The pee bath didn't seem to deter Wormy. I know my audience and soon he was emptying his gonads until they were as shrivelled as a raisin on a bonfire.

Not all of my subbies get to enjoy such great rewards but I particularly look after those that pledge their allegiance to me and time after time show their dedication and loyalty.

They know their place and love the mantra, "My Mistress always knows what's best for me."

Lady R: I would just like to thank YOU the reader for getting this far in the book without putting it down in disgust but if you are having your dinner or have a weak stomach I suggest you stop now and skip this chapter as things are about to get quite messy.

Now watersports is one of the most popular kinks that I perform on a regular basis that falls into the toilet play kink category, which Kaz has described beautifully above but the example I'm going to give this chapter covers skat aka poo and vomit play.

The client who had this unique kink was an educated and well-groomed man in his 50's who told me he was a film director. Often when waiting for a new client I would spy out the window to check that they are who they say they are for security purposes and this client who we will name James turned up to the appointment in his brand new Porsche looking rather dapper.

Now before his arrival we had discussed the appointment in detail as James wanted me to vomit on him while he lay on the floor to start followed by skat play which we will go on to later. Like most people I simply cannot vomit on demand so I ordered him to run to McDonalds to pick up a couple of large vanilla milkshakes on route to mine, so he arrived in his spanking red Porsche clutching the Maccy D cups for dear life.

When the formalities and money had been exchanged I ordered him to undress and took him through to the wet room in the back of the building so as to not make a mess, I gulped the shakes down and I was gagging already. Next thing you know the sick is falling all over his body and James is just lapping it up and rubbing it all over his torso and cock in delight. This was making me feel even more queasy as this was the first time I had ever done a session of this nature. Next up was the skat, so the night before knowing that I might get stage fright on the day I had prepared a shit by pooing in a Tupperware box and leaving it outside my flat in the cold overnight.

After 15 minutes of James rubbing my vomit into himself he begged me to shit in his mouth, I grabbed a stool and positioned my bum on the edge as he opened his mouth near my anus awaiting the gift, unfortunately for him I just could not go! I tried for a good 5 minutes to at least get a small nugget out but nothing, not even a fart.

So out comes the Tupperware... As I opened the plastic box the smell hit my face, 16 hour old poo left overnight outside fucking stinks, so without his request I was sick on him again from the smell. I put on my plastic gloves and scooped the excrement from the box and placed it on his chest, James immediately grabbed it and rubbed it seductively into himself then started to use it as lube on the penis rubbing my shit and vomit all over his cock. Picking up pace he finally let out a huge sigh of relief and his whole body trembling while I just stood quite frankly in shock.

After he finished his whole personality changed as he jumped up in disgust obviously reality hitting him after his orgasm that he had done such a vile thing to himself. He jumped straight in the shower, dressed and left with minimal dialogue and eye contact.

This was a different session for me and as mentioned nothing I had tried before, let's just say you shouldn't try everything just the once.

Chapter 22
Forced-bi

Forced-bi refers to ordering at least two of your submissives to engage in bisexual activity with each other. Of course, the bi play is never actually forced. The subs request this as if it's going out of fashion and generally can't wait to get their naughty lips wrapped around a nice hot rod. The role play aspect, however, requires some play acting and verbally commanding and often physically pushing your slave to carry out sexual acts. Sometimes kinky games are involved and might involve competitions to win a prize - such as a blowjob from the other slave! Condoms are provided and safe, sane and consensual play is always recommended.

A double domme session with Lady R and Mistress Kaz

We decided to write this chapter together as we have done many forced-bi sessions together. Lady R has always known how to throw a fabulous party and put on an elaborate spread! On this night in particular, she's picked up a selection of decadent treats including Halkidiki olives, sun-blushed tomatoes with mozzarella and pesto, wood smoked salmon blinis, topped with caviar and some fresh crudites with home-made dips. Oblivious, the boys brought the Bolly!

The room was lit low, a large triple wicked Candle which smells of the Seychelles permeating the air. Motown classics set the mood perfectly. Romance was in the air, at least for our three beautiful sissy ladies arriving.

To avoid our ladies-to-be from bumping into each other, we

asked them to arrive in intervals. Our first servant was greeted at the door and invited into the bedroom with a smile and invited to glam up. Lady R and Mistress Kaz pulled out an array of beautiful garments such as; a chiffon, pink baby doll that was barely there, a tight-fitting little red number, black satin girdles and panties, silk stockings, and of course a selection of glorious wigs and make up.

Danielle was one of Kaz's favourite sissy slaves. She was well behaved and had dutifully attended over the course of many years. At first, she was a little shy as she had never sessioned with two Mistresses before but once she studied herself in the mirror, with her freshly made up face and glam new look, she was ready for action. A little sniff of Poppers had her feeling hornier than a certain famous Truther/Youtuber at a swingers party!

Angela arrived next and was the absolute opposite to Danielle, with her already being a zen master in forced-bi. In fact, if forced-bi was a martial art she would be the black belt and she knows this! She is always eager to drop to her knees in an instant and needs to be constantly told to wait for instruction.

Sandy arrived last. She had some experience but wasn't overly eager and knew how to wait for permission.

After a mingle and some nibbles, it was time for the games to begin. The ladies were told that they would enjoy a delicious three course meal tonight. Lips were licked in anticipation.

Upon instruction, Angela poured us a large flute of Bolly each and we then ordered our ladies to sink to their knees, while we got comfortable on the sofa surrounded by cushions. We tossed a coin to choose who would go first and surprise surprise it was Angela, much to her delight! She was ordered to pick out her entree, a single olive, using only her mouth and pass it to Danielle. Her eyes glinting, she did this and was swiftly reprimanded when her hands went to reach for Danielle's penis. A sharp strike from Lady R's crop soon put her in her place and Lady R dragged her down to her knees with her hands behind her back.

Next, we revealed a surprise and announced we'd bought 6 cans of spray cream and they were to all be consumed before the subs were allowed to leave. We selected Danielle first as we knew she could be trusted to take it slowly, not rush into an orgy of sweaty, writhing bodies within minutes, unlike our dear Angela.

We both took a can of the cream and lifted the hems of our subbies dress and pulled their panties down. All three of their flaccid cocks twitched a little in excitement. This made Kaz giggle and Lady R snort with laughter as she nearly choked on her Bolly!

A generous helping of squirty cream was applied to Angela and Sandy's now semi-erect penis.

"Hope you are feeling hungry girls," Kaz teased and Lady R mocked, *"That's all you are going to get to eat until I've seen some cock sucking."*

Laughing amongst ourselves, we taunted our pet Danielle, saying, "Wait, wait, good girl, who's a good girl. Are you a good girl?" She nodded her head frantically.

"Ok, good girl, go, go, go, go on!" we hollered like cheerleaders egging them on.

Danelle slowly made her way to Sandy first , tentatively reaching her tongue out for a taste. Lady R then used her palm to push Danielle's face straight into the creamy mess so that her face was covered. Miss Kaz roared with laughter at this, rolling around the sofa as the night's antics unfolded. After gaining her composure, which took a while she demanded, "why aren't you eating it slut?"

The slave remained silent which caused Lady R to snap, "Are you not listening to her? She asked you a question!"

In a session, we always enjoyed egging one another on - a natural good cop/bad cop. Can you guess who played who? You probably can! However, sometimes we'd plot beforehand, giggling to each other and switching roles temporarily to confuse them, which worked a treat.

Without further ado, Danielle started to lick her delicious cream main dish and palate cleanser ready for the final course. Obviously, if you hadn't guessed, this consisted of her lapping Sandy's now hard, cream covered cock. Sandy's hands were on her head and she was starting to moan sounds of pleasure. It was time for some serious action now and Lady R said to Miss Kaz, "Sweetie, would you mind spreading Danielle's peachy cheeks for me so I can fill her arsehole with cream."

"I'd love to," Kaz grinned, "Let's pop some cream on her little cherry and turn her into an ice-cream sundae. The girls could do with a sugary treat, I'm sure."

At this, Lady R who had taken a sip of Bolly laughed and sprayed it onto the subs arse and took a long drag on her cigarette, making sure to flick her ash on his pasty, hairy arse.

Miss Kaz popped on her shiny, black, latex gloves and spread Danielles cheeks wide open to expose her chocolate starfish. We gave each other a knowing look and Lady R inserted the nozzle slightly into her quivering hole, before pushing the lever down and releasing its powerful jet of cream. The cream was cold and Danielle flinched in surprise, then returned to her licking duties.

Our highly enthusiastic Angela was ordered to lick the cream and without hesitation she leapt to it, slowly winding her tongue around the crease before sucking the contents out like a ravenous dog with a loud, slurp. (Also known as felching).

Now with their bellies slightly satisfied, we embarked upon a game of musical cocks. This is exactly like musical chairs but instead of choosing a chair when the music stops, the subs must put their mouth around a cock. Lady R and Miss Kaz were practically crumbling with laughter at this point watching the slaves bump into one another, fumble around and try to go for the same cock which led to a few stumbles. This game was mainly for our personal entertainment as not much cock sucking was getting done, so after refilling our glasses, we decided to engage in the main event.

Angela is such a slut that she loved nothing more than hot spunk on her face, so to finish the little soiree, we instructed Danielle and Sandy to lift their dresses and let Angela juggle their cocks, as Lady R would say, do a bit of downhill skiing. She couldn't get enough of these, greedily devouring one hard penis, then the other, using both her hands, her thirsty lips sucking as her head bobbed back and forth in a frenzy of cock lust.

Danielle, who was already in a state of excitement, was struggling to hold back after her creamy blowjob and asked for permission to come. We agreed that she'd earned it and it took less than 30 seconds for her to release a huge jet of cum over Angela's face - her dessert. With a shit-eating grin on her face, she certainly looked like the cat who got the cream.

Sandy being the dark horse she was, took some time to get to the edge. Lady R then whipped out a pink, vibrating buttplug, which she slid into Sandy's waiting butthole to stimulate her senses - or her backside at least anyway! Meanwhile, Miss Kaz, sidled over to Sandy and started to whisper all manner of filth into her ear. "I bet you love feeling that naughty bitch's slutty lips around your hard dick don't you? I hope you are going to spunk hard all over her face and give her the creamy treat she deserves. Come for me and Lady R, you dirty subby!"

We winked at one another in that symbiotic way they had developed and gently cupped a hairy ball each and gently started to tickle and tease.

Within seconds, Sandy's whole body was jerking and he released his hot load, which splattered heavily across Angelas face. She made no attempt to wipe it away and simply said, "Thank you Mistress's, I needed that." All we could think is what a greedy bitch Angela is today.

Chapter 23
Timewasters

So we have divulged in detail the ruthless, warts and all details of BDSM, the highs, the lows, the downright filthy and now let's hear from real life submissive men, dommes, fetishistas and their thoughts on their BDSM journey.

Q&A between Kaz and Lady R

Question 1: What's the weirdest way a slave has wasted your time?

Lady R: Over the years I must have heard just about every single excuse! I had guys that would say they were five minutes away, only to disappear and later send pictures of a smashed up car and claim they were in a crash. Funnily, I never heard from them again so I know they were just your stranger types of timewaster!

I also heard from another domme that she was in a session with a new sub and his Mum came home early! She ended up having to climb out of his bedroom window! He later asked me to do a session with him to which I replied, "I'd love to but you haven't got a good track record and my ability to shimmy down a drainpipe isn't what it used to be!"

Kaz B: When I was a baby domme, I did fall prey to a couple of the more weird and wonderful scams as I was quite naive to them and couldn't quite believe the lengths some men would go too just to get a bit of free chat. A classic example is the Amazon scam.

A guy will buy you gifts from your Amazon wish list so that you chat to him online. Shortly afterwards, the order is cancelled and no gifts arrive. Obviously, they can only pull this stunt once and they target a new domme every time as you wise up to it fast! It's pretty desperate and pathetic and I feel a bit sorry for them that they have to pretend to send a gift to get someone to chat to them when they could have just joined in with some of the banter I have on Twitter - now known as X!

Another example, which is too obvious to fall for, is subs that ask if they can pay for chat by buying your online movies. This means that as well as getting the movies they paid for, they would get free chat too. This was met with a resounding no!

What is the most common and frustrating excuse that subs use to cancel last minute?

Lady R The most common excuses are the cars broken down, a family member in hospital and some have even gone as far to say that a relative has literally just died.

Kaz B It's amazing how many grandparents these subs seem to have isn't it Lady R!

Lady R The funny thing is, if they were honest and just said they could no longer make it, I wouldn't mind so much but the terrible excuses were so frustrating. It got to the point where I had lists in my phone with entries going up to Timewaster 452!

Kaz B Haha - I tend to save them as things like Timewasting twat-nob or Crap-for-brains TW as I lost track of the numbers!

Lady R The no shows were the worst because you'd be sat there all dressed up and ready with the equipment ready to go and they wouldn't arrive.

Kaz B It's completely disrespectful and they lack common courtesy and manners. I found that subs would usually use work as an excuse to bail, which was probably true in some cases but the more obvious timewasters would wait till 5 minutes before the booking to say, "Oh sorry, I thought you were in Manchester/ Dundee/Aberdeen - basically anywhere at least 100 miles away!

Would you ever see a client that wasted your time before and would you punish them harder for it?

Lady R First of all, they would be paying me an extra fee to make up for last time and I think there would be an air of attitude as they walked in. As they were tied up they would get a few more extra cracks of the whip - 100%! One time my cleaning slave let me down at the last minute. The next time he visited, needless to say he was cleaning my toilet - with his tongue as I supervised!

Kaz B If someone let me down last minute, I wouldn't see them again without a deposit, unless it was a regular that had a good and believable reason. They would need to start the session naked on their knees, apologising and begging for forgiveness. I might forgive them if they carried out some jobs around the house that needed doing but if I was really upset, I think only eating a dish of the stinkiest cat food would redeem them!

Lady R Do you remember the sandwich fucking session?

Kaz B That was hilarious! We buttered slices of bread and he had to make love to it while moaning like a girl!

Lady R I think we need to write another chapter after this!

Kaz B I know, some of the insane humiliation duo's we did were next level!

Chapter 24
Humiliation

Humiliation is an aspect of femdom that is a strong joint favourite! To be fair, each chapter drips beautifully with heavy doses of humiliation, so it may have gone unnoticed but we couldn't resist the opportunity to relive some of our most favourite moments of dishing out humiliation, for you lucky readers to enjoy!

Allow us the pleasure of taking you through one of our favourite sessions! New Sissy Sam visited us for a humiliation session and had requested we dress him up as a woman and laugh at him. We chose some exotic lingerie consisting of a pink, lacy bra and a crotchless thong that did little to hide his modesty! Amid peals of laughter from the two of us, Sam shook with excitement as we giggled at his little appendage swinging in the breeze! Attaching a sparkly, pink collar and leash to his neck, Sam was ordered to all fours as we took turns in making him walk to heel as he crawled on his hands and knees behind us. He didn't make a good pet puppy at all and when we put a doggy dish of our fresh piss on the floor he lapped at it pathetically until we popped our feet on his head, ordering him to drink and make little doggy chuffing noises between every sip.

We were vaguely amused but the role of a humiliation sub is to entertain his Mistresses as much as possible and make them laugh out loud. This was how we assessed the session, by how much we laughed during his antics. By this point, he was barely raising a chuckle as subby worshipped our feet and licked our toes, whimpering as he switched from foot to food, slobbering all over our toes.

"Make more effort! We are not impressed!" We admonished our slave.

"Sorry Mistresses, I skipped lunch and I'm struggling to focus."

"Oh, did you miss your lunch Slave? Were you expecting to be fed?"

"No Mistresses."

"Did you hear that? Subby needs feeding? Shall we feed our pet?"

"He'll have to work with it if he expects his lunch!"

Mischievous looks and whispering to each other followed while Subby tried to make out what we were planning. We led our slave by the leash into the kitchen and threw two slices of bread and some butter down on the counter with a box of wafer thin ham and some salad cream. Slave stared at it dubiously, wondering what we were up to.

"Go on then, make your sandwich bitch!"

Do you have a knife please Mistress?" The slave mumbled.

"Of course not! As if we would allow a sub to play with dangerous objects. You'd probably end up losing a finger or thumb. You must use your pathetic, little penis to butter the bread!"

Sam was clearly enjoying being humiliated by two dommes as his little member was standing out firm and erect and made a suitable replacement for a butter knife as he enthusiastically stuck his penis into the butter tub and scooped out a table spoon worth of butter and proceeded to smooth the contents over the two slices of bread with his erect penis.

Next he placed several slices of ham that were arranged on the bread to look like a clitoris. Finally, we told him to apply a generous serving of salad cream to ensure the sandwich was nice and moist.

"How do I cut the sandwich Mistresses?" Sam muttered, his eyes wide.

"You don't, darling! You will fuck the sandwich now and how well it holds together is a good measure of your sandwich making skills."

"You aren't really going to make me fuck the sandwich are you, Mistresses?" Sam's jaw dropped.

"Bitch, you either fuck the sandwich or go hungry and stand outside in the cold in nothing but your bra and crotchless panties! What is it to be?

"OK, OK, sorry Mistresses! I'll fuck the sandwich now!"

We laughed as Sam tried to slide his cock in between the two bits of bread and he struggled to get inside of it. Soon enough, he figured out that he could open the sandwich and pop himself between the bread and the ham and with that Sam began to thrust his hips.

"Faster bitch!" we hollered! "Grunt for us!" "Oink like a piggy!"

Our commands and demands for more speed and ridiculous antics increased and Sam ended up on his knees thrusting into the sandwich as if his life depended on it as he squealed like a pig and thanked us profusely for the privilege!

"Oooh uggh. Mistresses! I'm going to come, please let me cum, I'll do anything!" Sam implored us as we cracked up laughing at his predicament.

"If you come piggy, you eat the whole sandwich!"

"Yes Mistresses, yes, I'll eat every drop!"

We gave Sam our permission and he hammered away at the Mighty White sarnie as if it was Nicole Kidman in front of him and not two bits of soggy bread. He groaned, caught up in the moment, his swollen ball sacks popping out from below the now - tattered looking bread, with every pump of his pitiful penis.

"You have 7 seconds to come, or you are going home with blue balls sissy bitch and you won't be given your clothes back either!"

We began our countdown, 7....5....3....6...2...Sam panicked with every number we enunciated.

"1...0...cum for us bitch boy!"

With that, as we hit 1...Sam started to buck and moan the house down as he pumped that sandwich full of a month's worth of warm, man juice. The now sodden sandwich was hanging by a thread! It seemed only right to whip out a tea plate, pop a napkin on the side and serve Sam his "lunch!"

"Best eat up hungry subby. Make sure you eat all your lunch and make sure you finish every   fucking crumb!"

Under the watch of our beady eyes observing him, Sam reluctantly held the sandwich to his mouth and took a bite. As we continued to humiliate and belittle him, he realised that his best bet was to get through the sandwich as fast as possible and bite it down in big chunks, his hot man juices merging with salad cream and spilling down his chin with every mouthful. Well, let us tell you this, he was extremely grateful for that napkin! He used his tongue to lap up the final crumbs and the suspect, creamy looking substances on the plate, then wiped his mouth and grinned, a proud expression on his face!

It seemed he was expecting some praise but instead we informed him that next time it would be a tuna and mustard sandwich, and to get dressed and get out before we changed our minds about returning his clothes!

And another disgustingly fun day was had by all!

Kinksters Stories

If you've made it this far in the book, it's only fair that we reward you with some truly unique and interesting stories from other side of the BDSM community. Remember, indulging in legal and consensual kink should not bring any shame and can be part of a healthy lifestyle. We hope you enjoy the stories and don't forget to leave us 5 stars in the reviews on Amazon.

Spanks and kisses

Love Kaz B and Lady Rampage.

Story 1
Human Teller submissive male with Gynoid fetishes

Gynoids are feminine robots, appearing in the sci-fi genre. Other nouns used are fembots, femdolls, cyber dolls and female androids.

Gynoid fetish along with associated mannequin and freeze fetishes are far from uncommon. They're often lumped into a general 'technosexual' and 'asfr' (alt sex fetish robots) umbrella. This is an attraction to people/your partner acting and moving like a robot or frozen like a statue or mannequin. How did I get into it? Thinking back as a youth I was always turned on by robots (particularly Androids) in any Sci-Fi shows or films. It was only after I'd known my Mistress for a while that I felt confident enough to mention it to her without feeling embarrassed. It's roleplay isn't it? Not too dissimilar to a 'sissy' wanting to be feminised really when you think about it. Just acting out fantasies within roleplay. Having read about it online there are two camps within 'asfr,' 'built' and 'transformation.' I'm very much within the 'built' faction, - i.e. in that I want to be an Android, a machine with no humanoid components. 'Transformation' or as you know 'Trans Humanism' is when you're turned into/upgraded into a cyborg/ robot. A big part of it for me is my deli packaging (shrink wrap mummification), also the box - again deli and my dreams to be on a conveyor belt/baggage carousel. I think that comes from when I've seen cars or washing machines etc being built in a factory on TV, i.e. having my limbs or head etc being applied to my torso by industrial robots as I travel down the conveyor belt. A huge part of it is my Domme playing as a sexy/evil scientist in her lab coat. That's a fairly common trope of many sci-fi films and obviously I have it in my subconscious from childhood. I.e. you are activating and programming me. As I say, it's a common scene from 'Robo Cop,' 'Terminator,' etc. If you were to look into it, Gynoid fetish and an attraction to fembots are far from uncommon. I've spoken to other technosexuals about it online and they are jealous that I have somebody understanding enough to help me with my fantasies being acted out. Check out how many robot clips there are on 'clips4sale' and 'I want clips.' In my youth, there was a really cheesy awful sci-fi flick that had a scene that really turned me on called 'Battle Beyond the Stars.' It's a knock off of 'Seven Samurai.' Anyway in this one scene, a beautiful scientist forces an Android to enter a force field or vortex type thing and knowing it will be destroyed it still has to follow its programming. I just remember it was one of the first times I was aroused. Essentially in my mind we're playing those parts I guess. To a certain degree, I also like the mannequin side of Gynoid, but I'm not turned on by puppets. My ultimate dream is being a (male) blow up doll and being inflated by my domme, then punctured by her high heels and deflated. Generally my fantasies end with me being destroyed.. Android - deactivated or better still you activating my kill switch will detonate my hard drive, punctured (see above) or consumed after mating - the sexual cannibal thing, or similar and a Zombie Mistress chewing on my thighs or eating my genitals, sorry - not sorry!

Story 2
Mistress Sophie Of Hertfordshire
– Transgender Autistic Dominatrix And Goddess

What can I say about Mistress Kaz B, (Princess Kaz_DOM to use her official Twitter handle). From my own point of view, meeting Kaz for the first time was a special moment in my life, and one that I'm not likely to forget about in a hurry.

This was in 2016, a time long before COVID had ever reared its ugly head. At that time, I'd just started to experience not just the BDSM and kink community, but also had started to take action in regards to my own gender identity. My own working position had just become stable from years of uncertainty around job security, so I was starting to come forward and think to myself about what was making my mind tick. With the arrival of my own gender identity from being a woman trapped inside a man's body, came the rise of another set of feelings, that of a sense of vulnerability.

Enter the scene where I'm now googling terms such as 'bound and gagged', 'damsel in distress', 'tied up and gagged' etc. When you place these terms into Google now, the first major barrier that you encounter is coming face to face with the links to porn videos, (no surprises there). But in-between the sexy videos of half-naked scantily clad ladies and general pornography depicting acts of depravity that some might vomit at, comes a whole new line of interest. When the terms BDSM and domination came floating into my mind's eye, it didn't take me long to realise that this was a whole other world that I just never knew even existed.

Being one of the many taboo subjects that the vast majority of society prefers to just brush under the carpet and pretend not to have noticed. Or else when seen or heard about by others, was something seen as seedy, perverted and to be avoided like the black death. (Something of which I've had first-hand experience on, as even though I'm happy in my Sophie state of mind, I still wouldn't walk down the street in a latex catsuit).

"What is this new and wonderful world I've stumbled across" I thought to myself, as I scrolled down the countless list of dominatrices on the page, in wonder and awe of how sexy and powerful these ordinary everyday women could be with just a simple change of clothing.

In my own mind, that was when the seed was planted in my sub-conscious of how I would want to look, in which I would picture in my wild imagination to be as gorgeous and divine looking like these all-powerful goddesses were. Then the unmovable and depressing reality would hit where I would stare into the mirror and see a towering well-built biker with

short cropped hair, with little to no chance of ever passing myself off in the image as a charming and beautiful fairy-tale princess.

It was at this point that I thought to myself that I would chase down my other passion that I had in life, in which I'd been crossdressing behind everyone's back since I was a small child.

The same went for LGBT matters in mainstream education, where Margarets Thatcher's poisonous Section 28 policy had done absolutely nothing but screw over entire generations of young people. (Well, everyone born from the late 1970s onwards at any rate). Having been brought up in quite a conservative narrow-minded neighbourhood, it was still a bit of a mystery to me as to why I was feeling a certain way, having had no form of teaching about LGBT matters, let alone kink and fetish play.

From an early age, I was always led to believe that being tied up and gagged was something only seen on the television or during an

abduction. So, I had to ask myself the elephant in the room sized question of why I felt the need to feel rope, tape or even zip ties around my hands and feet. As well as the sensation of being unable to speak with a gag in my mouth, struggling at the tightness of the restraints as I lay there in the dark and quiet.

It was a mystery that puzzled me, until my own line of work at the time presented me with more of an opportunity to think about this point of view more often, as well as the assistance of a well-known internet search engine which we've all come to rely on in our day to day lives. Because of the sensitive nature of what I was doing, I'd adopted the strategy of always going further afield of my hometown when it came too, attending cross dressing agencies and kink sessions.

Hence why in late 2016, I found myself attending my first ever kink session with the stunningly gorgeous, intelligent and highly charming Mistress Kaz B, who at the time owned a small flat in the area of Reading town centre. When I saw Kaz for the first time, I just couldn't stop thinking of how stunning she was, although with an air about her of a lady who knew how to control people just with a swift expression and glance of her eye.

On that occasion, Kaz had gone for a black leotard style outfit with a jet-black corset and thigh high stiletto heeled boots, which was an outfit that suited her right down to the ground.

When Kaz had quizzed me about what kinks I wanted to explore, I'd told her of the ambition of wanting to know what it was like to go through a military style interrogation. Having been a former member of Her Majesty's Air Cadet Corps by this point, I was curious to know how I would far up under interrogation, having done the theory on basic mental torture survival techniques during basic training. Kaz being the outstanding actress that she

was, rose to the challenge with magnificent splendour, delivering a session that I would never forget for a long time.

I'm sure that Kaz herself won't mind me saying this, but when I first sat in her presence, I got the unearthly sense that I was the presence of a lady who knew how to understand those like me.

Through a personal reason that I won't divulge, I found out that Kaz and I were connected in a way which neither of us at the time knew or even understood. For a bit of a backstory, it might be a good idea to tell you all that I was diagnosed with Asperger's Syndrome, now known as high function Autism, when I was just three years old. In recent years, this has become something which has defined me as a domme, because I do see that the kink, BDSM and fetish community attracts so many of those who are from the

Autism, ADHD, ADD and LGBT communities. Being Autistic myself, I feel that I do have a somewhat unique view into the mind of a submissive within the above listed communities, so this is a target market that I have zoned in on and have had a great success in, while aiding and assisting said individuals on their journeys into subspace.

The same went for myself and Kaz, despite the fact that we'd only just met, I couldn't help feeling that there was a more powerful connection in motion. You see, being on the Autism Spectrum, I'm inbuilt with a lot of hypersensitivity, so allowing a complete stranger like Kaz to tie me up and then use me however she liked was a pretty big deal. Kaz seemed to adopt what you might call a 'killing with kindness' approach, which meant that she would stroke and caress me one minute, and then violently slap me across the face or in the

cock and balls. But it was when Kaz's finger made contact with my skin and stroked me up and down in a way that made my penis stand on end, a strange sensation shot right through me. But it was a sensation not just of a romantic nature, but also that of mutual respect and supernatural understanding. The best way I could describe it, as being a jedi knight and having the ability to detect other jedi knights around you.

(Mind you, Kaz would be easily powerful enough to be able to

THE RUTHLESS GUIDE TO BDSM

pass as any one of the jedi masters in the Star Wars multiverse, or Mistresses in her case). This is what happened the moment Kaz touched my skin,

because normally in any other circumstances I would've hit the roof in shock, as sensitive tactile touch is something Autistic individuals find difficult to do. It was from that moment onwards that Kaz and I would start seeing more of each other in sessions, as I tried to come to terms with my new love of BDSM and kink. One session turned into two, which became three, and then four; although all good things had to come to an end at some point. In 2018, I was finally forced out into the open as being transgender,

which began a spiral over the next few years and put an end to all forms of BDSM activity for an extended period of time.

My last ever session with Kaz was during a special triple domme event, in which I was dressed up as a stunning bride and picked on and abused by three highly powerful and manipulative goddesses portraying the jealous bridesmaids, Kaz being one of them, (all in the name of fun of course). It was certainly a high to go out on, as I began to fade into the background, content on not upsetting my family anymore due to the violent nature of my outing as Sophie.

The result of the workplace attack on me that had outed Sophie to the world didn't just lose me my job, but also forced me out to my family as transgender.

My transgender outing had a fallout which lasted for months, where I ran away from home for a week or so and was nearly reported as a missing person as a result of the whole affair. This was alongside a failed suicide attempt where I contemplated deliberately crashing my motorcycle at high speed, which never worked out thank goodness.

'Every cloud has a silver lining' as the old saying goes, because being outed to my family as transgender made me realise that my family were a bit more open than I thought they would be.

Of course, the name I'd chosen for myself was 'Sophie', so my male name became just a name used by those who weren't aware of my transgender state. I started therefore to explore my transgender side from 2018 onwards, but a lack of funding and a desire of not wanting to bring my kink side to the surface meant that Kaz and I slowly drifted apart into the ether. Although Kaz's thoughts of being a playful and interesting submissive to her hadn't

quite gone completely away. While being out as Sophie had come with an interesting series of suggestions that I'd never thought of before. It was then in 2018 that I found the social media site called FetLife, which overnight exploded my understanding of the BDSM, kink and fetish community.

As a bit of an experiment, I decided to do a photoshoot with a good friend of mine wearing a domme style outfit, setting myself as the alter ego of 'Mistress Sophie', aka my true domme self. And just like that, the lady that you all now know today as Mistress Sophie was born. What I hadn't expected was the explosion of messages I would get, in which countless numbers of unknown male slaves would contact me via FetLife, begging me to dominate them, in the same way that Kaz had done to me all the way back in 2016.

Lacking any kind of dungeon facilities, I was unable to do any kind of professional sessions, but yet I started playing with subs at clubs and events. Then of course came the Covid-19 pandemic in 2020, which overnight shut down any kind of play whatsoever, putting a huge strain on the mental and physical health of us all. Skip forward to 2022, where Kaz and I were suddenly thrown back into communication with each other via email.

The subject matter of said email was my recent move into the world of writing, whereby I'd put a suggestion to Kaz about a new BDSM novel, knowing of Kaz's legendary fictional literary work into the realms of creative writing with her kinky and fetish book series, (confessions of a dominatrix being by far my favourite). Kaz later admitted to me that I'd gone about trying to convince her of a novel writing collaboration the wrong way, (hashtag slap yourself in your own face), so a typical failure on my part there of seeing the world in a different light; DOGH. Although in hindsight, Kaz appeared to change her mind less

Then a year later, in October 2023, we finally came face to face together for the first time in years. To give Kaz her due, her memory was bang on about me, having remembered so much from 2016 and when I used to session with her as a submissive.

The event that we bumped into each other at was the Birmingham Fetish Weekend, where I was attending as a host being my true and authentic Mistress Sophie self.

To my great surprise however, as I stood there having a much-needed drink at the bar, there she was, the one and only Mistress Kaz, her face hidden by a fancy and lovely designed sex cat mask. I just couldn't believe it, after all these years of being apart, the one person who had helped me on my BDSM journey was standing mere feet away. The temptation was just too great, as every nerve in my body told me to approach Kaz to say hello. Of course, Kaz herself had never seen Mistress Sophie before in her domme-like deminer, so it was hardly surprising that Kaz didn't have a clue who I was. With the equivalent boldness of the StarShip Enterprise, I gingerly approached Kaz from where I was standing at the bar, making sure to place myself in a position where I didn't scare her.

This was easier said than done, as some of my previous training from years gone by had enabled me to be able to sneak up on people completely undetected, in the same way as a special force's unit would track and hunt down enemy units. "Hello stranger" I said right beside Kaz after I'd moved into position, which naturally made Kaz start with surprise, wondering with curiosity who this strange lady was that'd just

popped up right beside her out of the blue. "Oh, hello" came the response from Kaz, in which I saw the natural eyes narrow slightly behind the cat mask, as Kaz tried to make out who I was.

"You probably don't remember me, but we met a long time ago" I replied as Kaz's eyes widened with interest, intrigued to know more, as I could see the journalist in her spring into action.

Even though Kaz didn't speak, I could see the questions exploding out of her like fireworks, as Kaz is a kind natured and curious lady bless her soul.

"Oh OK, I can't make you out, but I'm sure it will come to me" replied Kaz as I started to flick through my phone trying to find a picture of my male self. "Well if you don't remember me, you're likely to remember this guy" I replied, showing Kaz the picture of myself all the way back in 2016 with my short-cropped hair and slim build.

I have of course grown my hair since 2016, in which I Immediately after seeing my 2016

picture, Kaz smiled broadly and uttered something along the lines, "oh I remember now, how have you been, wow, you've changed".

"Yeah, I've been great, it's amazing to see you again, as I know we drifted apart and everything, how are you doing" I replied, as the rest of the conversation was sadly lost to the

channels of history.

Kaz was simply amazed at how well I'd done since we'd last seen each other, in which

I'd told Kaz all about my journey from going from a submissive into a domme.

Although I would later confess this to Kaz herself, being back in her presence was soothing and reassuring, to the point that we ended up having some interesting conversations and becoming solid hard friends to boot. At the time of writing this, I can safely say that Kaz's influence has been the main driving force in my life, with my soul promise to her that I will assist her in any way that I can. The fact that I'm writing this piece for her even now shows that Kaz has much cemented herself as a key pillar in my lifetime and

her contribution to it. In recent times, I look at being in the kink community as a case of progressing from a submissive to a dominant, or else in some cases feeling dominant for years and then taking a step back to be more submissive. It's like the analogy that goes something along the lines of, 'the best managers are the ones who start on the factory floor', in other words, the ones who work their way up through the ranks.

I've always had that thought process in my mind, as I have indeed worked in companies where I've had to start from the bottom and work my way up.

What I later learned was that the true power of a domme is not too just be a domme, but be both dominant and submissive simultaneously. During sessions, any pro-domme will tell you that no matter how much it looks and feels as if the dominatrix is in charge, it's actually the case of the submissive being more in command than the dominant. If it was the case that the submissive was less in control in real life, then it would completely undermine the safe word system. Even though Kaz would never use those exact words to me in any of our conversations, I would still get the feeling from

Kaz's teachings that this way of thinking was what was expected from a dominant in a submissive and domme style dynamic.

From my own point of view, the one thing that Kaz had granted me wasn't just a lifelong friendship or a shared interest. What Kaz had really given me, was acceptance, because I have come across a number of people in society that think that transgender women are not real 'cisgender' women, (in otherwise, the term used to describe a naturally born lady). The fact that I still had a set of genitals between my legs and no natural breasts despite being a female domme, didn't bug Kaz in the slightest.

It's certainly made life exceptionally difficult for me to try and fit into female clothing, knowing that it was designed for flat front and hourglass figures, which I most certainly don't have. Kaz not only saw through this, but also saw it as a way of acceptance, because I did bring one great advantage to the table. Kaz herself knew her kinks, no denying that; although there were some kinks that I had that could be combined to her own collection.

They always say you can't teach an old dog new tricks, but

with Kaz, you most certainly can, because instead of rejecting my kinks, Kaz instead told me that she was willing to learn them and even implement them into her own sessions. I certainly brought a lot to the table that even Kaz admitted sounded pretty cool, like for example my skills in sissy maid training, the ability to perform a fake kidnap or abduction, as well as having a certain skill for inflicting what I've come to call, 'psychological warfare'. All of which when performed in safe and kinky settings make for some interesting fun indeed, which certainly appealed to

Kaz's way of thinking. As of the time of writing this, Kaz and I have embarked on a domme tour, playing with submissives from all over with our dominant and sadistic twisted ways, (in a good sense mind, never a bad one ha-ha).

One of the most common questions I get asked is, 'what do you like about being a domme', for which I always reply, 'being mentally creative, and having the ability to think on the spot'. You see, it's interesting to just drag a submissive in through the door, beat seven bells out of them and then push them out of the door again; that would be properly sadistic. A major part of being a domme is all about having the ability of shaping a persona that others can believe in, but still at some time maintaining dignity and humanity. Because let's face it, yes while in session I can be Mistress Sophie, a sadistic evil bitch that can crush some cock and balls without thinking twice about it. But that doesn't mean that I'm then going to go into the street and then do a Miss Piggy style karate chop on a fellow human being in the goolies, in the same way as I would do in a dungeon play space.

(Which just for the record, is the fastest way of getting arrested, no matter how much you bat your eyelids at the police officer who's snapping the handcuffs on your wrists and reading you your rights).

Mind you, I suppose from a kinky and rather romantic sort of view, having a hulking great male police officer show up and snap handcuffs on you would be pretty sexy, (especially if you loved bondage, because you'd be begging the police officer not to take them off). One of the many viewpoints that I've come to see while being a domme is knowing when to draw the line. What I mean by this, is the ability to know when a play session can go too far, hence why we have a thing called, 'safe words'. Because I set myself up as a female domme who can perform kidnap and abduction sessions on submissives, I do regular messages from submissives saying something along the lines of quote, 'please kidnap me Mistress Sophie'.

(Well, who am I to deny a submissive of the opportunity to feel like the abducted actresses in the movie series 'Taken', starring legendary actor Liam Neeson).

It's when said submissive then comes out with a comment along the lines of, "and can you please do it in public", that I need have to slap my hand across my

own face in exasperation. The law states that kidnap's, false imprisonment and abduction are illegal, although if the person being kidnapped gives consent, then, well, what then? It's certainly not illegal if you don't press charges of course, but then at the same time, all it takes is for a passer-by to see a domme snatching the submissive off the street, and the next thing they know, their being swamped with half of the countries armed police officers who fully believe that an actual series abduction has just taken place. (Which in case you wondered, has very much happened before in the UK when a kidnap session went wrong).

So, my answer in this sort of situation if a submissive client was to message me with an enquiry on this front would be, "well if you have a huge farm which is not overlooked by anyone, has access to a dungeon play space and a van, then yes, I can help you achieve the session you want". In reality, most people don't have access to these sorts of resources, so they just instead content to me sneaking up behind them, clamping a hand over their mouth and pointing a water pistol into their back to make them comply. (Of course, if you

were rich enough to own private land not being overlooked by anyone and wanted to be kidnapped by me, well send me an email and I can get the ball rolling). From 2018 to the present day, I can say that my kink journey has gone from strength to strength, with a few minor points that I've had to get used to. Although I may feel like a female domme, I'm still having to fight the transgender label, which is a bit of a bummer.

Another large drawback is that even without heels, I'm still a towering six-foot giant, and am well-built enough in physical appearance and weight to even make a freight train cry with envy. It's always a pain not being able to show too much skin or body shape, which after all is a key aspect of being a dominatrix. I do still have my age on my side which is a good thing, so I'm just trying to make the most of it while it lasts. It may interest some of you to know that from an early age, I have suffered from hormone deficiency, which has made me think that it's a key part of my gender dysmorphia. Either way, when you go to certain

events and people are staring at you like you're the most stunning object on two legs, it does really lift your spirits. I'm sure my fellow female dommes will agree with me here, but being female is about feeling good in yourself, especially in your appearance.

When you're transgender, being told that you're quote, "one of the girls", is the great compliment that anyone can bestow upon you. That and the fact that my Autism has always been a barrier to exploring any form of social scene, it pleases me to know that acceptance is something that can be found in the BDSM, kink and fetish community. In 2023, I coined the term to renown kink podcaster Mr Nicholas Tanek of, 'there isn't a single topic in the world that can't be a kink', and I stand by those words, because I do believe that kink is just that. Another interesting point about the BDSM, kink and fetish world, is that it's far easier

to interpret what is considered consensual and non-consensual. For those with learning difficulties, this can be a huge bonus, as not only does it help navigate social cues, but also gives a clear line of communication between the different players in a kink scene.

Many times, I've had Autistic kinksters approach me and ask about how to go about being in the fetish scene, as they are either too afraid, or else unsure how to approach a submissive of a domme. Well, my message to those reading this is, 'don't be afraid, it takes a lot to shock a domme, so just talk to us openly, as we are here to help you', (just don't be a dick around us and ask us anything that we've clearly told you not to do). If you do see me around, don't be afraid to come and say hello, as I don't bite, (well, not unless you

want me too at any rate he he).

Story 3
B - Submissive male

Many people reading about BDSM and female led relationship will ask why would you want to do that? In my case I can offer some strong arguments in favour of why would you not do that? Before going into details about my own choices it might be worth touching on some general points about the average man and how they impact on lifestyle, these are broad-brush high-level observations, not tablets of stone.

The demands of masculinity make it difficult for men to express emotions and share their needs in relationships. Men tend to form functional relationships, he can help me with work, play sport together, go to the pub etc, rather than enduring and deep friendships that ladies form

Many men grow up to be stoic, lonely and isolated with few friends. As a consequence of the above for many men the opportunities to relax, let go and de stress are missing and these pressures are carried into their work and home life. A lady visiting a spa regularly is seen as therapeutic and healthy, a man seeing a Mistress to achieve the same sense of wellbeing would be frowned on by many, why?

Entering into a relationship with a skilled Mistress can help a man deal with many of the masculine characteristics that impinge on their lives and prohibit them from becoming the person that might strive to be. Having been involved in the scene for more than 40 years, I can say with complete confidence that this is the case if you allow yourself to let go

It didn't start this way, like all things in life when you look back there are a couple of moments that set you on a path, in my case, it was this around 1970/71 aged 16 one of the guys at school got hold of an "underground magazine", from his older brother, these were written and produced by an individual, a few copies made and then circulated to a small group. This particular one contained 2 stories, all illustrated and lots of detail. The first and this is where it starts was about 2 Mistresses and a latex slave who was dressed in multiple layers so that the gap between suits could be inflated turning him into a giant ball that could be bounced round the room.

The second was a detailed water sports story, about a chained slave and a Mistress whose bladder would "soon be empty".

Once I started worked, in London, I was able to turn these initial thoughts and dreams into some sort of reality, you have to consider that there was no internet or mobile phones, the only real options trying to see a Mistress were contact magazines and telephone box roulette where you would see small cards in telephone boxes promoting all sorts of possible delights, these rarely lived up to the image, but some contacts were made, some good and some not so good but the journey had started.

After a number of false starts I met a Mistress who offered much more than a quick caning and some leather clothing, this was a lady who understood both her role and the need to explore with her subs their needs and expectations, for the first time I was with one someone who could help tease out the need that I had for surrendering to someone, being in a situation where I did not have to take charge, make decisions etc, my mind was liberated.

Perhaps at this point we should look at two words with different meanings but ones that those outside the community many see as interchangeable. Slaves and submissives, slaves don't have a rights, choices or freedoms they are there to serve their Mistress in every way, a submissive and I consider myself as such, has some rights and sets limits but the Mistress has complete control within the agreed framework.

Limits will be explored and pushed and new experiences tried but within a consensual relationship. I have over the last 40 years met some wonderful ladies, my preference has been to get to know and serve a lady for a number of years, these relationships evolve and grow. I have for the last 5 years served the same Mistress (do you want to be anonymous?)

It's not wrong to enjoy your kink, it's actually healthy, it allows you to relax and enjoy experiences that are crucial to your own mental health, embracing kink has made me a much better husband, father and whilst I worked "boss"

I would like to expand on this point and bring in another couple of expressions that are used in the community, Subspace and Sub drop, I will start with the latter, it's generally seen as a mental and physical low, that starts after the end of an intense session and can last for hours or days, I am not qualified to speak on this issue as I have never experienced this, I can however expand on Sub space and the mental wellbeing from sessions.

At some point during the session a sub who is working with an empathetic Mistress who understands their needs and can guide them and challenge them further, may experience the mysterious Sub space, it's different for everyone it might be an out of body experience, or a trance like state, whatever the feelings the sense of euphoria is a key element of the experience.

This sense is associated with an increase in endorphins, these hormones are released during pleasurable activities and help relieve pain, reduce stress and contribute to a sense of wellbeing.

It is these latter feelings that for me last for weeks and are one of the many reasons I enjoy the scene, this sense of wellbeing is carried into my day to day life, I am fortunate that I have never suffered with mental health problems, or stress related illness, I have an escape valve but also this form of escapism is great fun, yes there is some pain involved but it's consensual and controlled, a good Mistress will read her subs reactions and adapt to them and help guide them to this special place.

I would like to add a few final thoughts:

Be honest about your experience and what you enjoy, your

Mistress is not psychic, she can build a session around your needs but only if you communicate with them.

If you are taking any medication and use poppers tell your Mistress, I have spoken to many subs who have no idea that the most dangerous effect of the combination of Viagra and poppers is a serious drop in blood pressure that can be fatal sometimes even for experienced subs and Mistresses the session does not work, talk about it afterwards, it might be expectations or just a lack of chemistry but it happens and it may be best for both sides to move on.

It's not wrong to enjoy your kink, it's actually healthy, it allows you to relax and enjoy experiences that are crucial to your own mental health, embracing kink has made me a much better husband, father and whilst I worked "boss".

No sensible person would turn their back on those benefits.

Story 4
Zara Du Rose – pro-domme and award winning fetish performer

For me, kink is all about exploring, release & finding your personal boundaries.

My journey started from when I was young by tying up dolls and playing games, but of course at that age it's an innocent exploration. It wasn't until later in life I realised the kink within me was always there and that it began at such an early stage.

Through exploring my kinks, I've learned a lot about how to set boundaries and clearly explain what I do and don't like.

I've tried everything that I ever wanted to (starting as submissive and moving to being dominant) and even though some things aren't to my liking for what I enjoy now, I'm glad I've had the journey to truly say I've given it a go!

Latex has always been a big part of my life. The fascination started in school with swimming caps. I used to make latex clothing for a short time and I am glad that my work gives me the opportunity to have such an extensive wardrobe of latex outfits. The look, the smell & second skin feeling is incredible.

Rope play is another key kink for me, tying others and thinking of ideas of how ropes can be used to enhance a play scene. However, sometimes it's fun to just start tying and see where it ends up for aesthetic purposes.

I also love being bound in ropes, but only by trusted people who know what they're doing and not as a 'submissive' role. I love watching someone else work though their process of tying and different styles. The hug you get from being bound is comforting and the marks left on your skin afterwards are satisfying to see.

My experience has been a positive one. I wouldn't still be involved in the lifestyle if it wasn't something I enjoyed!

I first started exploring as a submissive and pushed my boundaries to try new things. Over time with a girlfriend, I discovered the other side as a Domme and found I was more comfortable in that role.

I worked as a dominatrix for a few years which was both rewarding and exhausting.

I took a step back from doing purely Domme sessions as I stopped enjoying them on a personal level. But I love doing kinky GF experience meets and still enjoy exploring kink in my private life.

I feel that through BDSM a lot of people learn how to communicate boundaries, which helps in life outside of kink and can make you grow stronger.

It's often that people in high powered, stressful jobs need a release to submit and let everything go for a short time. Without that, real life can be overwhelming and become too much, BDSM is the escapism that's important for many.

The endorphin hit during and after a play session is euphoric & having those moments as memories is always something that stays with you.

Are there any negative sides to BDSM?

Unfortunately, there are people out there who use BDSM as an excuse to be abusive and manipulative or push people into doing things they wouldn't usually do for a power trip.

I remember being called weird a lot because of my interests when I'd mention it to friends or co-workers when things came up in discussion. I was often made to feel like something was wrong with me. BDSM is definitely more in the public eye now and there's more of an acceptance about it now, since 50 shades was released (which I despise for a few reasons…) people have started exploring more and it doesn't feel as taboo as it did.

My first experience with anal fisting was for a session (I'd only ever fisted my GF vaginally at the time). When I arrived for the booking, the client had a room which was covered in black plastic sheeting and proceeded to show me his collection of toys, lubes and gloves. Some impressive toys!

Fast forward to the action part & I had one of my arms in him up to just past the wrist, he then asked for my other arm to be inserted! I tentatively eased my way in and ended up with both arms inside him almost to my elbows!

At that point I realised "this is my life now" and loved it! It's surprising what you can fit with enough practice. Everyone needs a hobby, right?!

Story 5
Miss Kat –
Trans Woman and kink switch

A switch is a person who enjoys elements of submission and as well as displaying dominance, so they switch between the two depending on the play dynamic.

My name is Miss Kat, a trans woman and a switch that leans vastly towards my submissive side. I have been involved in the kink and BDSM lifestyle for over 30 years and was in a female led relationship with my late Domme for about 10 of those years.

For me, kink is an outlet. As a submissive, it is a way of relinquishing control to another and following a Mistress' direction. My favourite kinks are bondage and impact play. There is nothing more enjoyable to me than being blindfolded, restrained, and eagerly anticipating the sting of a riding crop, the slap of a paddle, or the lash of a flogger. I have thoroughly enjoyed every scene that I have been part of.

My fondest memory was also my most cathartic. Years ago, before I transitioned, my Domme and I were engaged in an impact scene. I was restrained on a St. Andrews cross, my back to her. The scene started with a riding crop and light impact. When she moved on to her favourite nubuck leather flogger, she intensified the impact of each stroke. When the session continued for longer than expected, she asked if I was OK. I affirmed that I was and she continued, hesitant. She noticed that I was crying and stopped again to ask how I felt. Through the tears, I told her I was fine. She continued, but increased the time between each lash. Finally, she brought things to a stop when my crying became more pronounced. As the restraints were removed, I collapsed and began sobbing uncontrollably, repeating that I was sorry. She walked me over to the couch in the dungeon. Still crying, I kept saying that I was sorry. She said that it was OK, that there was no need to be sorry. It was then that I told Her that I wasn't apologising to her, but to my Dad.

I had lost my father at a young age, 8 years old, and only days before my 9th birthday, I was the one that found him. He was born with a congenital heart defect and had suffered a major heart attack at the age of 29. After hearing a thud, in the bathroom, I had investigated and found him there on the floor. My apologies were because when I found him, I was in shock. As an 8 year old back in 1976, I had no idea what to do and simply stood there, rooted to the spot.

That femdom session helped me come to terms with his passing. That it wasn't my fault and there was nothing anybody could have done.

During aftercare, my Mistress simply held me and assured me that it was OK.

My domme and I had a romantic but non-sexual relationship. And I think many people have the misconception that kink and BDSM is always about sex. This isn't the case. Simply being held in Her arms was perhaps one of the most comforting things I have ever experienced. And it showed how humble she was in her dominance. She told me that night something that will always be with me. She said, "Though you may kneel before Me, you are NEVER beneath Me."

Story 6
PDSF - 42 year old submissive foot fetishist and trainee masochist

A masochist is someone who is aroused by
elements of pain play and receiving pain.

Saturday, 3rd September 2022. What made this day the day, I can't say. This, however, was the day I finally jumped over the edge, having spent 30 years yearning for the courage to take the leap....

I'd known that whole time that I was a submissive man, but struggled to accept it. As a young man, in the pages of magazines like Cruella, The Governess and Miss Sadie Stern's Monthly, I saw images and read stories that resonated with me so deeply. Sadly, they were so far removed from reality for me.

I didn't know anyone else who was submissive. I didn't know anyone else who had a foot fetish. I was an anomaly. An outlier.

As the internet age bloomed, access to Female Domination became easier and easier. Like the proverbial kid in a candy shop, I devoured anything and everything I could find. I found the websites of a few Dominatrices but I was too scared to approach any of them.

My head was full of unfounded fears. How would I cope being in the presence of a man hater? How would I cope with being beaten within an inch of my life by a crazy, sadistic Domme? Would I immediately regret embarking on this journey?

My teenage years, my twenties and my thirties all passed

without me pursuing my fantasies. They remained buried, hidden away. My secret shame. I felt like I wasn't a "real man," because "real men" weren't submissive foot fetishists. I didn't tell any of my partners about it. I didn't tell anyone.

Now, into my forties, the toll of not being my true self had started to weigh heavily. My mental health had begun to suffer, to the point where I had to take a number of months off work. I sought help from my doctor, and my employer helped me with access to a counsellor. I was veering dangerously towards a dark path, such was my low self-opinion.

Things had to change.

Counselling helped me to be kind to myself, to treat myself as a friend and to talk to myself kindly. Slowly, gradually, I started to accept my true and honest self. It's still a work in progress, but it's progress - enormous progress - nonetheless.

I joined Twitter under an anonymous name (PDFS) and slowly began to follow people in the kink scene. I followed Dominatrices and subs alike, watching and learning from their posts and interactions. I learned about terms like SSC (Safe, safe and consensual guidelines) and began to understand how things worked in reality. I joined a sub support group and learned from experienced subs about etiquette, the rights and wrongs, how to approach a Domme and what not to do.

Slowly, my confidence grew. Nerves turned to excitement. In 3 months, I'd achieved more than I'd managed in 30 years.

I'd followed Goddess on Twitter for a few months. Something just told me that She was the one. Something that transcended her clear beauty. I'd spent months reading her posts, looking at her website. I had to act. It was time.

My heart raced as I clicked "send". I'd written my application and re-read it twenty times or more. It was polite, concise, respectful and honest. Still, I had no idea whether it would be acceptable, despite my best efforts. I was excited, nervous, terrified of rejection.

A couple of days passed. I tried to keep calm. I'd received a message back to say that replies could take up to a week, so I knew not to panic. Just need to keep calm and accept whatever happens next.

A couple of days later, I received an email notification. "From what I have read so far, I would be happy to see you for an appointment". My heart raced. I literally punched the air with joy. It was an enormous sense of achievement, just taking that first step.

A couple of weeks later, I arrived on the doorstep of Goddess' dungeon. I was naturally nervous, but the overwhelming emotion was excitement. I stepped inside and my life changed forever.

In that 2 hour appointment, I experienced everything I had dreamt of for 30 years. It was mind blowing. I experienced sub-space, which was a wonderful, floaty experience. I finally felt like I had come home to my true place. All thanks to this wonderful, beautiful Goddess.

Most importantly, she made me feel entirely safe and looked after the whole time. I was able to express my submission without judgement for the first time ever, and it was truly life changing.

I walked out of that dungeon a different person. Well, the same person, but changed forever, for the better. That was just the first step on a wonderful journey.

I've had two more sessions since then which have been even more wonderful than the previous. The effect on my mental health has been phenomenal. To be accepted without judgement and to have permission to express myself in the presence of such a beautiful woman has been a tonic for my soul.

I've also made some incredible friendships with fellow subs, who have provided such amazing support. I've found the folks in kink world to be the most open, non-judgemental people I've ever had the fortune to connect with.

Though I still haven't been able to tell my friends or family about my kinky life, I'm no longer ruling out doing so. The self-acceptance and confidence that has come with being in this world has been amazing. Even if I don't tell them, I know I have a brilliant support network with my little kink family that I've found.

So, why am I writing all of this? Well, to perhaps reassure you if you've not taken the first steps on your journey yet. Don't wait too long, but don't jump into the first opportunity either. Do your research. Find someone who practises SSC. Make friends with other experienced subs and learn from them.

Most of all though, don't judge yourself harshly. Something I have learned is how wonderful, wide and varied the kink world is, and how friendly and welcoming the vast majority of people are as well. You may feel like you're on your own; that you're a freak or an anomaly, but you soon find out that there are a hundred, a thousand other folks just like you out there. With that comes the most amazing reassurance that you are, in fact, entirely normal, and that you will be accepted for everything that you are.

It's life affirming stuff.

Story 7
Krissy – Submissive male

Leather first rose to popularity in the 1940's when gay men who served in the war pursued companionship and company amongst like-minded people. Leather became in higher demand throughout the decades with entire club nights and events devoted to its appreciation which lead onto leather becoming more mainstream by the 80's and worn by those exploding onto the pop scene, film industry and consumers.

My favourite kink starts with leather. It is the basis of the fetish and creates this rebellious vibe. It may have all started for me in the 80's, being a staple in hard rock music. I was always attracted to women wearing leather because you knew it meant they had a sultry edge to them. This of course got me to where I couldn't get enough of just magazines. I started my road to crossdressing because I craved the feel of it more often than most people. This led to me being put into several embarrassing predicaments through the years, either through my own will or female dommes. And yet here I am back for more. I come to realise I can never escape my love or the control it has over my life. I have leather dresses and over 12 pairs of leather pants and wear them every evening when I get home. I even sleep in them or wear them to get groceries or work outside. When I see a woman in leather I fall out. I would pick a woman in leather any day over one that wasn't regardless of the other attributes. It's like a spell. Can I break it? Answer remains to be seen but 25 years later it still has me mesmerised.

On other occasions, practising my kinks alone has proved more worrying. Self-bondage be aware! Saturday started as any other day except I knew my significant other was going shopping out of town, at least an hour and half away. This obviously gave me plenty of time to dress up in a sissy dress and bondage. The thing about self-bondage is that each time it requires a heightened risk to get a high. Eventually this would put me in dangerous territory. Once I knew she was gone for a while I knew I had time for a hard to escape scenario. After dressing in a leather slut outfit I proceeded to hood myself with only holes to breathe through the nostrils. I decided to use 2 sets of cuffs to bind my hands behind my back. One pair had a chain and the other was a rigid hinge style. To make it more daring I faced the sets of cuffs against each other so that the key holes were inward. This turned out to be a bad mistake. With the rigid set on I could never get enough room to get the key entered. I was locked in a leather bondage hood and couldn't get out. I started to panic so now I was really scared with my breathing. I managed to find a sharp butcher knife blindly in the kitchen to somehow cut part of the hood so I could see a little. I soon realised there was no way I could get the cuffs off and my wife would come home and not only find me bound but also as a leather slut. I had one terrifying option…. I had a side grinder in the toolbox. I would try to cut the cuffs off with limited visibility, movement and while cuffed with my hands behind my back. I tried several times nicking my bottom and wrists. I couldn't cut in the same spot. The metal started to heat up and was burning my wrists. Extreme pain and panic set in as I now gave in to the idea my wife would find me as a bound sissy. I started to run the cuffs under the sink to cool off the metal and kept retrying until an hour later I broke free. My hands and wrists were burnt and cut as well as the floor and vanity. I made it out with only 15 minutes to spare. I don't remember the story I told but I don't think it was too believable. Let this be a lesson on understanding the situation and being safe when performing self-bondage. Besides the scars for life and humiliation I almost ended up in the hospital or worse. Practice caution and don't go too extreme.

Story 8
Sammie Switch

(a switch can be dominant or submissive depending on the
relationship or roleplay dynamic)

Twitter: @sammie_slut

As a Child who grew up in the early 80's, I was subjected to every
strict gender stereotyping and restrictions, with any infractions
resulting in severely violent punishments or emotional abuse. This
included but was not restricted to; trying on clothes that did not
enforce a masculine stereotype, playing with dolls, having long
hair, having piercings and not wanting to fight people or play
masculine sports etc. I'm extremely grateful to the kink scene for
giving me an outlet to explore my femininity and experience things
that didn't fit these strict stereotypes, in addition to helping me
reframe some of the trauma that came from being a disappointment to my parents, or in other words, being a cis male child that
was called "weird", "a mistake" and "wrong" for merely wanting to
explore my feminine side. I guess it follows that my favourite kinks
are feminisation, strap-on play and cuckolding. The feminisation
finally gave me a chance to explore dressing up and playing with
makeup, in a safe environment, while strap-on play gave me an
opportunity to experience penetration and further turned those
inflexible gender stereotypes upside down. I also have a deep love
for cuckolding as I feel that it's the most intimate act that you can
experience with a life partner, although I often wonder how much

of it also comes from wanting to deliberately subvert the strict rules of monogamous relationships that are sold to us from an early age as being the only possible "valid" relationships available to us. It has occasionally caused issues when emotions outside the session have filtered in but even when it doesn't go well, it's usually still the hottest form of BDSM play.

My experience of BDSM in general has been really good, there are a lot of really lovely people on the scene; there's no judgement, preconceptions, or animosity for the most part. The only time this has ever really been difficult is while playing with life partners in a session following some sort of unresolved disagreement. I feel that BDSM is incredibly beneficial to your mental health. For me, it has given me a chance to take abuse that I had suffered as a child and reframe it in a way that makes me feel happy or horny. Obviously having good boundaries and using consent driven play is integral to this but I've been really lucky to play with some of the most caring and down to earth people within the scene. There can occasionally be negative sides to BDSM. BDSM can create a long running power dynamic that spills over into all of your vanilla interactions; From a submissive perspective, it can occasionally lead to you agreeing to things that you're not comfortable with and ends with you feeling pressured to do everything that's asked of you in your vanilla life outside of scene play, in the same way that you would submit to your play partners whim within the context of a session. My view of submission is that it requires an enormous amount of trust. To give your body and being to someone else is an intimate and somewhat terrifying act that takes a lot of good communication and care on both sides. Obviously, you have a safeword if things really get out of hand, but by the time you use the safeword the psychological damage may have already been done. When this is done right, it's a feeling of absolute nirvana, however if it's done wrong, it can introduce feelings of distrust into a relationship that didn't previously exist on any level; It's a delicate balancing act and I feel that the only way to do it is to be brutally honest with people about the way you are feeling. If anyone oversteps a boundary or goes against your consent, it's always best to discuss this and highlight the issue as soon as possible; it may be that they just forgot; we are all human after all. It can also be difficult sometimes at parties if your Dominant leaves you under the care of another Dominant individual, if this happens, you need to have talked about this as a possibility and consented to being left. In addition to having discussed consent and limits with the person you are being left with. When this doesn't happen it can be a terrifying and traumatic experience with what could essentially be a complete stranger. As a Dominant, I suppose the difficulty is dealing with the somewhat obsessive nature of submissives; especially if you have a lot of them.

Once you have played with someone that you have a connection with, that connection is massively amplified which makes you both feel good. If you have many submissives all calling for your attention at the same time, it can sometimes be difficult to see them as being on the same level as you which can cause you to dehumanise them in some way, forgetting about the enormous amount of trust they have placed in you and thinking of them as less than you in some way, even outside of a scene context; which is crazy really, given that we are obviously all human, and all equally important. I have known Dominants in the past that have capitalised on these powerful feelings in order to manipulate or destroy aspects of people's vanilla lives outside of session play that they had no right to meddle with; this can be traumatic for everyone involved. It's always a shame when you see people weaponizing aspects of these feelings to deliberately hurt people. An ex-partner of mine outed me as trans, bi, and a sex worker, to everyone that they were able to contact via my Facebook. I pray this doesn't happen to anyone else as it caused an enormous amount of painful trauma and hardship at the time. From a pro-Dominant perspective, the negatives tend to come when submissives turn up for sessions in an unclean or unhygienic way, demanding that you play with their bodies despite the pungent and downright unsexy aromas that they then refuse to clean from their body before play begins. I feel that Sessions always work best when people are equally prepared to make the effort, making it much more fun for all. The more effort that everyone puts in, the better the experience is likely to be. In my experience, society tends to treat people involved in BDSM as different or abnormal in some way; this is now starting to get a bit better but it used to be abhorrent. In the past I have been verbally abused, sexually abused, beaten up, and in one instance bottled, just for wearing a dress in public. It's always been a scary experience to be different but I like to think that we are still evolving as humans and I have certainly seen a dramatic improvement in people's perceptions and comments over the last 20 years.

I remember renting an Airbnb some years ago to go to an event, which turned out to be just a room at someone's house. It didn't seem like it would be much of an issue when I first arrived as I was only greeted by one person. Unfortunately, as I went to leave, fully dressed in my; slutty dress, wig, makeup, fishnets and high heels, I found that I had to walk through a room of about 20 devout Muslims who, it's fair to say, did not agree with my life choices that evening. I was verbally abused on the way out of the house and told that my stuff would all be burned. I ended up going to the event and trying to have the best time I could with all that worry but then wasn't able to get back to my stuff again afterwards. I did eventually manage to get all my things back through Airbnb, and even got an apology but still had to find somewhere else to sleep that night, and then make my way back home, halfway up the country, still dressed in my slutty Sammie attire. London can be a scary place at night sometimes. In conclusion, good, honest communication is the key to any BDSM relationship.

I love being cuckolded but without good communication this can go horribly wrong and can be incredibly traumatic. I'm Polyamorous but I would say that one of the most emotionally difficult sessions I've ever had was with a partner and her lover, who I didn't realise had become her primary partner during the time that we had been unable to see each other during covid. There were a lot of unresolved emotional issues that had sprung up from a lack of proper communication and so much time apart. When we met each other for the first time following the lockdown, things were super awkward and neither of us properly addressed it. I had arranged a lovely hotel and meal night that I thought would be fun but my partner wanted to spend time with her new partner so she suggested a cuckold session. I wasn't at all in the right headspace for that at the time but have always adored being cuckolded and didn't want to be a killjoy so I agreed. After getting dressed up, and meeting her new boyfriend in Sammie mode, I was restrained in four point bondage and an enormous ball gag was put in place to keep me quiet. I'm unsure if it was the tight bondage, the gag, the unresolved emotional issues, or the fact that I was unable to safeword, but I felt totally disconnected from the session that it gave me feelings of being less than human in some way. Unfortunately, it was also difficult for her new boyfriend too, which resulted in there being little sexual contact between them both. After about two and a half hours of watching them talk, cuddle, and do drugs together, having completely forgot I existed, I realised that our relationship was fundamentally over and shifted myself into a position whereby I could at least try and get some sleep. It was a devastatingly painful realisation. Several hours later when they noticed that I had fallen asleep they untied me and I couldn't get my body out of a freeze trauma response. This then turned to a fawn response as I was made to feel like I had completely ruined their evening. I still feel like I should have done something different but I couldn't control my body or feelings and couldn't say a safeword either. I often lament the fact that we didn't have an honest and clear discussion about our relationship before starting a session as intimate as that but I feel this anecdote, although hugely painful, highlights the importance of good communication and honesty within BDSM relationships. A lack of open and honest communication can be the downfall of any BDSM relationship.

Story 9
Tall Ian - Submissive man

When I visit a Mistress, I tend to go for small, but fierce ladies, and love to be humiliated by them. The sessions are always filmed, and there is always a script. This adds to the fun, and when I watch them on web sites it's exhilarating to see that other people are enjoying the sessions.

Walking through a door, and having a 5ft'4 lady rip your clothes off, then order you to do all sorts of silly things, and push your boundaries? This is exhilarating, exciting, always memorable, and very, very naughty! This has to be good for your mental health, as you are having an incredible, and unique experience!

When I was a novice, I had no idea what I was getting myself into! I looked through the web, and found a Mistress, left a comment on her Twitter, "Can I be in a filmed session with you?" To my surprise she actually replied! My comment was only a joke! So, I had to book a session. Travelled to her lair, and nerves were going mad. Walked up to the door, and when she opened it, standing in front of me was a sexy, 5ft, blond hair, and dressed in an amazing sexy outfit! Purple leather skirt, high heels, and glossy, nylon stockings.

The session started with me standing naked, and my mistress on the bed. I had to do a silly dance, waving my little willy in the air. Getting loads of small penis humiliation, and much to mistress amusement! Then I had to suck some dildos. Constantly being ridiculed. After that I was strapped to the bed, and tickled. Got spanked till my bum was red. Towards the end my nerves got the better of me, and my little willy stayed little! Mistress did like to giggle at it. Somehow I came without an erection! When the session ended I knew I would be back for more!

I now have had many great BDSM experiences with my Mistress and friends. All sessions are filmed, and have a role play theme. My favourite things have been stripped while strapped to a St Andrews cross, dick slapped, humiliated in many different ways, spat at, pegged, pinched, rode like a horse, laughed at, nipple pinched, and look forward to trying to push it further in the future.

Story 10
Podopheleus – Submissive male, advocate for men's mental health and author

Hello kinky folks,

Before I get started, please allow me to introduce myself. I am Podopheleus, the author of two novels:

'Triple-Formed' and 'Sexual Equanimity'. I also run my own website, where I host blogs, podcasts, interviews with the BDSM community, pro-domme testimonials, and poetry. Furthermore, I am an Advocate For Change, working towards the liberation and normalisation of topics related to submissive men, femdom, and sex work. Within the community, I am known as a kinky journo and poet. In addition to that, I manage three support groups for submissive men and co-host Twitter spaces alongside the wonderful Kaz B.

Being a submissive man: finding a pro-domme and being true to yourself is one of the challenges of being a submissive man and a novice. Wanting to embrace your submissive tendencies is all about finding the right pro-domme. Now, let's delve into the specifics to gain clarity on how one can go about finding the right Domme while also understanding the type of submissive they are.

1. What type of Submissive are you?

It is essential for a submissive man to establish what type of submissive they are. For example, are you super obedient – a "yes, mistress" type of submissive? Or perhaps you are a little more on the mischievous side, maybe a bit bratty. Maybe you are into sensual play, or you enjoy being a slut, or you are a hedonist. Are you specifically interested in humiliation and degradation? Knowing what type of submissive you are will help you communicate your desires to your Mistress.

Secondly, there are many Mistresses out there, and certain Mistresses specialise in specific activities. It might be worthwhile to do some research about the Mistress you are thinking of contacting to find out if she is a specialist in any particular activities that align with your desired kinks, fetishes, and play style.

2. Are Dommes dominant 24/7?

Spoiler Alert! It's important to remember that Dommes are real people, just like everyone else. The persona you see on social media is often a marketing tool. In reality, being a pro-domme doesn't mean being dominant 24/7. Some Dommes even have Submissive roles in their personal partnerships or have vanilla partners. You might be surprised to discover how many Dommes share similar interests with you, whether it's music, books, food, cuisine, TV shows, or movies. So, when reaching out to a Domme, don't let the fantasy element cloud your judgement. Remember that you are communicating with a human
being, not a mere fetish dispenser.

3. What are your limits and boundaries?

As a submissive man, it is imperative to know your limits and boundaries and be clear about them. This is not something you should keep to yourself or shy away from expressing. If you have not communicated your limits to your Mistress and she crosses them unknowingly, it can lead to a negative experience for both of you. Therefore, it is important to communicate clearly, openly, and honestly about your limits and boundaries.

4. Is Aftercare important to you?

Aftercare is an area in femdom that is often highly neglected. Some dommes offer extraordinary aftercare and take the time to ensure that their subs leave a session in good spirits. They dedicate additional time to help their subs wind down. On the other hand, there are dommes who offer little aftercare, sometimes due to back-to-back appointments, leaving little room for additional aftercare since the next client is on their way. This can cause the submissive to experience an immediate drop that can last for days.

It is also important to consider what type of aftercare works for you. For example, do you seek affectionate gestures like cuddles, going out for a meal together, or simply having a drink and a chat?

Each Mistress may offer different types of aftercare, so don't be afraid to ask a Mistress about the kind of aftercare she provides.

5. Can you be open and honest with your Mistress?

This is something I hear quite often, "I don't feel comfortable speaking to my Mistress about certain things." If you find yourself constantly walking on eggshells around your Mistress and feeling unable to openly communicate with her, it may be an indication that the relationship is not suitable. A submissive should not fear their Mistress or be constantly worried about her reaction. What kind of relationship is that?

If you find yourself in a relationship where you feel unable to be open and honest with your Mistress, it might be time to consider moving on.

6. What happens if your Mistress disrespects you? Do you just accept it because it's femdom?

Let's clarify something here. As a submissive man, you are not a mug. If your Mistress constantly talks to you in a disrespectful manner that goes beyond consensual play, where she abuses her power and continually disrespects you outside the boundaries of your dynamic, that is not all right. Submissive men should have the courage to speak their mind when they feel disrespected, as long as it is done in a respectful manner.

You can articulate your concerns respectfully and assertively, without being an asshole or

confrontational. The issue is that submissive men often avoid confronting their Mistresses out of fear of upsetting them. However, allowing a dominant to abuse their power will only have a detrimental impact on your mental well-being in the long run. It's time to start standing up for yourself and expressing your thoughts honestly, while maintaining a respectful approach.

7. Communication is key

Communication is key to resolving most issues. If we examine history or arguments between friends and family, most of them can be traced back to either a lack of communication or the mind-set of "I am right, you are wrong." When it comes to communication, the responsibility can fall on both parties.

Every Mistress is unique and may have different preferences for communication. Some prefer written communication, such as messaging or emails, while others may be open to voice notes or scheduled calls. Regardless of your preferred method, make an effort to communicate clearly using your Mistress's preferred method of communication.

Sometimes Mistresses can be busy and things may get missed. If that happens, try not to hold it against them. Instead, work together and show empathy. Mistresses often receive a substantial volume of emails, along with managing sessions and other tasks like marketing and accounting. Remember, efficient communication requires understanding and adapting to each other's preferences and constraints. By doing so, you can cultivate better communication with your Mistress and build a stronger connection.

8. What should I do if something goes wrong between us?

It all depends on what exactly happened. Was it a miscommunication? Something you did? Or something your Mistress did to you? In my opinion, unless it's a major issue, most things can be resolved through a one-on-one discussion.

However, it's important to note that some Mistresses may not have the time or willingness to engage in a one-on-one chat, especially if they are not being compensated for it. They may also refuse to book another session if you have done something to upset them. This can be a grey area, and it's crucial to understand your own Mistress's boundaries and preferences.

I recently came across a Twitter thread discussing a similar subject matter. It suggested that if a submissive man upsets his Mistress, he should send her a huge tribute as a way to show sincere

remorse. Personally, I'm not entirely in agreement with this approach, as simply throwing money at a situation does not make it disappear. If I upset my wife, I wouldn't buy her an expensive gift to mask the issue. Instead, I would opt for effective communication, discussing what happened and how we can overcome it to strengthen our relationship.

In my view, the best course of action is to have an open-hearted conversation with your Mistress. Clearly express what happened and work together to determine the steps needed to resolve the issue and improve the relationship.

9. Gratitude, Gratitude, Gratitude

When you finally find a Mistress who aligns with your style of play, with whom you can speak openly and honestly, and the dynamic flows smoothly, it's like a ship with an optimised hull design on a peaceful summer's day. Everything feels harmonious and without obstacles standing in the way, akin to a ship gliding effortlessly through serene waters. It is essential to express your gratitude, but be mindful not to overdo it and avoid overwhelming others. Express gratitude without becoming excessive, as it can turn

into a nuisance, akin to someone having a good ol' chinwag in the middle of a swimmer's lane. It's essential to find a balance so that your gestures of gratitude are respected and appreciated without disrupting the flow of the situation.

Gratitude can be expressed in various ways, such as a simple thank you after the session, a thoughtful gift, a voucher, contributing towards your Mistress's expenses, creating a meaningful present, writing a poem, or even writing a testimonial about her.

Mistresses put in a great deal of effort to ensure that we have the best possible experience, and a lot goes into it, from responding to our messages to planning the session and even cleaning up afterward.

Therefore, it is essential to consistently show some form of gratitude as a way of acknowledging their efforts.

10. Are you happy?

Above all else, it is crucial to ensure your own happiness before visiting a Domme. If you seek out a Domme as a form of escapism without truly loving yourself, it may provide temporary relief. However, in the long run, it can potentially worsen your well-being, especially as a new submissive. The initial experiences may become something you rely on and develop an addiction to, as you constantly seek that

feeling to feel better about yourself.

That's why it's important to prioritise inner work and

self-acceptance. Find love and acceptance within yourself, so that when you do find the right Mistress, the sessions won't become an addiction, but rather an enjoyable experience—comparable to engaging in something you are passionate about. To achieve this, you need to work on your own happiness while also finding a Mistress who aligns with your personality. Take the time to do the necessary inner work and research to ensure a fulfilling and healthy D/s dynamic.

Wishing you all the best on your journey in finding and embracing a healthy, consensual BDSM dynamic.

Much Kink Love,

Podopheleus

Story 11
Tom's Kinky Journey –
Submissive male

Hi, I'm Tom as this is my name in kink life. I'm from Germany and my Mistress knows of course my real name, nevertheless she continues to call me Tom because that's the name with which I introduced myself on our first date.

It's also a symbol of my double life as a man in his 50s, both married to a vanilla wife and the servant of a smart and stunning British dominatrix living in Berlin, who is also successful in her freelance civil job.

I can remember the exact date when my kinky journey with Mistress A started in 2019 and I haven't seen any other dominatrix since.

I have felt submissive tendencies since my teenage years, especially attracted by feet, and dreamt of being sexually dominated by older women. Foremost by a particular teacher at school and the older sister of a friend.

During my student days and afterwards as a bachelor I began to see different sex-workers and have been to some dungeons as well though I wasn't overly impressed or built up a deeper connection with one of the ladies.

After some years on the job I fell in love with a wonderful woman and finally got married, now for more than 20 years. Over time the marriage fell a bit apart for different reasons - mostly my fault I guess - but without being unfaithful at any time.

How I met my Mistress

Due to my job I have the opportunity to travel to Berlin and other major German cities for conferences and congresses a couple of times a year. I always loved these little breaks from home.

So being a bit naughty after all, and having done some research on online platforms, I finally applied for a soft domination hotel room session with a Mistress on one of my Berlin trips.

I felt utterly nervous overall and a bit curious that she was British as I always had a preference for the UK and the English language.

From today's perspective I know that Mistress speaks German quite fluently. Nevertheless she feels more at home in her native language and became the best English teacher ever whereby my English without doubt has improved over the years.

On this evening in November something I hadn't expected happened. When I met my mistress for the first time I instantly fell for her natural beauty and her soft voice with that slightly demanding undertone. After we had a wonderful conversation and a drink at the bar she introduced me to the pleasures of sub-mission and female domination playfully but strictly with much understanding for her victim. It was easy to build up a kinky connection and when she left I was as much confused as flashed and definitely wanted to see her again. We met two months later on another trip to Berlin.

Development of the D/s dynamic

From our third meeting on we met for longer dates, mostly spending at least one night together. Having a lot of social time filled with sightseeing, cinema, museums, shopping and also open talks about all sorts of things, including my family situation, we built up a deeper connection and a kind of friendship developed.

I remember well the corona pandemic and its different lock-downs. In Germany only business travellers were allowed to stay in hotels and so I organised some (fake) business trips to Berlin and Hamburg. After doing online work from the hotel room, my Mistress and I strolled, pretending to be a working couple at the hotel, through the empty streets of zombie-like Berlin.

Looking for some fun besides searching for corona test stations and showing our vaccination certificates was like a paperchase. These very naughty times really strengthened our D/s dynamic.

The first time I ordered breakfast to the room, was with my Mistress due to the fact the hotel restaurant was closed during this time of the pandemic. It was so much fun doing forbidden things beyond kink.

Kinkwise our dynamic developed over the time as well. Starting with mostly feet and boot worship Mistress introduced me to so much more as light CBT, nipple-torture and even spit-play and watersports.

And I became addicted to the riding crop, the collared and leashed horsy for some pony training. Nevertheless it's still more soft domination, without inflicting serious pain or long lasting marks.

Initially, watersports was a hard limit for me, but soon became one of my favourite kinks after I had the courage to ask my Mistress what she really favours. I love the humiliating aspect as much as the special intimacy between Domme and sub. On the other hand the discussion about favourite kinks saved my anal virginity so far.

Generally, I like to be humiliated and exposed, for example by being put on display, only wearing a collar, harness, in the window of the hotel room. Nevertheless I still totally fancy foot and boot worship, naked feet with red painted toenails in the end as the absolute trigger.

A slightly humiliating touch can add an extra layer of excitement when out at dinner.

Looking for sizes during shopping sprees, waiting patiently at the dressing room, carrying sometimes heavy shopping bags - recently we bought a big plant for her flat with a quite massive flower pot I had to carry through the city, the bag handles really painfully cutting into my skin, - and I have to organise our joint activities. When off with Mistress, there are also her witty though discreet innuendos of my slave position to others in my presence.

What kink means to me / Benefits and problems

For me kink and our D/s dynamic is a wonderful and much needed escape from everyday life. Because of all the activities besides being trained in the bedroom it feels like a most delightful, female led relationship for a time.

I'm feeling free, relaxed and open minded when together with my Mistress. I can give up control even though I'm still responsible for organising social time as a kind of her personal assistant.

There were also remarkably funny moments we shared together.

I was tied up naked as the Mistress wanted me to watch her yoga exercises in the morning. But I didn't put the 'Do Not Disturb' sign on the door of the hotel room. Therefore room service came in and found me in my unpleasant position on the floor. Mistress had to save me, at least still wearing her gym gear. Needless to say that I got punished later when she had finished her exercises and changed to her full dominatrix outfit.

I also remember open and helpful conversations about personal matters concerning both of us.

When I had some serious problems on the job, having to eat plenty of humble pie to keep my head above the water, she encouraged me by saying that she is the only person who shall humiliate me. Everything ended up well.

Mistress also taught me the wonderful idiom 'You made your bed, now lie in it' when I was a bit whiny about my family life. And she instructed me, with the authority as my Mistress, to be a good and attentive marriage slave when at home. I love her humour and indeed, following her instructions, I had the best time with my wife for years on a short trip to Hamburg recently.

I have already mentioned that I'm living a double life. My

wife mustn't know about my kink activities as I'm absolutely sure she wouldn't understand or accept what I'm doing. The marriage would inevitably come to an end. As I'm dedicated to only one Mistress and because of the long duration of the dynamic I sometimes feel guilty of cheating on my wife, which I do without doubt.

On the other hand it's sometimes difficult for me to see her as a Mistress and not as my mistress. I have had a crush on her since our first date and I have to keep constantly in mind that no matter how the dynamic has developed it is, and will stay, a client/provider relationship.

I'm sure she knew about my crush on her from the beginning on as she's a smart woman. I even admitted once having a little crush on her. Guess she also knows that this was an understatement.

Being too much concentrated on my secret escapes I had some problems valuing my everyday life, which was neither good for my marriage nor for my performance on the job. Mistress found out during one of our conversations and told me off, encouraging me to pull myself together and value my vanilla and family life more. Doing so worked and was really helpful, also for the time I spent together with Mistress, as I feel more relaxed again. Sometimes borders or boundaries have to be (re)defined.

Final thoughts

Kink and the D/s dynamic with my mistress unquestionable has enhanced my life despite all the problematic aspects of keeping everything secret. Mistress definitely changed me for the better in most parts of everyday life. I am thankful that she made me more attentive and open minded, treating other people now with more respect and friendliness than I did before. I draw strength out of my kink adventure, feeling calmer and more resilient.

What I really miss is the opportunity to share my thoughts and experiences with friends in real life though I'm glad to have found a fantastic Twitter community with wonderful people, mostly located in the UK. This may be good for my language skills but makes it difficult to meet in person, as I found no good reason so far to explain a single trip to London to my wife.

As a hotel room kinkster, I wish a solid cage were standard in every good hotel as this is the only thing I miss - a bit of dungeon equipment. Generally I have experienced German hotels as quite kink friendly.

The chambermaid who found me tied up and naked on the floor seemed not to be traumatised as she didn't report the incident. So there were no consequences after all. Maybe she had a secret talk with Mistress A and started a dominatrix career by herself.

During the pandemic, when room rates were low, I managed to stay two nights with Mistress in Berlin's five-star Ritz Carlton. After a training session we left the room for shopping and lunch but forgot to put away all of our toys and outfits. When we returned to the room everything was well cleaned up including my harness and Mistress's riding crop properly arranged on the bed. (-Ed: While we chuckled at this last comment, we dread to think how it affected the poor Maid, who hadn't consented to being part of someone else's kink. Please always be mindful about consent when practising kink!)

Shortly after I had finished the summary of my kinky journey, Mistress A decided to end our D/s dynamic. Even though I felt, and still feel whilst writing this in summer 2023, devastated and heartbroken, she did so for good reasons.

I mentioned before that I was emotionally attached to my Mistress, fighting my massive crush on her for several years. Nevertheless over time it became obvious that she and our extended meetings a couple of times a year were the main focus of my life, more than anything else, and that I had neglected my marriage and family life.

Despite a lot of open conversations on this topic and clear orders to focus more on the relationship with my wife, taking our dates as refreshing escapes from everyday life, I wasn't able to do so. Honestly, I was living just for these moments and didn't care much about anything else. Finally Mistress ended up somehow feeling pressured and that she couldn't meet my dependence on our meetings in the long run.

Also writing to her while on holiday with my wife has proven to her that I'm definitely not focussing enough on my marriage, a task she had given me with her authority as my Mistress. Mistress A therefore told me that she wouldn't appreciate being in my wife's shoes and doesn't feel good about meeting someone when it's causing problems for another person.

Her analysis; That it would be better for me to focus on other things in life, rather than her being the main focus and that she thinks it isn't good for my wife to be in a relationship with someone who is so much focused on another person, nailed it. Guilty as charged!

As Mistress A has proved to be the wise and caring person I always thought she was, she may have saved my marriage and prevented a major crash in my life, but when a dynamic ends, no matter if vanilla or kinky, it actually hurts.

Though there are lasting memories and I'm grateful for all the time, experiences and fun we had together.

So to end with a kind of witty remark; I cannot recommend falling in love with your Mistress.

Story 12
Alexander G - Submissive

I adore BDSM and when I am strapped down to a whipping bench, the first stroke of a whip or cane hitting my skin erupts my soul. This is due to the fact I am blind and I rely on sounds and smells to paint my world and tell me what's happening. I love when my eyes are closed and all I can hear is the sound of my mistress, the sound of her heavy boots coming closer, and I feel that first tentacle of her whip swish through the air, till it finds its target and slices into my back.

BDSM also helps me to finally be myself, for years I have to hide that I love to act like a woman and called myself Anna. When I am with a Mistress I can show this side, it is impossible to do this in my vanilla life. I would be ridiculed .

I wish I could tell those dear to me what my kinks and likes are but I know that the minute you tell somebody that you like being caned or dressed in tight woman's clothes, they will instantly desert you, so I hide and lie about it. I make up names so my family don't think I am weird.

BDSM is part of my life, and I wouldn't lose it for anything. I know that the minute you tell people that you enjoy domination and kink they look at you funny. As a blind man, people already pity me, and I would rather go to somebody who sees me as a full person for enjoying the same things as them, than being seen as a half person who doesn't deserve to enjoy life. So I will continue to be on the scene, I am not saying it's perfect, and I have seen how if you upset one person in this lifestyle, the whole world falls around you and throws you to the lions, but I have also seen kindness towards me, that I would never get in the normal world and I would rather have that any day.

Story 13
Red Heaven Media –
Fetish Producer and kinkster

Behind the Camera

A day in the life…

I'm running late. It's raining. The car didn't start, I couldn't get an uber, so I am using public transport.

Good start to the day.

I'm carrying a bulky case with cameras and a huge bag full of lights. This is a special day in my life as a fetish/BDSM film-maker and photographer. I had been commissioned by Darkside Magazine (an online BDSM journal) to shoot a South African domme at Peacock Parlour – a beautiful dungeon in North London. But this is a BDSM shoot with a difference.

Today the slave is Danish. His mistress wife sends him all over Europe to be the plaything of dominants in a variety of countries. Today he is flying from Copenhagen. He will be the plaything of the Mistress.

The shoot will be extreme BDSM and made for her website and for the Danish couple. I've never shot extreme BDSM before. So I am a little nervous.

I arrive, wet with the rain, tired and slightly stressed plus nervously excited. Mistress opens the door and greets me in a friendly way. I relax – she is warm and smiling and chatty. Dressed in all black, she doesn't wear the usual latex, rubber or leather – her look is stark and simple. Her short blonde hair gives her a stern or austere look. She makes tea and we talk about our backgrounds, waiting for the slave to arrive. She normally works in her South African home, but enjoys travelling and combines this with holidays and her great love – extreme beatings of willing slaves. I tell her I've never shot extreme BDSM

before – my background is shooting "erotic" fetish/BDSM. In other words, mild to mid strength BDSM. I'd shot mild fisting, anal play, watersports, humiliation, flogging and other aspects of the BDSM lifestyle but never where blood is drawn through beating.

She explains she's a trained first aider and knows limits and how far she will go. I will be outside my comfort zone today. Then, the slave arrives.

The Mistress and slave greet each other and immediately the slave goes to change. I prepare the lighting and check the cameras. I'm using three cameras – one fixed camera on a tripod, one handheld and one stills camera. We discuss the best positions to record and adjust lighting over a bench, where the Mistress intends to carry out her skills. She shows me her collection of canes and floggers. They all look evil.

The (naked) slave enters and the Mistress fixes the swing. Slave lowers himself on the swing, his arms tied back and his legs tied open. He is then blindfolded. I started videoing.

Mistress introduces herself and the slave. She explains what she intends to do to the slave and that it is all consensual. She indicates his beautiful cock cage. This is custom-made and costs a great deal! She starts by using some lube on his hole and easing various small toys into the orifice – gradually widening it so the dildos get bigger and bigger as the sphincter relaxes. The last toy is huge and I have to stop myself gasping as it's slowly pushed the

full length into his arse. She leaves it there for a while – meanwhile telling the slave how good he is and how his arse is there for her pleasure, gently rocking him on the swing. She regularly speaks directly to the camera, advising her subscribers how the scene is progressing.

The dildo is removed and she puts on long rubber gloves. She announces to the camera that the slave will take a lot more than just dildos. She tells me to bring the camera closer so her audience can see in close-up. She doesn't realise my camera has already zoomed into close-up but she's in charge so I move closer to the slave. Fingers first, her hand enters and then the palm and up to her wrist. Occasionally the slave makes a whimpering sound but the Mistress continues sliding her arm until the elbow is reached. It is hypnotic to watch. Through the lens, I see her other hand moving into shot – she inserts the fingers

alongside her already buried arm. I am starting to perspire. She leaves her arm and hand in his arse for at least a minute. Then slowly withdraws until her fingers are the last to leave his anus. This is the end of the scene, so she removes her gloves and rubs some cream onto his open rectum. She indicates to me the scene is over. The slave is helped out of the swing. Off camera – both the Mistress and slave chat normally and we all discuss the next scene. This is to be a severe caning.

The Mistress lays out on a leather couch her canes and floggers. Although the dungeon owners provide a good assortment of BDSM paraphernalia – this Mistress prefers her own implements. Understandably, as she knows the "swing" radius, the weight and the damage they can do – for this type of BDSM she won't risk using untested canes.

This scene, I am told, will last about 30 minutes. I had already taken some photos of the preparation and I asked when she would like some more stills taken. She tells me to take some before the beating and then some after. A before and after look she wants. She also asks me if I can tolerate seeing welts and blood. She doesn't want anyone to faint or even be nauseous. I say I have a strong stomach and am privileged to record her skills. I think she likes this little flattery. The slave is positioned on the flogging bench and blindfolded.

The Mistress speaks directly to the camera once more. She explains to her invisible audience that they will see a "true" caning and she thanks them for subscribing to her channel. She goes over to the sofa and holds up each cane. They are all different lengths and thicknesses. Some have small carvings on them and a mix of colours. I focus on an exceptionally lethal looking cane with a snake as the handle. The Mistress says, "I see you notice this cane" and she holds it up. "This is my Black Mamba," she adds. "It's the last

cane I will use on him". She takes the thinnest cane and I move back with the camera. She announces "Slave will receive 6 strokes" I focus on her face before she casts the first blow. It is full of concentration. Her eyes are unblinking. There is a "swish" and a "thwack" as the cane finds its mark on his buttocks . A straight pink line is marked across his arse. More strokes followed and the pink marks accumulate until a pattern emerges. Each line is exactly parallel to the one before so by the end of the cane's usage, there are six clear pink lines across his arse. "very skilful" I think.

The Mistress takes the second cane and, as before, tells her viewers its purpose. It is heavier and shorter than the one before. She takes her position, the cane is lifted high above her head and the other arm is extended – her legs slightly apart giving her balance. She remains in this position for a few seconds, then, with great aim, brings the cane down so a mark is left between the original pink lines. She does this six times, leaving another six lines so his arse has alternating pink and red lines. Twelve in total. I'm amazed at the accuracy.

Over the course of the next 20 minutes or so, she uses three more canes – each one looks like it will do more damage than the one before. Each one does. The slave's poor arse has now become speckled with blood and the marks, lines and welts look angry and painful. The Mistress checks with the slave after each cane is used and he doesn't complain or moan. My own pain level is low – a slight knock will have me yelping in pain – but this man has a pain level beyond my imagination.

Finally, She picks up the Black Mamba.

Looking directly at the camera and glancing at the slave, she talks briefly about the history of this cane – where it came from, its weight and why it's called the Black Mamba. The Black Mamba snake is the fastest and one of the deadliest in the world. She checks with the slave and says she will deliver one blow and ask again if he wants to take more blows. Stepping back, she assumes the same position when using the previous canes. For the first time, she asks the slave if he is ready. He confirms he is. After a long pause, she brings the cane down hard on him. This time he grunts – clearly feeling the shock of pain.

Very slowly, she delivers more blows – again, skilfully – checking that the slave is OK after each one.

By now, the slave's backside has welts which are bleeding and I can see loose skin forming around the cuts. Not a word of complaint can be heard from him. He lies there, naked and prone with an arse – which I think in my innocence – will need hospital treatment.

I'm expecting the Mistress to end the scene at this point but I do not receive a signal from her indicating this. I am hoping the poor man won't be put through further torture. The camera stays on as she opens a bag and takes out some medical equipment. "Now" she says, "You will see how a good slave who receives a punishment like that is rewarded". I have visions of her using her medical knowledge to torture the slave further. I am wrong. She takes out bandages, creams and various other things. She then asks me to stop recording and take some photos of her with the slave's lacerated arse. We then continue recording as she speaks to the camera about the aftercare of his wounds and abrasions, explaining about cleaning and sterilising. She gently medically deals with all the "injuries" she has afflicted. I record most of this as she believes strongly in showing her audience how it's essential to know limits and to ensure slaves are treated with respect.

The recording is stopped and she spends the next 20 minutes attending to the slave. He has removed his blindfold and is actually smiling and chatting amicably with the Mistress while she bandages his wounds.

She regularly asks him how he feels. Once finished, he goes to the bathroom and I help the Mistress clear up and pack my cameras and lights away. I ask her if she is pleased with the session. She says it was excellent and is pleased the slave has such a high pain acceptance level. She adds that she will compliment the slave's wife in Denmark on sending her husband to the UK for her service. I ask if this is unusual in her experience. She confirms it's irregular, but knows of other couples where the husband is loaned out to Mistresses internationally.

The slave is now dressed in a suit and says he will be returning to Denmark tomorrow and is intending to visit a BDSM party that evening. The Mistress says she will want the raw videos and stills (i.e. unedited) as her partner manages her site and will edit for her. We all exchange numbers and social media details and I take my leave.

It's still raining as I make my way through the crowds returning home after a day at work. My head is spinning with images and flashbacks of what I'd just seen. Had I really recorded a man getting his arse beaten, literally, to shreds? Willingly. While I jostled with the home-goers, I wondered if anyone had spent an afternoon similar to the one I'd just witnessed. Perhaps the man who sits next to me on the tube is an avid BDSM player who indulges in wild fantasies with dominants. Maybe the woman sitting opposite me on the train is an experienced dominatrix with a retinue of slaves at her command.

Tonight I have to prepare for a shoot at the Murder Mile.

Another day, another film, another meeting of pain and pleasure.

Final thoughts

I am a producer and photographer and have made many "fetish" style films. I set up a website ten years ago so people could watch my movies. I specialise in Female Domination or FemDom – but the fetish is mainly where one person controls another – not necessarily through pain – more with mind control.

Eroticism is vital I believe. So, shooting something far out of my comfort zone was an education. I realise the word "fetish" can mean countless aspects and BDSM itself contains numerous sub divisions. It was the first time I dipped into another area of BDSM. We are always learning.

Was I keen to repeat the experience? I know some of my friends enjoy "blood-play" and I'm told of various scenes which go off the scale (for me). However, I don't think I would voluntarily watch or even take part in such a scene in the future. I'm freelance, so if offered more (commissioned) extreme BDSM scenes to record of course I would take the work. I consider myself an artist and it is up to my skills to ensure the best recording is made of this and any event everyone has likes and dislikes and some prefer the outer reaches of BDSM while others experiment and find their tastes becoming more tolerant.

Because I was able to work with a highly skilled domme and a pain tolerant slave, plus see what I saw today, my tastes have certainly became a lot broader.

Story 14
Mactawser – Switch kinkster

Living with BDSM – Looking back on my
journey through life with a kink

Intro.

I am a spanko switch. I enjoy being spanked. I enjoy spanking others. I enjoy watching others being spanked. I like to photograph the results of a spanking. This kink has had a significant influence on my life, behaviour and relationships for what seems like forever. For years, I have been wondering why I have my kink – where did it come from? Was I born with it? Was it brought on by experiences in childhood? This not knowing, and the existence of the kink itself, has troubled me for a long time and has taken its toll on my mental health, not in a dreadful way, but certainly enough to have caused me a fair bit of anguish and soul searching.

With some time on my hands, I have now looked back over my life, trying to identify clues as to when my kink came into existence, or that perhaps it already existed from birth. Inevitably this has involved going far back into my childhood, and in subsequent paragraphs I describe certain childhood experiences. I would like to make it absolutely clear from the outset, that as an adult I have no sexual or pornographic interest in children or under-age persons, nor do I approve of any such interest or activity – I describe some of my childhood spanking punishment experiences purely as potential clues to the origins of my own kink. Nowadays, with corporal punishment of children almost universally banned, it may be difficult to understand its common-place nature in the home and in education in years gone by, based on the dictum of "Spare the rod and spoil the child." I hope my musings may help others to understand that they are not alone in their kinkiness, a feeling that troubled me mentally for many years before I discovered that quite a few otherwise perfectly "normal" people are "afflicted" with the same kink. (Back then, there was no internet, hence, unlike nowadays, there was no simple way of finding or identifying like- minded souls).

Life Events

The following are happenings in my life which I remember well and which I think probably relate to my kink. They are not vaguely recollected memories, nor fantasies, but memories of virtually photographic or cinematic visual quality, and it is for this reason I feel they are related to my kink. What I cannot say is whether these events were instrumental in bringing about my kink, or whether the kink was already there and my feelings engendered by these events resulted from its pre-existence.

Brenda

I am three years old, nearly four. I am with my little playmate Brenda. We each have a bag of crisps, which we are happily munching while our mothers chat in the warm morning sunshine at the side of my parents' house in Gloucestershire. Suddenly Brenda does something (I won't say what) which causes her mother huge embarrassment, whereupon she says something along the lines of, "You disgusting, filthy child!", apologises pro-fusely to my mother, grabs Brenda and takes her away towards their home, a short distance away.

That afternoon I went to Brenda's house and asked if Brenda could come out to play again. Her mother says she can come out, but that because she had been so naughty in the morning, she can only come out to play until half past three and that she is going to be sent to bed early.

When Brenda comes out, I can see she has been crying, but she seems happy to see me and we wander off together into their large back garden. Brenda tells me that she couldn't help what happened earlier, but that her mother had spanked her very, very hard. She says her bottom is still sore, and at that point pulls her knickers up "wedgie-style" to show me two very angry-looking red buttocks, which, in my mind's eye, I can still see to this day.

I feel a strange sensation at this sight – I feel sorry for my little friend, but at the same time I am somehow excited at the view. The sensation soon passes and we wander off along the lane to see if we can find any minnows in the brook, then head for the farm to look at the Piglets.

Gillian

I am now four years old. One fine evening, a little group of us are playing in the street – Brenda, Sally, Gillian, another girl (can't remember her name) and me. I have no boys to play with, the only boy living nearby being Brian, who is a bit older than me and a real bully. We are playing a sort of cricket-cum-rounders game and it comes Gillian's turn to have the bat, when suddenly she says she must go home. We try to persuade her to stay, but she says that if she doesn't get home on time, she will "get the stick" – I don't really know what she means, but as she leaves us, Brenda says that Gillian will be spanked if She gets home too late because they have a cane at their house. Again I get that strange sensation – sympathy for Gillian that she might get punished, yet some excitement at the thought of her being caned. We carry on our game without Gillian until my mother calls me in and the others drift off home.

Me

It's a few days later. Brenda and I have been playing all afternoon in our front garden in my parents' 2-man, pale green tent which my father has erected for us on the front lawn before leaving for work. It is hot and sunny. We've been having a great time. Brenda is wearing a little blue swimming costume and I'm wearing dark red bathing trunks. We have been pouring water over each other from a watering can, watering the flowers in the garden and just generally having innocent fun. Brenda and I both have our tea at our house, then we go back out to play in the tent again. Eventually Brenda's mum comes round for her and they head off home.

I continue to play in the tent for a little while and say I want to stay in the tent until it gets dark. Mum has other ideas. She wants me to come in and have a bath before going to bed. She has run the bath and doesn't want the water to go cold. She keeps trying to get me to come in, then finally tries to grab me, but I run away round the garden. When she finally gets hold of me, I turn quite nasty and kick out at her, just as my father comes out to see what all the fuss is about. Dad takes the leather belt out of the loops on his trouser waistband, grabs me, pulls down my bathing trunks and gives me three very painful wallops across my bottom with the belt.

This is something new to me. I've had the odd slap from my mother, but my father has never punished me before now. After a shocked silence, I burst into tears and Mum grabs me and comforts me, telling Dad he didn't need to do that. He says I deserved it and that His father used the belt on him when he was young. Mum is not happy. She carries me upstairs to the bathroom, puts me in the bath and washes me. My bum is still sore when She's drying me and I ask her if it's red. She says that it is, and lifts me up so that I can see it in the bathroom mirror – three neatly spaced scarlet welts across my buttocks. I am fascinated. I touch them, feel the ridges. Again, although I am sore, I have that same almost pleasurable feeling I had when I saw Brenda's spanked bottom. In my head, I can still see those marks to this day.

Sally

I am now five years old and have a posh new trike, which my parents bought me (along with a beautiful ginger kitten called "Whiskers") for my fifth birthday. I ride it out on the road sometimes, but always have problems with Brian, who keeps pulling me off my trike and taking it from me. Sally wants to ride my trike and take it out on the road, but I tell her she can't do that because Brian will take it from her. Anyway, I'm not sure I want Sally riding my trike (selfish of me, I think looking back). Sally is seven and says she isn't really afraid of Brian. I say OK, that Sally can ride my trike, but only on our house drive, not out on the road. She promises she'll stay in the drive and goes up and down the drive a few times before shooting out the gate onto the road and zooming off towards the council housing estate, where, from a distance, I see Brian knock her off the trike then ride away on it.

Sally comes back to me crying, but I am angry with her for breaking her promise and riding out on the road, resulting in my trike getting into Brian's thieving hands. Sally goes home with her tail between her legs while I run to tell my mother what's happened. She is annoyed with me and Sally, but heads off to Brian's house, confronts Brian's mum and comes back with my precious trike. She says Brian's mum has slapped his legs, but that he will be getting belted by his father when he comes home. I am delighted Brian is going to get his comeuppance, but again I get a strangely pleasurable feeling when I think of Brian being belted by his father.

About a week later, Sally comes round to our house and asks if I can come out to play.

Mum says that's OK, but she isn't going to take my trike anywhere out on the road. Sally says she's sorry, she won't do that again. It's raining a little bit, so Sally and I go into the garage, which is empty apart from my trike, because my father has gone off to work in our car. Sally wants to ride my trike again. I say she can't, because of what she did the last time. She says she's really sorry and she'll be good. I still say she can't ride my trike. She says she could just ride it around inside the garage. I say no because she'd been naughty the last time.

After some pleading, she says that yes, she was naughty, but if I let her ride my trike, staying inside the garage, maybe I could spank her for being naughty, like her parents sometimes do. I say no, but she pulls her panties down and off, then bends over the trike's saddle. I'm taken aback, unsure what to do, but I end up giving her bare bottom a few slaps and she giggles. She says my little smacks are nothing and to spank her harder, so I try a few harder slaps. She giggles again and I pick up a small garden cane and give her a couple of half-hearted strokes, leaving two faint red marks across her bum. She yelps, then laughs and says that's enough, can she ride my trike now. Without waiting for an answer, she jumps, still bare-bottomed, onto the trike and rides it round and round inside the garage, clearly enjoying every second of her ride. After a while, she says I can spank her some more if I'll let her ride the trike again. I say OK and she bends over again. This time I try to hit her a bit harder with the cane and it obviously hurts her a bit, but I continue until she's had five or six strokes before I ask if she's OK. She laughs and says she is, but she wants to ride the trike again now and I say she can. She goes round and round inside the garage again. Meanwhile I feel the strangest sensation, which I simply cannot describe, but which I now recognise as being associated with my spanking kink.

After a while, Sally gets fed up riding my trike that day. The rain has stopped and we wander off to the farm to look at the pigs and piglets, meeting Brenda on the way. Nothing is said about what Sally and I have been up to in the garage.

Later, this "You can spank me if you let me ride your trike" transaction between Sally and me becomes a fairly regular thing. We always do the spanking in the garage where we won't be seen, but in time, I let her ride my trike on the house drive. She never attempts to go out on the road.

It all ends when Sally's parents buy her a proper two-wheeler bike, which she won't let me ride because it's far too big for me, which is indeed the case. Ah well, our little arrangement was nice while it lasted.

First School (Gloucestershire) - The Girl in the Class, then The Twins

Being five years old, I am now at my first school in our local village. I like school. The (female) teachers are nice and seem to treat us all quite well, although they do warn us from time to time we have to behave properly or we could get punished. The type of punishment is unspecified and is an unknown to us children, until one day in the playground, a little girl in my class is spotted by our teacher when she punches another girl, making her cry. When we get back into the class, the teacher walks up to the miscreant's desk, tells her to put her left hand flat on the desk, then without warning gives it a whack with a school ruler. The girl bursts into tears and the teacher tells her that was the hand that punched the other girl, so the hand has been punished, and she should think herself lucky she's not getting both hands punished. The rest of us are somewhat taken aback at this and keep quiet. The teacher tells us that this is the sort of thing that will happen to us if we misbehave, especially if we bully someone or get involved in fighting.

We all choose to behave.

Later on in the school year, we are all out in the playground. It's a warm and sunny playtime and some of us are playing around the big tree in one corner of the playground when there's a bit of a commotion further along the front of the school and the two "terrible twins" are walking towards us, crying their eyes out. They are older than us, in the year above; and I refer to them as the "terrible twins" because they are boisterous kids and can be a bit disruptive, but they are not bullies and certainly not malicious. It turns out that a teacher caught them fighting each other in the playground, and, considering their behaviour to be unacceptable, sent them to the Headmaster, a mysterious figure, rarely if ever seen, but held as a threat, as in "If you do that again, you'll be sent to see the Headmaster!"

In the case of the twins, this proves to have been no idle threat. They are both holding their bottoms and wailing that they've each had six of the best from the Headmaster. In righteous indignation at his treatment, one pulls his short trousers and underpants down and bends over to let us see the result of this punishment. We all stare in awe at the six absolutely parallel, closely spaced, angry red welts across his bum. * He hastily pulls his pants and trousers up again and they both race off when they spot a teacher, who has noticed the commotion, walking towards our group. We are all horrified at what could await us if we misbehave, but again I get that strange feeling, partly of horror, partly of pleasure and partly half-wondering what welts like that would feel like on my own bum.

* Decades later, as a result of bumping into a fellow professional (nothing to do with S&M), I discovered that he had attended the same school around the same time, and that the Headmaster's idea of six of the best for boys was a single, really hard stroke across the bare buttocks with an instrument consisting of six wooden rulers, loosely bolted together at the "handle" end, spaced with washers, with the edges of the rulers forming the impact areas. This chap had actually experienced it for misbehaviour when at the school and said he remembered it "hurt like buggery" as he put it. Apparently the device was not used on girls, who instead were punished on the hands with a whippy cane.

Primary School in Scotland

I am now six and we have moved to Lanarkshire for my father's new job in Glasgow (my parents are both Scottish and are effectively moving "back home" to Scotland). I am sent to the local primary school, part way through a term. In order to assess my ability level, I am temporarily placed in the "baby class" (otherwise these days known as "Reception"), where the teacher is a fearsome woman who is Deputy Head and seems to find my mixed Gloucestershire/Scottish accent most amusing. I am surprised at how threatening and bossy she is to the Reception children, who all seem a bit cowed by her.

After assessing my reading, writing, spelling and arithmetic abilities over a morning, she assigns me that afternoon to a class with a young female teacher, who seems quite nice, doesn't mock my accent and appears to be interested in my abilities, which are apparently well up the scale in her class. Suddenly, part way through the afternoon when we are practising reading, she snaps, "Lynda, come out here!" A girl with long black hair gets up and walks out to the front of the class. "Put it in the bin at once!" says the teacher. While Lynda removes a sweet (or a "sweetie" as we would call it in Scotland) from her mouth and drops it in the wastebasket, the teacher lifts the top of her tall desk and takes out a really nasty-looking piece of dark leather strap, split in two for about half its length. Without prompting, Lynda holds out a hand and the teacher draws back her arm then brings the strap down firmly on Lynda's palm, making a loud crack. Lynda winces, but doesn't cry.

She stands still until the teacher says she can go back to her seat. "Unless you can offer e one in the class a sweetie, you mustn't eat them in class!" says the teacher. I am kind of horrified. This is the dreaded "tawse" or "strap" or "belt" that my grandparents, uncle, aunts and parents have mentioned at various times – and obviously, it's not used only on boys, but on the girls as well! Again I get that strange feeling of excitement which I can't explain, but somehow, although it terrifies me somewhat, I would like to see more of it.

In fact, as I settle into the school, I realise that I will see the tawse used most days, because although officially intended to be used only as a punishment for bad behaviour, it is in fact used for every single detected breach of the school rules and (frighten-ingly) as a teaching aid, with practically every mistake being an excuse for punishment. Failure to be able to read aloud correctly a passage from last night's reading homework, failure to be able to spell one of the words in last night's spelling homework, failure to provide the correct answer to a mental arithmetic problem, messy written work, all seem to merit at least one stroke of the tawse, not necessarily a hard stroke, but quite painful nonetheless.

Other reasons for punishment are things like late arrival (even by half a minute), having dirty fingernails, not having a clean handkerchief, forgetting to bring your "gutties" (plimsolls) or a particular book to school, etc, etc. All detected infringements of this nature result in summary punishment with the tawse, regardless of whether you are a girl or a boy, although boys, being boys, are probably more likely to get walloped than girls, and probably walloped harder than girls.

Again, I get this odd feeling when watching someone getting the tawse – on the one hand I'm sorry for the "victim" (although sometimes I think, in the case of bullying, for example, that the punishment is well deserved); on the other hand I feel some excitement within myself about the whole pain and punishment thing, especially when a girl is on the receiving end, although I still don't understand it and absolutely detest my own hands being tawsed. Strangely I feel I might prefer my bottom to be tawsed or caned.

Apart from a couple of significant events mentioned later, the remaining years of my primary education passes without much of obvious potential "kink" significance. I have new interests – Meccano construction, motor cars, electricity, amateur radio, photography and cinema (mainly Cowboys genre!). I no longer feel anything much when boys receive the tawse, except if it's for bullying – I detest bullying. I still get some sort of strange thrill seeing girls tawsed, however, and I still don't understand why.

Gillian again and two other friends

I am eight years old. I have come back to Gloucestershire with my parents who are visiting old friends and neighbours, including various "aunties" of mine (no relation, really, but they were definitely better and kinder aunts to me than my real aunts in Scotland). While my parents visit some old neighbours, I play in the street with Brenda, Gillian, Sally and that other girl whose name I've forgotten. Gillian has a two-wheeler ladies bike, which is far too big for her, but she and the others are taking turns riding it on the road.

I have never ridden a two-wheeler (in spite of regularly begging my parents for one), but out of bravado and a burning desire to cycle, I claim to have a bike and I get a turn on this one. I wobble along the road in great excitement, before finally falling off, much to the amusement of the others. I say it's because the bike's too big for me, and the others rib me about it, because they've all managed to ride it without falling off.

Suddenly Gillian says she must go home because last night she had the stick for coming home late – she lifts up her skirt to show us three fading welts across the backs of her thighs. I get that strange feeling of excitement again and ask her what this stick is like. "It's a green cane," she says, "and it hurts." Then she rushes off home. Sally gives me a strange look, but neither of us mention what we used to get up to in my parents' garage.

It's another evening during the same visit to Gloucestershire and my parents are visiting some old friends in another town a few miles from where we used to live. I am left to play with our hosts' son and daughter, Geoffrey and Ruth, both around my age. We play with a ball in the garden for a little while, then come inside and go to the boy's bedroom, where we listen to music on the radio (no iPods, iPads, iPhones, CD players, or cassette players, etc in those days) and talk about our schools. The subject of punishment comes up. The boy has been caned a couple of times on his bottom. The girl has been caned on her hands. I tell them about the frequent use of the tawse in Scottish schools and they are horrified and fascinated at the same time.

In a drawer in Geoffrey's bedroom is a stock of upholstery supplies belonging to his father, who has been repairing some chairs. Geoffrey takes out some webbing and asks if I can make a tawse to show them what it's like. With a pair of scissors, I quickly fashion a couple of tawses, one two-tongued, the other three-tongued. Then we play at Scottish schools, pretending to be pupils and teachers, regularly walloping each other with these tawses. It's quite fun and we laugh a lot about it all, although I point out that the upholstery webbing is much lighter than the leather used to make real school tawses, and hurts hardly at all, whereas the real thing is painful. They say the school cane is painful too, and we all agree that it's best to avoid getting punished because it hurts. Our game is interrupted by my mother shouting up the stairs that it's time we left, so the "tawses" are stuffed back into the drawer of upholstery supplies, we say goodbye to our hosts, and leave to spend the night at the home of one of my "aunties" mentioned earlier.

My idiotic plan for a perfectly behaved gang

We've returned home from our holiday now and I'm lonely and a bit bored, in spite of my various hobbies. The girls I used to play with no longer come out to play with me, even Sheila, who is a bit mad, I think, and always wanted to play with me in the tent (erected on the drying green, otherwise, euphemistically described as a "lawn" or just "the grass"). She liked to strip off and play Nurses and Doctors. She also wanted me to strip off so that I could be a patient and she the nurse, but I'm a bit embarrassed and not so keen. After my refusals on several occasions to take all my clothes off, she has decided I'm not as much fun as she would like and decided not to play with me anymore. I'm a bit annoyed at losing her company, but also a bit relieved, because I didn't want to undress for her and thought if I did I might get into trouble.

I'm now sitting in my "den" which is the loft of my father's garden shed, thinking too much about my lack of company. I foolishly decide I would like to form a gang of some sort, and after a bit more thinking I start drafting in a little notebook my proposals for the "D Gang" – I write out all expected behaviours for members, then a couple of pages detailing punishments for failure to show these desirable behaviours, including getting tawsed for the more serious ones. I'm initially quite proud of my proposals and a few days later, I manage to get a school friend, Donald, to come out to play (Donald originates from Peebles, which he annoyingly insists on calling "Pebbles", and that's not far from Biggar, which he even more annoyingly insists on calling "Bugger"!). I tell him about my thoughts. Naturally, he is horrified and says, "So ye mean we're gonnae be in a gang where we've a' tae behave wursels, an' if we don't, we get walloped? Jist like bein' at schule, ye mean? Ye're mad! Ye'll get naebody tae join that sort o' gang!" I see his point and we head off to the nearby woods to climb a few trees and float sticks in the river. The notebook, and my daft idea of a disciplined gang of conforming members, is thrown into a corner. *

* Decades later, while clearing out some old stuff from my parents' house, I came across the notebook. Looking at my "D gang" proposals, I was extremely embarrassed to have produced them, although the desirable behaviours were all good, kind, friendly, respectful and thoughtful, whereas the prohibited behaviours were definitely undesirable. In fact my ideals practically mirrored those of the Scouts or the Boys Brigade, but with punishments for failing to maintain the prescribed standards of behaviour towards others – as young Donald had said, much like school, really. I immediately shredded the notebook, wishing to forget about my silly ideas. That said, it's worth remembering that similar regimens are the subject of books such as "Children of the Void" and "The Feminine Regime" albeit that they involve females rather than males, so perhaps my silly young ideas weren't uniquely odd.

High School Years Transition

I am three months short of being twelve years old. I now have a nice bike and a piano! My hard work at primary school (mainly engendered, I suspect, by fear of the tawse) has paid off, and I'm at the High School, not, I'm pleased to say, at one of the other secondary schools nearby, where, if rumours are to be believed, the regimes are particularly harsh, with lots and lots of vicious use of the tawse.

Because of when our birthdays happen to fall, we are in a "transitional" class, which is a bit like still being at primary school, in that we spend most of our time in one classroom with the same teacher, instead of moving round to different classrooms and different teachers for different periods of the day. Our teacher seems quite fair. She uses the tawse only for misbehaviour (as demonstrated firmly on one "smart-ass" boy on our first day), not for making mistakes in our work. I notice her tawse is considerably heavier than the ones at primary school (except for the headmaster's one there), and that she can really lay it on. I approve of the fact that she comes down particularly heavily on bullying – we have all been bullied by older kids on our arrival at our new school, with so-called "initiation ceremonies" like having our heads stuck down the toilet while it is flushed, and so on – not nice!

The "transitional" few months pass fairly uneventfully. Our class doesn't suffer from much tawsing punishment, although often we can hear walloping sounds coming from elsewhere in the school; and we have discovered that although our teacher seems fair and restrained in the use of her tawse, some other teachers are not so, and it is easy to get punished by one of them for infringements like lateness for school (even by a few seconds), shouting in the corridors, being caught in the wrong playground (can't have boys and girls mixing, you never know what they might get up t0 - forgetting to bring gym shorts and plimsolls on the right day, etc. I no longer feel anything much when I see boys tawsed (although I might occasionally wince at the severity of the punishment), yet seeing the much rarer event of a girl receiving punishment still causes some sort of excitement somewhere deep inside me.

Onwards via puberty

With transition behind us, we're now properly in High School education. We discover that our teachers' natures range from really kind and nice, to really horrid, nasty, sadistic and vicious. The kind and nice ones never use the tawse, or only if severely provoked by seriously bad behaviour. The sadists seem to look for every possible excuse to use the tawse, and when they use it they use it most viciously, some even explaining how they ensure it's as painful as possible, both by their treatment of the leather and their mode of wielding it. Some maths and science teachers also love to explain the physics of the whole process, talking about moments of inertia, force per unit area, acceleration, and so on. One night I woke up suddenly with a most peculiar sensation. My pyjamas and bedclothes are all wet around my crotch area. I don't know what has happened, but I seem to have wet the bed. I tell my mother the bed's wet and she says it was probably my hot water bottle leaking – she'll change the bed and give me clean pyjamas for tonight. This all seems strange to me, as I've never been a bed-wetter. I don't tell anyone else about it, but worry that I may have some strange disease. It doesn't happen again for a while, then it happens twice in one week. Mum says she needs to get me a new hot water bottle, because the one I have is obviously leaky. I'm more worried than ever now that there is something seriously wrong with me. The wetness doesn't really seem like urine, nor water from my hot water bottle, but it is sticky. Then one day something happens at school that provides at least part of an explanation.

We are in a French lesson with our fairly young, quite attractive, female teacher, who has not long finished her teacher training. She stands no nonsense, but is not "tawse-happy" although she does have a fairly hefty Lochgelly two-tongue tawse. Suddenly she calls one of the boys out to the front of the class and takes out the tawse. "Get them up, crossed," she says, "you disgusting, filthy, dirty little boy." She then gives him four harsh strokes, drawing the tawse right back each time to give maximum swing and impact.

The boy is already blushing and has great difficulty holding back tears. The rest of us kind of look at each other in puzzled silence because we don't know what the punishment is for.

Later, in the playground, a group of us are discussing this event, speculating about what caused our French teacher's ire, when one of the boys who was sitting near the "victim" says what sounds to me like, "She caught him lankin' under his desk!" Some of the others nod wisely. Some look puzzled. Naively I say, "What's lankin' then?" Some of the others burst out laughing, saying, "It's no' lankin' it's wankin' we're talking aboot." None the wiser, I say, "Oh, right, what's that then?" More laughter from some of the others, although I now suspect some of that was mere bravado. The first lad, the one who explained the reason for the punishment, exclaims, "You don't know what wankin' is yet? Ye're just a baby though, so I suppose ye're no' grown-up enough tae know. It's spunkin' yersel' up, ye know, touchin' yer cock to mak' spunkum!" I don't know where to look, and am wishing the ground would open up and swallow me, when the bell signals the end of the interval and we troop back into school.

That night in bed, I think about the day's revelations. I recall one of my friends having said to me, sometime previously, that he "liked wee babies, but wouldn't fancy the dirty things you have to do to get a baby." I'd had no idea what he was talking about, and he had responded with something about getting the seed into the woman to make the baby. Again, I'd had no idea what he was on about and so changed the subject to talk about budgie breeding (his uncle was a bird breeder). Now things are beginning to dawn on me, however, and later, thinking about it all, I begin to connect my apparent bed-wetting, this "wanking" thing, and the "seed" thing. The bible story of Onan (in the Book of Genesis) suddenly comes to me, and I at last understand what "spilled his seed on the ground" meant. Now, I reasoned, as Onan was put to death for that act, spilling your seed must be a mortal sin, and sins need to be punished, or I might go to Hell.

The next time I wake up all wet and sticky, I know what has

happened. Obviously, I have sinned in my sleep and must be punished, but there is no-one I can tell about it, and therefore no-one will punish me. Hence I decide that to avoid going to Hell, I will need to punish myself. In some books I have read, there are references to nuns and monks self- flagellating to cleanse their sins, so, in order to avoid going to Hell, perhaps I should do the same. Initially I do so by smacking my hands with a wooden ruler, but it's painful and makes it difficult for me to hold my pen at school the next day. About a week later, when I have another "wet dream" as they say, I decide I need to be punished on the bottom, so I creep off to the garage, close the door behind me and wallop my bottom with a heavy wooden ruler my Dad uses for marking out his woodwork. This provides quite a lot of pain, which will obviously last a while, but doesn't hurt my hands, and I feel I am in some way washing away my bedtime sin of seed-spilling.

I now have a slightly different view of the world. I feel more grown-up and I know a lot more than I did, although, in reality, sex is still something of a mystery to me.

* I continue to have the odd wet dream from time to time, and every time it happens, I punish myself hard across the bottom with the heavy ruler. As time passes, though, I begin to find I actually get some pleasure out of the punishment. I convince myself that this beatific feeling is because I am purging my sin. In time, however, I find myself creeping away and having a wank in order to provide an excuse for punishing myself, and decide that in fact I am probably now committing further sins, therefore requiring more and more painful punishment. I have now discovered that instead of using the ruler, I can use some industrial machinery drive belting that my father has in the garage. Some of this is heavy leather, some heavy rubber. They both provide lots of pain.

* It must be difficult in these days of the internet, social media, readily available pornography, etc, for most people to understand the sexual naivete of children back then. Obviously some managed to get the information, or work it out for themselves, probably picking up snippets from older friends or siblings, or perhaps from

some "dirty book" or "dirty magazine" they'd somehow managed to acquire. With no internet, no sex education and a general taboo on anything remotely connected with sex, it wasn't easy to gain the relevant knowledge about human reproduction and "normal" sex, let alone any form of sexual deviancy. My only "sex education" was that my mother told me girls had a "slot" and that I'd know what to do when the time came; and from a male teacher who told us boys that we needed to respect girls when we dated them and, "as your mother was once a girl, never do with a girl anything that you wouldn't do with your mother" – obviously good advice except, perhaps, for those with an Oedipus complex!

As time passes, I begin to look forward to punishing my bottom, and do so more and more severely. I also find that after punishment, I feel like relieving myself again with a bit of masturbation, which obviously is even more sinful, so I come round to the idea that it's better if I punish myself first, then I have a "masturbation credit" and can have a wank afterwards without committing further sin, as I've already been punished. Somewhere in the back of my mind, though, is a feeling that I shouldn't be doing any of this, that I am weird and that no-one must find out because I'm sure no-one else has these feelings. This significantly affects my mental health – not hugely or particularly badly, but somehow there is always some sort of black cloud of sin and shame lurking in my brain and I worry that I am uniquely odd, possibly evil. Nevertheless the urges are so strong that I convince myself that it's OK, because I'm potentially harming only myself, not anyone else.

As time goes on

I carry on through High School, doing well academically (again, working hard because I am keen to learn, but also, in the subjects I find less interesting, spurred on by fear of the tawse). I don't have a lot of social life, although I do have a few male friends for company. A couple of them I go cycling with. One shares my interest in photography, electronics, radio and music, and we build (and even sell) audio amplifiers, speaker cabinets, etc. I now find witnessing severe tawsing of boys just a bit upsetting, unless the punishment is for bullying. Seeing a girl tawsed, however, is a different matter and excites me, especially if she has chosen the tawse over some other method of punishment. For example, when a girl has been given, say, one hundred "lines" to do and comes in the next day not having done them, she is told that she can hand them in the following day, but now there will be a hundred and fifty to do. Instead, the pupil opts to ask the teacher to substitute a tawse punishment. To me (and to some of the other boys) this shows a certain bravery on the part of the girl, and is admirable and somehow sexy. Interestingly, female teachers rarely, if ever, oblige, but will suggest that if the increased punishment lines are not handed in the next day, the pupil will have to discuss it with the headmaster and risk being punished by him. Male teachers, on the other hand, always oblige and will subject the girl to a (usually) fairly moderate tawsing.

Generally speaking, boys get tawsed more frequently than girls, partly because the girls are generally a bit better behaved, but also because there are recommendations from the Education Authority relating to the physical punishment of girls, especially by male teachers. Most teachers pay at least lip service to these recommendations, and to the overall recommendations encompassing the punishment of both male and female pupils. Some teachers, however, basically do exactly as they like, hiding behind the principle that a teacher is always in loco parentis and can do anything a parent can in terms of punishment. This gives them pretty well carte blanche to adopt any punishment they fancy. A few of our teachers appear to have sadistic tendencies, some choosing from time to time to apply the tawse to a boy's (clothed) bottom instead of his hands, although given the thin material of our gym shorts, they provide negligible protection when our gym teacher gets a boy to bend over and support himself on the wall bars while he applies the tawse firmly to the lad's bottom. This never happens to me, by the way, only to certain boys to whom it seems to happen perhaps more regularly than it should.

I will never know if there is any sort of sexual motive for that type of spanking in the gym, but one of our other male teachers worries me a bit. He uses his tawse at what seems to be every opportunity, and uses it viciously, with a "whip cracking" action, which makes it extremely painful, usually causing the victim to jerk their hands away, often resulting in an additional stroke, or two if they have the misfortune to utter an involuntary expletive at the pain. He likes to explain, from a physics point of view, how he ensures his punishments are particularly painful, how it is for the pupil's own good, and that they should not complain to their parents about being punished as, if they do, they will probably get further punishment at home (which is certainly not true for many of us, but might well be the case for some).

It is noticeable that while most punishments this teacher administers are on the hands, there are three boys in our class that he nearly always punishes by getting them to bend over and touch their toes. He then reminds us all what a parabola is and demonstrates the shape by running his hand lightly over the victim's bottom (it's not clear if he actually touches their trousers or not, but if he doesn't he certainly almost does). He then applies either his tawse or his nasty, heavy, metal edged ruler to the taught bottom, causing the pupil to leap forward in great pain. He never applies more than one or two strokes, but it's clear that it leaves the victim in considerable pain. One boy, who is the most frequent victim, is always resentful about this punishment when it happens to him, and always shows the rest of us his marks when we are in the gym changing room. The angry red welts do look extremely painful, although I find them "interesting" to see. I take every precaution to avoid getting punished by this teacher, as do many of my classmates. It seems at times that he almost provokes the "misbehaviour" that merits this special punishment, for example by making some sort of half-joking quip to the class, but aimed at the intended victim, causing the victim to laugh a bit, or giggle, whereupon he is accused by the teacher of being frivolous, "Oh, so you think that's funny, do you, boy? Come out here and I'll make you laugh on the other side of your face!" This always seems unfair to many of us, although some of the girls in our class find it amusing, until one day after applying two firm strokes of the ruler to a particular boy's trousered buttocks, he calls out one of the giggling girls and tells her to bend over and touch her toes too. She blushes crimson, but compiles. He then gently runs his hand over her skirt and, ruler in hand, again talks about parabolas and the different parabolic shapes of boys' and girls' bottoms. He appears to be preparing to apply the ruler to her bottom, but after waving it about a few times, he places it on his desk and tells the girl she's lucky he's in a good mood and that she nearly got the same as the boy did. She goes back to her seat, completely mortified and looks close to tears. In one way I'm relieved he didn't bring that ruler across her bottom, yet in some other way I'm disappointed, because something deep inside was looking forward to seeing a girl get her bottom punished. Later, in the playground, a group of us boys are discussing this, and one lad (the one who long ago ribbed me about my sexual naivete) says, "Well, he's a pervert, isn't he? Some folk like wallopin' other folks' bums and some seem to like havin' their bum walloped. Ah don't think Georgina is a pervert, but ah think he must be. He shouldnae have been touching her bum neither!" Some of us question him about how he knows this stuff, and he replies that his big brother told him and that there are books like (what sounds to us like) "Auntie Justine" and "The Story of "O"," that talk about things like that. We ask if he's read them and he admits that he hasn't, but says that people who like that sort of thing do exist. We're still doubtful, but the subject of conversation then changes to a smutty discussion of who amongst us has touched a girl's bum. Later in the week I go to the local library to see

If I can find the books mentioned. I can't see them anywhere and finally pluck up courage to ask the librarian if they have them. I get a strange look and the librarian says, "No, We don't keep books like that. You usually take out books on photography, electricity and model engineering, son, so I suggest you'd be better sticking to them. We've got a nice new one here about the Rolleiflex that I think you'll like, so I'll book it out to you now." So off I go with a shiny new book about the Rolleiflex twin-lens reflex camera. Ah, well, I am really interested in photography, and the book might have some nice photos in it! Later in the term it strikes us that this maths teacher no longer gets any pupil to bend over for punishment, although he still frequently applies the tawse viciously to hands. We know that the girl he got to bend over complained to her parents, and we assume that they complained to the Headmaster, who has told the teacher to stick to punishment of the hands and not apply punishment to bottoms, especially those of girls. We also notice the gym teacher now punishes on the hands only, no longer getting boys to bend over and support themselves on the gym wall bars. We guess the Headmaster, severe as he himself is when he applies punishments, may not have realised what sort of punishments were taking place in some parts of the school. He has presumably offered guidance as to what is appropriate, or perhaps laid down the law as to how the teachers should behave. (Can you imagine the consequences if any of this happened nowadays). I'm sixteen now and I have a girlfriend, Rosemary. Well, sort of a girlfriend. Up to now, she has been the attractive girlfriend of one of my mates, and he has dumped her in favour of someone I find less attractive, but about whom he raves. I have been given a couple of tickets for a concert at the weekend, so my mate suggests I might like to ask his ex-girlfriend if she'd like to go. I nervously do that and discover that, being "on the rebound" from my mate, she is happy to accompany me to the concert. We get on quite well and agree to further dates. She is a weekday boarder at a convent school where the discipline is said to be strict, and I can see her only at weekends, which isn't a problem (they are allowed to go home from midday on Saturday, returning Sunday evening).

A few weekends later, sitting in another concert, I notice she fidgets a lot and looks uncomfortable. As we head for the train afterwards, I ask why she was fidgeting so much. She is a bit vague about it, but I press her for an explanation and she finally tells me she was punished that morning for something that happened in their dormitory last night. Pulling me into a close (for non-Scottish readers, that's a communal entrance hall to a tenement block), she briefly lifts her skirt to show me a nasty, angry-looking set of tawse marks across the back of her thighs. Apparently these are the result of four hard strokes of the tawse applied by one of the vicious nuns at the school. Rosemary is embarrassed about them, but won't tell me the reason for the punishment. I feel strangely excited and I stupidly persist in asking for more details, but she clams up. We sit on the train home in (almost) silence, then say goodbye at our destination. The next weekend when I wait at the station to meet her, she doesn't turn up, so I go to a phone box and ring her home. Her mother answers the phone and says her daughter probably won't want to speak to me, but she'll ask her if she does. Finally Rosemary comes to the phone and explains that she doesn't want to see me again. After some stilted discussion (her mother still in earshot, maybe?) I get the impression that she considers my interest in the welts on her thighs to be unhealthy and creepy, and anyway, she doesn't really like me that much, but she was on the rebound, so that's why she had been dating me. Ah well!

The rest of my years at school pass. I am now much more interested in girls, although in general they're not too interested in me, except for a couple of intellectual ones who make odd comments about liking me, but sad to say they don't really appeal much to me. They are fans of Jane Austen. I stick with my photography and become interested in cinematography. I still have this cloud inside my brain telling me there's something odd about my desire, in certain circumstances, to see and to experience punishment. I still tell no one about my feelings and I still worry that I am unique in my leanings. Although those remarks about books mentioning such things have eased my conscience a little, I still think what I do to myself from time to time must constitute a sin and that worries me. I also worry that my proclivities may affect future relationships with females, as happened with Rosemary.

Twixt School and University

Having done well academically in High School, I have now been accepted on a four-year university course and, against the Headmaster's advice, have left school at seventeen, as I can't bear the thought of another year of the place, sticking to arbitrary rules and being bossed around by teachers! One of my classmates with whom I have become good friends, has also left at seventeen to train to be an accountant, and we have borrowed his father's car to do a tour of the Scottish Highlands. On our way north, we have stopped near Pitlochry in an otherwise deserted picnic area to make bacon sandwiches washed down with tea (we have a nice two-ring camping stove with us). On taking our litter to a waste bin, we discover the bin contains a paperback, "The Carpetbaggers" by Harold Robbins. Fishing it out, just out of curiosity, we discover it's what we might call a "dirty book" as it flops open at various well-thumbed pages involving matters of sex – and there it is, a reference to what I now know to be S&M! At last I have, to my enormous relief, confirmation that my kink is not unique, that there are others with the same or similar. I might not be "normal" but there are others like me out there! We have a good laugh at some parts of the book and take it with us for further reading and (certainly in my case) further enlightenment.

At University then in my first proper job following graduation

I am a university student now, but have missed quite a lot of the first year through illness, from which I almost died, saved only by the skill of a local doctor who, as a last resort, decided to try a new drug, which pulled me back from the brink, much to the relief of me and (especially) my parents. I am back to my studies and I have a girlfriend again. We met at a St Valentine's Day disco where I was DJ. She had attended a different school from me, a school with a reputation for severe discipline, regardless of whether disciplining boys or girls, and she tells me she has been a regular recipient of severe tawsings at the hands of nasty teachers, for both minor and major breaches of the rules. We get on quite well and are beginning tentatively to explore each other's bodies. I have taken her to the University ball. She tells me she is a virgin.

A few weeks later, she goes all peculiar on me and finally tells me she's not really a virgin, because she has been intimate with a lad from her school. It turns out I know of this lad through the church and I have never liked him. She says she didn't like him much, but just wanted to lose her virginity and he was handy at the time. I am not at all pleased at this, but since we are heading towards making love in the near future, I say it's OK, although there might be consequences as far as our relationship is concerned. She is quite upset, but wants to remain my girlfriend. I say we'll see how it goes, but that I might need to consider punishing her somehow. She gives me an odd, puzzled look, then laughs nervously and jokingly says maybe I can sometime, but not on her hands, as they were always too sore when they used to be regularly belted at school.

A couple of weeks later, taking advantage of the fact that my parents are out for the whole day and evening, we end up in my bedroom, indulging in a session of "very heavy petting" and it becomes fairly clear that we are going to end up having sex for the first time. At this point I suggest that I am disappointed that I will not be taking her virginity. She apologises again for the fact that she is not a virgin, and (miracle of miracles!) suggests that maybe I should punish her now, although she says that when she went to bed with that boy, she didn't know she was going to meet me, so perhaps she shouldn't be punished too hard. I'm not sure what to say, but I suggest using my father's trouser belt (the one he thrashed me with when I was a toddler) on her bare bottom. She agrees to this, so I dig out the belt and we both strip off.

She bends over the side of my bed and I tentatively wallop her a couple of times with the belt. She says I can give her a few more strokes if I like, then we can make love. I give her another four, harder this time, then she lies on her back on the bed and invites me in. By this time I am extremely aroused and entry is difficult, much more difficult than expected, and she bleeds dramatically on my bed sheets. We both then realise that her earlier fumbles with that boy from her school did not result in rupture of her hymen, and that now she really has lost her virginity, much to her pleasure and mine. This, then, is my very first experience of S&M with a girl, as opposed to punishing myself alone in secrecy! We have both enjoyed the experience.

We kiss and cuddle in bliss until I walk her home to her parents' house after hastily changing my bedclothes and temporarily hiding the blood-stained ones so that I can deal with them covertly later.

The next time we meet, a few days later, we somehow seem a bit embarrassed about our previous session, but it's clear we both want more. My parents are out again the following Saturday, leaving the house empty, and we agree to meet again for a further session of love-making (or kinky sex if you prefer!). Come Saturday, after some cuddling, kissing and petting, we strip and get into my bed. I tell her it was very naughty of her to say she wasn't a virgin when she was, and that maybe a little more punishment is in order. She agrees by getting out of bed and presenting her bare bottom over the side of my bed again. I fetch the trouser belt and give her six strokes. She says, "Is that all you can manage?" so I give her another six, as hard as I can, then we have wild, hungry sex, both climaxing dramatically.

After a short rest, she wants me to make love to her again, but no erection is forthcoming. She expresses disappointment, then says she has read somewhere that some men can get excited by being whipped or otherwise physically punished, so would I like to try that. I can't believe my luck, so I agree and present myself over the bed just as she had. She hits me with the belt a few times, but it has little effect on me. She apologises for the fact that it's actually a fairly thin belt and asks if I have anything heavier.

Of course, hidden in my bedroom I have one of the industrial-weight leather belts I have used in the past to punish myself, so I dig it out and let her go to town on my exposed bottom – exquisite pain, with someone else wielding the instrument! It has the desired effect, of course, and soon we are indulging in more wild sex in various positions, much to the pleasure of both of us.

The next time we have an opportunity to be completely on our own, we indulge in another S&M session, only this time she wants to know what the heavier belt feels like across her bottom. Although initially taken aback at the severity of the pain (even though I have hit her quite gently), she does find it arousing, encouraging further strokes and ending up quite marked and bruised, as do I after we swap places.

To cut a long story short, our future as a couple indulging in S&M continues into a BDSM relationship, with light bondage at times (very light – always escapable!). After a few months, the initial excitement with BDSM wears off a little. Our straight love-making sessions become extremely frequent (at every opportunity, really!), while our BDSM sessions become less frequent, but still fairly regular, and all the more exciting because of the anticipation. Our relationship lasts for nearly four years before becoming a bit stale and she starts a sexual relationship with her (much older) boss, whom she eventually marries and they start a family. I am slightly relieved in a way because her parents have been pressing us to get married and neither of us was sure we wanted that. Some years later, my mother bumps into her in the street. She is pushing a pram with her new baby and looks tired but happy. She tells my Mum that we had a special kind of love, but that she could never have married me.

Back to University as a Postgraduate

I have now left my job and am involved in research for a PhD, with a group of my peers, many of whom I knew from undergraduate

days. We go to parties, go hiking, go climbing, play lot of munic-
ipal and private golf courses around the west of Scotland. I meet
a few girls, but have little success with any of them. I take out a
couple of my ex-girlfriend's friends – we have quite a nice time,
but nothing serious happens. I'm not too bothered, although I
would like to have a permanent girlfriend again, regardless of
whether she is interested in BDSM, but obviously that would be
a bonus. For some reason, my colleagues at university have started
to call me "Lash" and later "Doc Lash" because apparently I have
mentioned my S&M proclivities while slightly the worse for wear
having consumed too much beer and whisky. They laugh about
this, but don't seem all that disapproving. Unfortunately, any
girls in our social group seem to have heard about me as well and
either don't want my company or, if they do, it is only in a large
group situation. I remain without a girlfriend and start worrying
again that my BDSM tendencies are spoiling my chances with
the opposite sex. This starts to affect me quite severely, particularly
when would-be dates stand me up, apparently after hearing about
my kink. The busy St Enoch Square and the even busier Glasgow
Central Station can be lonely places when, as the old song says,
"Girl don't come." I am not a happy bloke and feel a bit of a loner.
Then one day I go on a blind date with a female friend of the
steady girlfriend of an old school-friend of mine. She has recently
split with her boyfriend and would like someone to accompany
her to another friend's wedding, although she isn't looking for a
relationship. She turns out to be a beautiful blonde with a great
figure and a lovely nature. Basically we hit it off on our first date.
She knows nothing about my kink and I don't tell her. We become
a steady, happy couple and get married just over a year later. We
have a fantastically loving sexual relationship, free of kink, and
strangely I don't miss the kinky stuff at all really.

The guilt about my kink lifts and I feel happy and "normal"
– whatever that means. One day, after a few drinks, my wife says
she has heard in conversation with an old university friend of
hers that I used to be known as "Doc Lash" because of a certain

propensity to kinky behaviour. She asks if this is true, and after initial denials I admit to my kink, although not to the extent of it, nor to how kinky my relationship had been with that ex-girl-friend. She doesn't seem at all bothered and says it's OK with her, as I've never been in the slightest bit violent with her or forced her to do anything she's uncomfortable with. I'm embarrassed and try to downplay the whole thing. The next few times we make love, however, I have, for the first time ever, some real difficulty, as I am subconsciously concerned about the revelation of my kink. My wife is pretty understanding and apologetic, saying that if she'd known it would cause problems, she would never have mentioned her conversation with her old friend. She intended it to be a bit of a fun remark, not something to cause problems in our normally great sex life.

Life together continues fairly happily, but still with some clouds associated with the mention of my kink and occasionally, when that conversation comes to mind at the wrong time, I have a bit of trouble during our love-making. She continues to be understanding and does everything she can to relax me and make everything OK, but still I sometimes have "issues" as one might say. It's my birthday. My wife gives me a lovely Colibri cigarette lighter (I smoked a little in those days) and two mysteriously shaped packages. I prod these packages about, puzzled as to their contents. "Go on. Open them!" she chirps, "I'm sure you'll like them because I think they're your sort of thing!" I tear the first package open to find a shortish, but quite heavy, leather bull whip. I'm stunned at this. "Go on, open the other one too!" she says. I do as I'm told, and find a nice riding crop, neatly tied with a ribbon and a gift card endorsed, "You might even like to try this gently on me, my darling! xxx"- still stunned, I don't know quite what to say, but I grab her and kiss her like mad. "I'm taking you out for a nice dinner for your birthday," she says, "and when we get home, maybe we can play with your presents ..."

I draw a veil over what happens next, but in brief, she finds that she quite enjoys indulging my kink and fantasies, albeit not too violently when she is on the receiving end. As two switches, we live happily and without guilt. As is often the case, I believe, we more or less suspend our kink for many years after she becomes pregnant and throughout bringing up our family. During this "suspension" period, I spread my wings a bit and start to spend some time in the local BDSM scene, finding my photography and cinematography skills appreciated to the extent that I become in effect a "painographer" working with other consenting adults in a somewhat clandestine world. * My wife has no interest in any form of BDSM activity except with me, and doesn't really approve of my extramural activities, but doesn't interfere, although she insists she doesn't want to know what I get up to.

* This was in pre-digital times, presenting many challenges which are much more readily overcome with today's digital video equipment, modern LED lighting, readily available, more sensitive and highly portable cameras, computers, etc. While I'm generally not in favour of the "Oh, never mind, we'll fix it in post" attitude of some producers, it is certainly much easier (although not necessarily all that easy) today to fix various things in post- production. Back then, certain things just could not be fixed later and things had to be, as far as possible, right first time. I could tell various amusing (and some not so amusing) anecdotes concerning happenings during shooting sessions, but this is not the appropriate forum.

Once the family has left home, our marital BDSM activities together start all over again and continue, with the odd break, throughout our married life. This part of our life together, when we resume activities after the "suspension" period, is probably in many respects the most relaxed and exciting of all. We have the time to experiment with a range of new instruments (assorted canes, whips, crops, floggers, tawses, paddles, birches and so on). We also try various "pervertibles" –everyday items that can be repurposed for BDSM activities (some of those silicone kitchen spatula-type tools can make wonderful spanking instruments!). We experiment carefully with electro-stimulation using a simple

TENS machine – it's surprising how much pain and pleasure can be gained from one of these fitted with some custom electrodes. I reduce my "painography" activities and instead start to make various custom BDSM instruments and equipment, and am pretty good at it, being fairly skilled in leather-work and woodwork. Life is good!

So What?

And that's it, really. What started out as an exploration of memories in an attempt to identify the origins of my kink (nature or nurture?) has morphed into a potted history of my BDSM life, from beginning to end. I don't know whether I've achieved anything through this exercise, although I'm tending to think that perhaps my kink was innate, but brought to the surface by early childhood experiences. Of course it could well have come to the surface without those early experiences – I just don't know, but the fact that those experiences are so clear in my memory does suggest to me that they may well be of some formative significance. Either way, I have been what I have been and I am what I am! Looking back, I feel that my kink has been a mixed blessing mentally. In some respects it has caused mental stress regarding the fact that I am not "normal" but somehow "different" and also mental stress that I might be "found out" by others who could not, or would not, understand my kink. On the other hand, at otherwise stressful times in my life, e.g. stress in my job, my professional life, it has provided the greatest pleasure and mental stress relief that I can think of, almost like a drug, I suppose. Let it be known that I have never, ever, tried any sort of recreational drug apart from alcohol and ordinary tobacco, but I guess my "drug" of choice, my addiction, has been BDSM; and as with all forms of recreational drugs have their pros and cons. Nevertheless, on balance, I think BDSM has, overall, probably been beneficial to my mental health.

I think the greatest problem with my kink has been the attitude of society to BDSM activities. That is why I have always taken steps to reduce the likelihood of being "found out." Those of us who indulge in such activities, however caring, consensual and in private, are seen as nasty, vicious, predatory, violent and perverted beyond redemption, much in the manner in which homosexuality was viewed (and indeed outlawed) in the past. Unfortunately, this perception is potentially reinforced by the levels of really extreme BDSM encountered in a wide range of really nasty video material available on the internet, and the fact that some of these horrors may well be associated with highly illegal and inexcusable activities such as real sla , human trafficking, non-consensual violence and extreme exploitation of potentially vulnerable people; which is not something the vast majority of BDSM enthusiasts would support, but sadly, as in practically every walk of life, We have to endure trouble caused by extremists.

In spite of the difficulties and the stress brought on by having to keep my proclivities hidden from most of the world, and still even now having some (probably quite unnecessary) feelings of shame from the "lone and sinful" actions of my teenage past, I am left with many wonderfully happy (if sometimes slightly guilty) memories from my BDSM activities, particularly those with my wife, the love of my life. I am also left with a significant collection of BDSM instruments, toys, whatever you like to call them, which sadly are no longer used. Some time ago I sold off some of the items, but I am still left with a lifetime's collection of tawses and approved school straps, most of which are genuine old Scottish leather ones, well used, plus assorted whips, crops, floggers, and so on. I cannot bring myself to simply scrap these items, as they all hold pleasant memories for me. I feel they should still be getting used regularly for their intended purpose and I would be happy to donate all or any of them to someone in the scene, preferably (although not necessarily) someone who produces videos so that others can see them in use, producing that exquisite pain with which so much pleasure can be.

Story 15
Sissy Boi Natalie –
Lover of frilly, satin dresses

I'm still reasonably new to the world of 'kink' and have only recently found a comfort level with a Mistress. For me, it's a difficult world to understand and to get into, getting taken seriously was a struggle for me. This was not down to the Mistress, but down to me for not dropping my guard.

My childhood clearly impacted my choices of kink and the biggest and hardest part of this was admitting to yourself what it is you want to achieve. For me, I always thought I was different. I'm sure it's a classic tale and certainly not unique in any way to me.

Around 10 years ago, I sat myself down and decided to stop hiding from my true desires. I had these thoughts in my head, and I needed to play them out.

After spending a fair while reading up on my fetish and subscribing to endless Reddit streams, I came across an advert for a local Dominatrix. I'd not seen this being advertised before and didn't really know what services they offer. Surely I'm far too mainstream and vanilla for this kind of thing? How wrong one person can be! So, I took some time to read up about this particular Dominatrix and the services that she offers in a session. Here are some of the services offered and my interpretation at the time:

- Strap-on I don't know why I'd need to wear one.

- CBT Being kicked repeatedly in the balls. No thanks

- Feminisation Dressing up! AH HA!

- Panty Fetish Oh wait, maybe that's it?

- Sissification I have no idea. Probably not for me!

- Anal Play It's an exit. No thanks

- Humiliation This sounds like a possible starting point!

- Degradation Something to do with building mainte-
nance? Maybe a typo!

- CEI Pretty sure it's to do with a crime scene.

- SPH I couldn't even begin to work it out!

So with this naïve and uneducated knowledge to hand I called the Mistress to discuss booking a session. This is verbatim and proof that I had a LOT to learn!

Me: Hello. Is that the Mistress A (name changed to save my embarrassment)

Mistress A: It is, who is this?

Me: Hello Mistress, my name is Mikey.

Mistress A: Hello Mikey, what can I do for you?

Me: Mistress, I'm looking to book a session with you please.

Mistress A: OK Mikey, can you tell me what you're looking for in a session?

Me: Hmm, I don't really know. I'm a newbie you see, and I think I need to be dominated!

Mistress A: Well, domination is a large area. Do you know what your hard limits are?

And here comes the most stupid thing you're ever likely to hear!

Me: Do you mean what hard foods l like?

Mistress A: Laughs. Oh dear! It's not quite what I meant. How about things you fantasise about?

Me: Satin Knickers!

Mistress A: OK, so you like to dress up?

Me: I've only done it a couple of times and it was nice!

Mistress A: OK. We can session, however, we need to identify your hard limits. These are what you do not want to do under any circumstance! Why don't we do an hour session. I'll give you a free 30 minute 'pre session' chat and we can play around and see what you like!

This was a turning point for me. Someone who listened to me. Didn't laugh at me. Just listened to me. I was taken seriously! Wow! Just Wow!

I wasn't going to put this section in; however, I think it give you a real insight into my mindset at the time. On the day of my session, I decided to go to the local supermarket. In my head, I didn't feel that I could arrive empty handed and be taken seriously. Now I know that you may be thinking that maybe I bought some flowers or maybe chocolates. That would be a nice gift! But no. I thought the right thing to do was to arrive with some women's underwear and pretend that it's the kind of stuff I wear regularly 'get off' in! I cannot express enough how painful it is for a man to buy underwear for his partner, now double that stress by pretending it be for someone else knowing full well that you're going to be wearing it soon! Women's sizes make no sense! It's really confusing! Ideally, I would turn up with some frilly, satin knickers and a bra that matches. The Mistress would certainly take me seriously! What I selected was a pair of cotton knickers, which I think are commonly known as apple catchers?? Definitely not sexy and potentially wouldn't fit either! Then a problem arose! Whilst skulking around the women's underwear section I was approached by a young, slender and attractive woman who asked if she could help me? This was an issue. I've got a couple of choices here. Run? Pretend to not talk English? Admit it's for me and hope she's not freaked! In the end I don't the right thing and lied. I told her it was for my girlfriend (why!!). She looks down at my basket and then looked back at me. Then came a round of questioning that made me squirm like a man in ill-fitting knickers!

Assistant: Is it practical underwear she needs?

Me: Who?

Assistant: Your girlfriend.

Me: Oh! Erm, what do you mean by practical?

Assistant: Are you buying this as a gift? Maybe a birthday present?

This seemed to be going well! Even I couldn't get this wrong!

Me: That's right, it's her birthday tomorrow!

Assistant: OK. Are you looking for something that would make her feel good in?

Me: I guess so. Something sexy! (Typical bloke answer and it's not the last time!)

Assistant: OK, so would you mind me saying that I'm not sure that the panties you've selected are the sexiest items we stock.

This was a problem. I pretty much knew that these items sitting in my basket didn't 'rock my boat' but it's the only thing I could find that may cover my fat ass!! I'm in a little deep now! How the hell am I going to get out of this!!?? I had a plan! Blag it!

Me: Can you point me in the right direction? (I don't even know what it means!)

Assistant: Can I ask what size you're looking for?

And here is where it all went wrong! I folded in the first line of questioning! My response should have been 'It's for me'. The likelihood is that this lovely assistant wouldn't have even battered an eyelid. She would have looked at me and taken a deep breath and led me to the kinky isle and that's that! But oh no! Not me!! I reverted to a typical bloke and lied. Well done me!!

Me: I don't really know the sizes I'm afraid. But (here it goes) she's about the same size as you!

IDIOT!

Assistant: Well then, this should be easy. What about the bra size? The same as me?

Me: (trying not to automatically look at her breasts). I think so. (I had already looked at her breasts!)

Assistant: OK, so we just need to decide on style, material and colour. Any thoughts?

Without hesitation

Me: Satin.

Assistant: OK. And a style? Thong? French? Full brief?

Now I won't detail the whole (and quite painful) conversation but it's fair to say that I made a complete arse of myself! I walked out of that shop £52 lighter but the proud owner of white satin knickers, size8 and a 34b white lace bra. And just to spice it up in the bedroom the wonderful assistant convinced me that white hold ups would really finish the outfit off nicely! Just so we are all on the same page. These are NOT my sizes!

I arrived for my session in good time and sent a message to the Mistress A to advise that I'm ready! A reply came exactly on the time we'd agreed to start the session. The message was a simple set of instructions on accessing the property. Look for this door, go through it, be quiet and head for the rear of the property, you'll see a white door. Knock and wait. I followed the instructions to the letter. I knocked on the white door and waited. Then I heard the distinctive sound of heels across a wooden floor. I really wanted to back out, I was nervous and started shaking! Mistress opened the door and welcomed me in. She had a warm demeanour and kind eyes. I'm not sure what I had expected? Maybe a larger woman with a whip in hand shouting abuse at me? Mistress A was wearing a latex catsuit. It zipped all the way around the crutch. She had a large cleavage that was clearly assisted by the latex being zipped slightly lower! Her boots had red long heels and she towered over me.

Mistress A: Hello Mikey, how are you?

Me: I'm well thank you Mistress.

Mistress A: That's good to hear. So let's do business first.

Me: I'm sorry?

Mistress A: The tribute. We always take care of it first so that there's no awkwardness.

The tribute is the financial element to a session. Each Mistress will request a certain tribute for her time. This is always agreed before a session so that there are no surprises. Mistresses will change their tribute amount depending on session length and possibly depending on what the client wants to get out of the session. Additional expenses should be covered by the client. Your mistress should never be out of pocket.

Me: Of course, Mistress, here you go.

Mistress A: Now then Mikey we are going to start by under-standing your experience, your limits and your expectations for today's session. You should be aware of a few things. There are two safe words. 'Amber' is used if you're uncomfortable with something and need to either slow things down or discuss what's happening. 'Red' is used to stop the session Immediately. If 'Red' is used, we may not continue the session depending on what the issue is. Please don't feel embarrassed by how your body reacts. No one in here is judging you and what happens in the dungeon stays in the dungeon. Your safety is paramount.

Me: I didn't realise a safe word would be needed.

Mistress A: They rarely are used though it gives people peace of mind. These sessions are a two-way street. Most mistresses enjoy the session as much as the client. Communication is so important. I'll know by your reactions when it's going well. So now we need to get an understanding of what it is you like?

Me: So, this is my first 1-2-1 experience. I like the idea of wearing women's underwear and being caught doing so and then maybe getting punished for it? That said, I'm not into pain! I don't like the idea of whips and canes. It just sounds too much for me.

Mistress A: What about strap-on play?

Me: I don't know what it is. How would I wear it?

Mistress A: 'Laughing'. I've not heard that before. It's not for you to wear. I wear it and teach you how to suck cock for me and then we could work on you pretending to be a girl!

It fell silent. Mistress A just looked at me and waited for an answer or at least a reaction. I suddenly felt really warm!

Me: Wow! I Had not heard of that before. I thought it was some-thing lesbians did, but now you say it, it makes sense!

Mistress A: So, can I make a suggestion?

Me: Please do.

Mistress A: How about we take it one step at a time. Let's try a few different things. Let's see how far we get and how much you enjoy it. This way we'll know for next time. It'll be slow and remember you have the safe words. I'm going to try and push your limits slightly. When we start the session, you must remember that I'm in charge. You'll always refer to me as Mistress. Any more questions or concerns before starting?

Me: I don't think so Mistress. I'm quite excited.

Mistress A: Excellent. So, in that case. Undress immediately in front of me!

And so, it started. My very first session had begun. Was this going to be what I thought it would be? How many times would I need my safe word? The panic started again.

I stood up from my stool and started to undress. Normally at home I just throw the clothes in different corners of the room. Not this time though. Mistress A watched everything I was doing. Then she stood up. She came up to me almost nose to nose. 'Don't stop' she ordered. 'And make sure your clothes are folded and placed in the corner'. I did exactly as I was told. 'Now stand still and let me look at you'. It fell silent as Mistress A walked around me looking me up and down. I felt slightly humiliated. I liked the feeling! Then the embarrassing moments started! I started to get aroused! WHY!!!! I am standing naked in front of a woman I've never met. There's zero chance of any sexual activity and yet 'mini me' was starting to show up. Mistress A noticed this immediately. She laughed and said that it was a useless and pathetic excuse for a cock, so much so that from now on she'll call it a 'clit'! It was turning me on. Humiliation again. I never knew it could have such an effect on me. I've never experienced it before. Mistress A had done nothing other than look at me and tell me I had a small cock! Yet I wanted more of it. I plucked up the courage to utter my first response:

Me: Sorry for my small cock mistress!

Mistress A: It's a CLIT! NEVER refer to it as a cock. It's useless. Now tell me what is it?

Me: A clit Mistress.

Mistress A: Exactly. A pathetic clit.

Mistress A really knew how to push these buttons of mine. She didn't have to say anything. Just a look either straight into my eyes or up and down my exposed body. As she moved around me her hands clamped onto my shoulders, and she pushed me to the floor. "From now on you must always be on your knees in my presence, do you understand?" I replied with a slightly wary "Yes Mistress". Mistress A walked to the opposite corner to where I was, and I heard a cupboard opening and then the heels against the floor coming back to me. I'm on my hands and knees with my head down as Mistress A straddles me. She sat on my back like a horse. I really had no idea what was happening. Being so out of control was yet another turn on! I could feel Mistress A moving and doing something, but I had no idea what. Then everything became clear. She grabbed my hair whilst still straddling me and pulled my head backwards. "Don't move," she instructed. A pink collar was placed around my neck and secured in place. Unbeknown to me, this collar had the words Sissy Slut across the front of it. Mistress A then clipped a lead to the back and paraded my naked self around the room. She made her way to a chair in the corner of the room where she sat down. "Sit back on your legs" she demanded. I was now upright and sat on my heels. It was uncomfortable and I think she knew this. "Now then sissy, it's time to dress for me". Mistress A opened a box to her left side and pulled out a handful of underwear. I could see straight away that it was mainly lace knickers of all colours (and hopefully sizes!). "Get over here and get these on you! There's many to choose from, just make sure you make the right choice!" I really didn't know what that meant. Was it a test? Is there a right choice? Grabbing the garments, I tentatively started to look at each pair and tried to get a feeling from Mistress A as to what I should choose. She was giving nothing away! Not a flinch. I finally found a pair that I thought would fit. They were not exactly what I would choose. A Black lace (not the 80's band) thong. Not very forgiving around the front! "Why have you chosen them?" Mistress A asked. "Because I think they'll fit," I replied. "I don't care if they fit, in fact that clit of yours doesn't need any room, does it?". I didn't know how to answer. Maybe my decision was based around comfort. It fell quiet before Mistress A said "your decision should be based on what pleases me. I don't care about your comfort. I want you humiliated for my pleasure. Seeing that tiny excuse squeezed tightly pleases me. Make a better choice!" The penny dropped. Of course, how stupid can I be! This session is trying to find my desires and deep hidden kinks. Mistress A was so on the ball. If humiliation is the key, and it seems to be pressing all the right buttons, then humiliating myself for her pleasure is a win! With this newfound confidence I re choose. This time I picked the French knickers. Pink with white lace. They were not small but certainly not my size. "Now put them on" Mistress A ordered. I pulled them up over my knees and then over my ever growing 'clit'. They were certainly snug. But wait, what's this feeling? This restriction on my nether regions was another turn on. I could feel myself bursting in the underwear, but it felt amazing. Like I was being controlled. Mistress A nodded at me and then opened the box again and pulled out another selection. This time it was a bra. The process was similar but I went straight for the matching colour. HOME RUN!! Mistress A stood up. "Stand up and turn around". She took the bra out of my hand and stood behind me. Putting her arms around my body she was able to do the clasp of the bra up. With her hands in the shoulder straps, she moved the bra up and adjusted it to cover my small cups! Then without warning, Mistress A slid her hands into the bra cups and grabbed my nipples hard! I groaned in genuine discomfort. "Don't make noises unless I allow it, understand?" "Yes, Mistress," I replied. She still had my nipples in her hand, and she twisted again. This time it was pain but more a relief. It's hard to explain this feeling. A little like when your pins and needles start to go away. Sometimes it hurts, sometimes it is pleasurable. I was all over the shop. Once again though, what I did realise is that my 'clit' liked it.

Mistress A certainly knew how to tease someone. There was a fair amount of flicking nipples and getting me to rub my clit through the knickers for her entertainment. Now though was the time that I really wasn't sure about.

Mistress A made her way across the room again and this time stopped at what looked like a rack of belts. How mistaken I was. These 'belts' where a harness. A harness with a hole in the front of it. The hole in the front served a special purpose, to house the cock that Mistress A was about to select. "What's your favourite colour Sissy?" Mistress A asked. I really had to make the right decision here. Thinking about it quickly, I replied with "pink Mistress". "That's a good answer although its wrong. When I'm selecting a cock for you, you must ALWAYS reply with black. A Sissy always craves Big Black Cock (BBC)". "Yes Mistress" was my tentative reply. This was the first real time in the session where I was questioning myself. Though I don't know what I was questioning. Mistress A had picked a small, black dildo which was now attached to her harness. It was realistic looking. It had a foreskin and thick veins down the shaft. It even had a large pair of balls at the base. As she walked over to me it bounced up and down almost nodding its approval! I panicked! "Amber" I said nervously. Immediately, Mistress A turned into a different person. Her persona became the caring woman that she clearly is.

Mistress A: Are you OK?

Me: I'm really sorry Mistress, I'm not sure about the strap-on.

Mistress A: Then we won't go down that route. That's what initial sessions are all about. What about the strap-on is worrying for you?

Me: It's the penetration. It's really going to hurt.

Mistress A: OK. I understand. Can I just say firstly that we didn't even get to that stage and its unlikely to have happened at all. This introduction and your reaction are perfectly normal. Is this the only issue?

Me: What if I'm gay?

Mistress A: Firstly, if you're gay it's not a problem. Secondly, are you attracted to men?

Me: No. I find us men quite disgusting to be honest!

Mistress A: So, there you are then. How about we restart and go in a slightly different direction?

Me: That's fine. Sorry to stop it!

Mistress A: Don't apologise. These sessions are your time, and we want to get it right for you. Our safe words are in place to ensure we get sessions right!

We reset.

I'm back on my knees and Mistress A is in front of me with her strap-on looking at me. You could say eye to eye! "Right now, Sissy boy, rub that clit for me. I want to see you enjoying it like you're a woman". I loved this. The fabric of the knickers created a kind of sexy friction. "Now then Sissy, whilst you rub that clit, you wank off this cock of mine. Take it in your hands and pleasure me!". My first touch of a strap-on and it wasn't bad at all. And you've guessed it, 'mini me' seemed to like it too! The verbal humiliation ramped up a lot from Mistress A.

Mistress A: That's it you dirty little bitch. Take that cock slowly in your hand. Don't forget to rub the tip. Now I want you go get your face closer. Why don't you kiss the end of my cock? Just kiss the tip.

This was the strangest feeling I could have ever imagined. The joy of rubbing myself was almost paved into insignificance when getting closer to the strap-on. I could feel myself getting harder and harder in the knickers.

Mistress A: Good girl. Now why don't you just slip the helmet into your mouth? Just the end. That's it, a good slut loves to work on the head first.

I had shuffled closer and forgotten about my clit and seemed fixed on the strap-on. Instinctively I grabbed the base of the cock with one hand before moving it onto the balls. Why did I do this? My head was spinning in confusion and euphoria.

Mistress A: You are a dirty little fucking slut, aren't you? Now put them balls in your mouth!

I did exactly as I was told without hesitation! This then forced me to have to move my head position. I was now kind of under Mistress A and looking straight into her eyes. I took the balls into my mouth and wanked the cock slowly.

Mistress A: Do you like my cock sissy?

Me: Yes Mistress. It makes me feel slutty, Mistress!

Mistress A: Good girl. Oh! What do I see in your knickers?

Unbeknown to me, in this high state of arousal my cock had leaked pre cum everywhere. The front of my knickers are clearly sticky.

Mistress A: My little slut has made a little mess, hasn't she?

I started to worry here. I wasn't sure if this was something that was normal in a session. Had I peaked too early? Should I use the safe word again so I can apologise? NO!! This was just another part of humiliation. My mistress had made me get so aroused with a plastic cock! A cock that I willingly was sucking!

Mistress A: Who's a naughty girl? Creaming her knickers! A bad girl gets punished, doesn't she? Are you a bad girl?

Me: Yes Mistress! I'm a bad slut!

I don't know why I said that! Again, was it the right answer? What the hell is punishment? Oh well, I'm here now, let's see what occurs!

Mistress A: OK your dirty little cock sucking sissy whore! I think you're desperate for some cock! I think your pussy is gagging for it!

Me: My pussy Mistress?

Mistress A: Yes sissy. Your sissy hole. Your virginity belongs to me, and I want it!

Here comes the panic again! I can feel it bubbling up inside. In my head Mistress A is going to shove a traffic cone up my arse! I don't think I can handle this. But then something happened that took away the worry and concern. Mistress A sat on the floor and I was in between her legs with my back to her. My head was resting between her breasts and her hands neatly lay over my shoulders whilst she squeezed my nipples. The squeezing wasn't harsh, almost seductive and considerate.

Mistress A: You're a very good girl Sissy. We need to give you a name, don't we? A name we use when you're a sissy. Do you have one?

I'd not given this any thought in the past. There are names that I like and also names that I associate with certain times of my life.

Me: Natalie Mistress. Is that OK?

Mistress A: That's a lovely choice.

Natalie: Thank you Mistress.

Mistress A: Now then Natalie you have made a real sticky mess in those knickers. Why don't you put your hand down there and rub your clit for your mistress? Get those fingers covered for me.

Natalie: Of course, Mistress.

Mistress A: That's a good girl. Now take those fingers and taste yourself for me. Taste that sticky mess.

Natalie: Mmmmmm.

Mistress A: (Whispering to me). Now then Natalie. I want to train your pussy. I promise that you'll enjoy this. We'll take this very slowly and one step at a time. Your pussy belongs to me doesn't it Natalie?

Natalie: Yes Mistress. It's your pussy Mistress.

Mistress A: That's right. Now move slowly onto the bench. Make sure you're on your back and your head is on the pillow. Do you understand?

Natalie: Bench Mistress?

Towards one side of the room was what can only be described as a piece of gym equipment though this one was black, leather and had attachments for locks! As I moved closer to it I could see that it had stirrup attachments, it could be adjusted for different heights and also changed so that someone could kneel on it and have their torso flat in front of them.

I lay down as instructed and Mistress A came over. Being on the bench made her tower over me which was intimidating in an excellent way. She reached above me and pulled down what seemed to be a selection of belts and clips. The first item was a ball gag. For those not familiar (and I wasn't) it's literally as described. A ball (with breathing holes in it) attached to two leather straps. The ball gag is used to stop noise from the sub. Mistress A attached this to my face and made sure it was tight. It was surprisingly restrictive. I'd assumed that it was easily moved around however this was NOT the case. She then took a long belt out attached to four cuffs. Firstly, the start of the belt went around the back of my neck and the first two cuffs attached to my wrists. I remember thinking that the other two cuffs were clearly for people with long arms! I quite quickly realised my stupidity when Mistress A pulled my legs in the air! She attached the two remaining cuffs to my ankles. When all was tight it caused legs not to be able to go down as they are now being held up by my neck! Excellent! I was very exposed. Helpless. Virtually immobile but more aroused than ever. Mistress A then made her way to my side and grabbed my nipples. Harder this time. So much so that I had to take a sharp intake of breath.

Mistress A: Poor little Natalie. Restrained and ready to have her virginity taken by me. Ready to have her pussy trained and ready to make me money! I'll have your pussy filled every day whilst I watch and take all the money!

She leaned in one last time and whispered "Your safe word is now a click of your fingers. Do you understand?".

I couldn't talk with this gag in place. I nodded my head enthusiastically.

Mistress A: Good girl. Now then, these knickers are no good on you are they? A slut doesn't have knickers covering her fuck hole, does she?

Natalie: 'Mumbles'

Mistress A: I'm going to expose your clit and pussy. Oh Natalie, that clit is throbbing isn't it!

Natalie: 'Mumbles and nods'

Mistress A: I think your pussy is begging for cock, isn't it? It needs training though! Let's get some lube there first.

This is the first time that I had ever had any exploration of my bottom. The lube was really cold, and it sent a shiver through me. I think the expectation was real.

Mistress A: Now then Natalie. I want you to take really deep breaths for me. Deep in and out.

I did exactly as told. I was looking up at the ceiling when all of a sudden the largest object I could ever imagined started to make its way inside of me. I was trying to remember what I had seen in the room this could be!! I'd not seen a Polaris missile, or a bollard all lubed up and ready and in my slightly panicked state I tried to get a look at this enormous object beginning its journey into me! Surely I'd have to start clicking my fingers before I tore in half!!

Mistress A: Slow deep breaths Natalie. You're a very good girl that's nearly a whole finger.

ONE FUCKING FINGER! Are you joking with me? Holy shit. I thought I'd feel Mistress A's wrist watch shortly!

Mistress A: That's such a good girl Natalie. Feel that finger taking your virginity. In and out. Slowly opening you up.

Natalie: 'Mumbling and nodding'

Mistress A: You're a dirty little slut Natalie. That pussy is begging for cock. I can feel you grabbing me tightly. There's a very dirty girl. Your pussy is being fucked.

I was unsure how I felt at this time. I'm not sure I liked the penetration but the domination side of this, the restraint and 'forced' side of this was a real turn on. I lay there being penetrated and there's little I could do about it. I could click my fingers, and this would stop, however I didn't want it to stop. I wanted more but I don't know what 'more' looked like!

Mistress A: Oh Natalie, your clit is getting bigger. You dirty whore. Do you like this? Do you like your pussy being stretched? Look at this clitty.

I managed to move my head up slightly and I could see my cock fully erect. I was desperate to touch myself but was retrained. My cock was twitching hard, and I could see the pre cum dribbling heavily and even starting to run down my cock. Mistress A looked at me and scooped up the sticky trail on her finger and smeared it on my ball gag. It then ran into my mouth and there was nothing I could do about it.

Mistress A: Eat that cum Natalie. You love that pre-cum don't you?

Natalie: 'Nodding furiously and mumbling'

Mistress A: I bet you want to cum don't you Natalie?

Natalie: 'still nodding and mumbling'

Mistress A: That's a good cum slut. I'm going to let you touch yourself, but you must NOT cum until I give permission. You must ask and then wait for permission. Do you understand Natalie?

Still furiously nodding in approval, Mistress A stretched over me, purposely rested her breast on my chest then undone one of my hands. She took my free hand and moved it to my erection and coerced me to masturbate. Whilst it felt amazing, there was an embarrassment to it. Being watched while doing this personal act, to me, is humiliating yet gratifying at the same time. Extremely mixed feelings were spinning in my head.

Mistress A: Now then Natalie, slow strokes! Make sure you enjoy this! I'm going to countdown from 10. When I get to 1, you MUST cum! No excuses. I'm in charge and you do what I say, do you understand?

Natalie: 'Nods in agreement'

Mistress A started to count down, slowly. 10,9…..each number was like a bolt of lightning through me. There was a nervous thought going through me. What if I couldn't do it? "7,6,5", I started hammering away hoping to achieve the desired goal! "3,2,1….CUM! You better cum you dirty cum whore!

Mistress A: What a let-down you are! Take your hands off your clit. I'm disappointed Natalie! My orders are clear. Don't ever let me down again Natalie, do you understand?

I tried to say sorry, but I couldn't get any words out. I was full of adrenaline and confusion. Had I done good? Or bad? I felt like it was the latter!

Mistress A then moved over to me and cradled my head whilst undoing the ball gag. As she held my head, she reassuringly whispered in my ear that the session had ended and to take some deep breaths. "Yes Mistress" I replied in a weak reply. I was drained. I hadn't really done anything, but I felt like I'd done a few rounds in the ring!

Mistress A undone my restraints and moved over to me. She looked at me directly and said "I have one last task for you Natalie, it's for my amusement. Are you ready?"

Natalie: Yes Mistress.

Mistress A: You're going to put a condom on that poor excuse for me, then I'm going to allow you to wank yourself until you cum. When you do cum, you will then take all the cum you produce and eat every drop. Do you understand?

Natalie: Yes Mistress.

Mistress A: Good girl. One last thing, I want you to make noises like a girl moaning and tell me how much you want cock, all in your best girl voice!

Natalie: Yes Mistress

This was a level I never thought of. Masturbating is something I'm pretty good at! I've practised a lot over the years but this idea of pretending to be feminine felt strange. I did as I was told. The condom slid on easily and I stroked slowly but firmly. Mistress A stood in front of me watching intently. I moaned in a high pitched voice and started telling Mistress how much I wanted her cock. "Good girl" she said to me. I felt a warmth pulsing through me and I started to gyrate in rhythm to my stroking. I started using more expletives and begging for cock and cum. What had come over me. Whilst I was clearly aroused I was overthinking this as I started to lose my erection slightly. Unbeknown to me, Mistress A clearly knew what was happening. I always had eye contact with her. She ran her tongue over her lips and mouthed the words 'cum for me' then pulled the zip down slightly on her catsuit. Her breasts heaved and she put her hand inside and squeezed her breast. This was too much for me and a came over and over again. The warm cum filled the teat without an issue. I had a massive rush in my head. It was an orgasm like I had never experienced before.

Mistress A: Oh Natalie, you filthy cum hungry slut! Now eat every bit for me.

Natalie: Yes Mistress.

I pulled the condom off carefully. Did this need to be seductive?

Erotic? I didn't really know. Mistress A clearly did! She tipped my head back, took the condom from me and tipped all the warm semen into my mouth.

Mistress A: Now gargle for me and swallow it in one!

I did what I was told. I loved it!

Story 16
Mister James W – Submissive male

Submissive male, mentor to other submissive men and active participant in femdom discussions.

What on earth would persuade a man to want to submit to a woman? To fly in the face of a patriarchal society where he should be the 'natural leader'? Is there something mentally wrong with such men? A psychological flaw perhaps?

Or perhaps there's something more profound.

"The way to a man's heart is through his stomach" said Fanny Fern in the 1860s. So why do otherwise materially content men stray from familiar paths? And, what possesses the type of men who explore the world of kink to submit to a dominant woman?

For that, we turn to another writer Helen Rowland: *"The woman who appeals to a man's vanity may stimulate him, the woman who appeals to his heart may attract him, but it is the woman who appeals to his imagination who gets him."*

But that is only the start of getting to grips with a complicated mind maze littered with magic and mines, equally equipped to excite, and exasperate both the submissive man – and the dominant woman he encounters.

I have witnessed first-hand the highs and lows of chasing the submission rabbit down its holes; often questioning my own sanity and those of fellow travellers consumed with the energy to put ourselves at the mercy of those who would seek to badger and belittle us. What is going on here? And are we playing a long game towards irreparable harm? Or are we seeking to escape something itself that is harming us?

The brain is an amazing pharmaceutical centre, and four chemicals are responsible for making us happy: Endorphins, Serotonin, Dopamine and Oxytocin. These get released into the body from all sorts of activities whether it's physical exercise or meditation or some other pleasurable pursuit. They don't judge. They just do. And what exactly gives rise to their release varies from person to person. To the extent they inform others of underlying behaviours is highly limited for they are outputs versus inputs.

And this matters more importantly not so much to third parties but to first parties themselves: *Why do I seek these things? Am I addicted to activities others find distasteful? And will I become a better or worse person as a result?* These are all valid questions and as in all matters of the mind, can either be huge weighty issues or passing fancies that delight the body carrying this organ.

To the issue of where this all matters when it comes to submissive males grappling with their appetites, this topic inevitably turns into one of seeking not just a willing partner via a dominant woman but also making sense of it all. So far so good. Where things go from there is another thing. All too often the dominant woman is leaned into as a surrogate therapist. And while it's true that her art presents as therapeutic, it's not therapy. Even those professional dominant women with formal training in therapy ought to tread carefully when engaging in both disciplines: Is it wise to have a client on board where domination that can lead to idolatry be also blended with support to address deep-rooted control issues? I'd suggest they make odd bedfellows and really should be kept apart as there are too many conflicts of interest here.

If the man can make peace with his appetites – and providing they are not hurting others or harming himself – then is there really a need to get to the bottom of why they are why they are? But if he's plagued with '*Why me?*' Then he ought to seek professional help from a kink-friendly therapist and keep these activities a separate pursuit away from any dominant woman he may be seeing. While many a dominant woman might be sympathetic to what troubles a submissive man, neither party is served well with a deep dive into what makes him tick.

And for those men who may be blinded to warning signs that they may need professional help? It's an unhealthy addiction if submission is taking up substantial time and resources beyond what are needed for a balanced lifestyle overall. Another sign is seeking to monopolise the attention of the dominant woman of the moment and wear out not just her welcome but her mental labour as well.

A profound tell is to confuse surrender and submission as one and the same. This could see the submissive failing to respect their own boundaries while in pursuit of that kink high. The red flags one is often advised to look for in others prior to forming a relationship may also arise from oneself. The engagement with a dominant woman may ironically help fuel this and could see abuse taking place on both sides especially if there's a high degree of co-dependency.

But it's not mandatory to seek out a professional if one is losing perspective. It's quite possible to pull back and seek reflection away within a vanilla pursuit to give one a chance to recalibrate. Not unlike a social media detox, taking a time out to explore other forms of stimulation away from kink can be helpful. It also can offer a breathing space to rethink one's engagement with play. Perhaps committing to personal agreements and limits with oneself on how far one should go while at play. It might prove even more useful to write them out as personal affirmations to help cement such commitments ahead of play.

My own personal guiding principle for healthy kink play is to liken it to a series of exquisite condiments, without which my overall life would taste bland. Similarly, I approach dominant women in a similar way: I see them as whole beings with agency and depth, not as one-dimensional dispensers. Any play with them is to be seen as engaging in a series of various seasonings that spice up our time together. And like all forms of cuisine, portion control and knowing when to politely leave the table, are essential!

May your adventures as a submissive male be a rich pursuit and that you never quite reach your destination because the journey IS the reward

Story 17
Kinkybee – Submissive kinkster

The word Kink to me relates to fetishes which are centred around being dominated by a woman and the sexual arousal triggers. Like sexuality, it is something you can't run away from, the sooner you accept it for what it is, the quicker you can control and enjoy all it can offer. I believe there is kink in all of us some more than others and if you are open to it, you can explore it to find its true meaning for you.

As I mentioned, being dominated by a woman is my biggest Kink. From this I am happy to partake in various Femdom activities which puts me in a submissive state against their dominance. It's not all about pain, more being made to obey, this can before her pleasure, amusement or both. I liken it to going on a roller coaster ride, letting go, taking control out of your own hands, entrusting the thrills and safety in someone else's hands, when you are on and it starts, you're on until it's over, it doesn't stop because folk are screaming. When it's done, you run around as quick as you can because you want to experience it again. If I try and narrow it down I'd say it starts as a fetish for women in high heels and goes from there, the clicking of stiletto heels on a hard floor will always attract my attention.

It took me many years of playing in the BDSM world, hours of session time, 20 plus different dominatrices to come to this conclusion of what really makes me tick. I have tried many of the Domme's activities from their interest lists, pushing my own limits. I have also been able to accept myself for being a kinkster, in the early days I saw what I was doing almost as somebody else, looking through a window, it wasn't me. Since accepting this, I have moved my kinkness to another level, I've never looked back, I'm now enjoying other engagements with others in the BDSM community, which I have really enjoyed and it's not just about getting off.

There are still negatives in BDSM, normally it comes down to lack of knowledge & experience. It's important to play with those who know how to play safely. Financial Domination or Findom as its better known is a growing concern of mine, bases around submissives sending money, some see this as a way to make a quick buck, there is a fear that the lack of care and diligence towards the submissive sending money, means that it can have a negative effect on them mentally and has similarities to gambling addicts. The unfortunate thing is that as it's a more underground movement, it will never get the same research or support used in the gaming industry. This does allow mentally vulnerable people to be taken advantage of, just to line some vulture's pocket.

In recent times, society has become more warming to some aspects of BDSM, such as what you can buy in Ann Summers, it still has a negative stigma attached to it around perverseness and "being a weirdo' as a whole. I would still not be comfortable being fully "out of the cage" and letting myself be known as a BDSM player to those not in it.

The funnies:

Don't remove your cuffs

When I went to my second ever pro Domme session, I was less than well versed in sub protocol. My mistress had finished the session and I felt really good. Being a polite and submissive slave, I wanted to help my mistress clear up after the session. I thought it would save Mistress a task so I proceeded to remove my wrist cuffs to save her from taking them off. I'm not an idiot, I could easily unbuckle them. Actually, I was an Idiot, my mistress turned to me and firmly said to me "A sub must never remove their own cuffs" I apologise straight away but I was strapped to her whipping bench, (I guessed the session isn't over) she took one of her canes in her hand, "6 of the best judicial". I had no idea what that was until after. It was so painful, hasten to say, to this day, I have never made the same mistake.

Metal chastity device in the cold

I once was put into chastity during a session, a metal CB6000 when put on it was a good fit, not too tight, not too loose. I was put to work in the garden, it was quite a cold day for naked gardening, I was also so worried the neighbours would see me. The cold then made it to my cock and balls, I experience cold shrinkage, the chastity device fell off, my shrinkage then deserted me, I tried for 10 minutes to get it back on but to no avail, my mistress came out, I had to go to her device in hand to her laughter and amusement.

Story 18
Exploration of BDSM –
Will Danielson

Being a teenage boy is a confusing time. Hair growing in strange places, girls no longer a nuisance but an intriguing attraction and hormones raging all over the place. As well as this, I had the added realisation that my sexual interests were not what you might call mainstream. Why did Sandy in Grease look so much more alluring in black leather? Why does a scene in a film where someone is tied up cause a twitch down below? Why do shiny black boots look so amazing?

After some research on the early incarnations of the internet, I established I was sexually submissive to dominant women. It was a relief to have a label, but even more exciting to have a starting point for further exploration. I've since learnt that many people don't explore such feelings for a variety of reasons but having a YOLO attitude, I decided to dive right in and embrace my submissive desires.

The first point of call was a munch. The strange term didn't put me off and despite some initial nerves I made my way to a local pub in my uni town and met up with a bunch of total strangers, whose shared interest was kink. I spoke with the organisers, met people of all ages and realised that my interests were the tip of the iceberg and that the kink world was intensely diverse.

A couple of vanilla relationships came and went with the missing kinky element being the elephant in the room. I found myself craving deeper submission. Sex with handcuffs or a girlfriend in PVC underwear, whilst lots of fun, was not meeting my deepening submissive needs. I took the bold step to put my student loan to good use and book to see a professional dominatrix. The lady in question was an adult actress who I already had a crush on, so to find she offered professional domination sessions was even better. This session, although only an hour long, helped me establish in more detail what my kinks were. I confirmed a love for bondage within five minutes of the start, but surprised myself with how much I loved being gagged and made to wear a hood. I found myself in a paradoxical situation of paying for submission and setting controls. My philosophical mind began musing whether true submission could be commissioned or whether there was a Valhalla I would have to continue searching for.

My newfound confidence took me a fetish club night, a definite step up from a munch and an absolutely hedonistic delight. Kink demonstrations, amazing outfits, equipment to make the eyes water, it was all there. I found myself suspended in a grope box for twenty minutes, my inhibitions very much left at the door.

As I fell down the rabbit hole, real life reared its head and I found myself in another vanilla relationship, learning no lessons from my previous experiences. A blind hope that kink would develop obviously did not come true, but the rest of the relationship was exceptional, and I made the conscious choice to try and suppress my submissive tendencies. Years passed, but there was always something missing. We had the conversation and she explained it wasn't for her and she couldn't even try it, it didn't feel right. I explained how intrinsically submission is linked to my sexuality, and we made the exceptionally tough decision to separate. I knew deep down it was the right call but it didn't make it any easier at the time.

I took my time in building back up but vowed that any future relationship would have to have a D/s element to ensure the best chance of longevity.

A series of short-term kink-based relationships yielded short term gratification but did not progress to anything more serious, so I continued to get my fix through visits to professional mistresses. I was heading toward the point of trying too hard, but also realising that the panacea of a female-led relationship was going to be hard to find.

So here I am in my mid-forties, confident of my submission, with few regrets on how I reached this point but still searching for that certain something. The horny teenager is now a realistic man who knows that it might be a case of scratching the itches when possible, but with the hope that a true submissive relationship is just around the corner.

The saving grace is the world in 2023 is a lot more understanding of the BDSM world than it was even in the late 90s. Whilst the dynamic in 50 Shades of Gray was bordering on abuse, it helped bring BDSM into the mainstream. When I took my first steps on to the scene it was scary, hidden and not widely understood, but having been to munches in the last year it is fabulous to see growth in attendance and a number of younger people there, confident and exploring their kinks in the same way the younger version of me had. BDSM is still an easy, titillating story for the mainstream media and you'll find the odd scoop featuring someone visiting a dominatrix, but I imagine the responses across the population are now a lot closer to 'so what' than 'urgh, that's unnatural'.

Story 19
Adult Baby Specialist Steven

To juxtapose Mistress Kaz's adult baby chapter, I would like to add sometimes there is a sexual side to it to adult baby fetish. Back in the day, when it was normal to see washing lines full of terry nappies and plastic baby pants before disposable nappies came along, many a curious boy would be excited by the shiny plastic pants blowing happily in the breeze and would steal a pair before running home to masturbate with them.

Many would have their first orgasms & this fascination with plastic pants would remain.

Some would naturally progress to wearing terry nappies with them.. again stealing them from washing lines!

That was back in the 60's and 70's and when mother's changed to disposables, that stealing spree ended.

Some adult babies lucky enough to have partners who indulge them in their fetish are often put into nappies at home and for the more daring ones, sent to work wearing a nappy & plastic pants under their clothes to add to the excitement.

Many wives have been known to take a new lover & keep their partner as babies, only allowing them to orgasm at nappy changes to associate the wearing of nappies with pleasure.

While it is rare to find a partner who will participate in their fetish (many men decide to not tell their partner) most men do this in secret. They often feel a sense of shame and will throw out their "baby stash" only to rebuild it soon after. And repeat this process over the years.

The types of nappies an adult baby prefers usually depends on their age, or more specifically, what they wore as a baby.

Those born before the 1980's were generally put into terry nappies and plastic pants, or perhaps rubber pants if they were born in the 1940's.

Those born after that would have worn disposables as these were popular then and saved on all that washing, so they choose to wear adult disposable nappies.

However, terry nappies & plastic pants are starting to become popular again as they are much better for the environment. So mother's beware as they may start going missing again!

Before the internet, many thought they were alone in their "baby desires" but these days there is pretty much everything an adult baby would need. From adult terry nappies, plastic and rubber pants to baby clothes in all styles, sizes, and materials including plastic and rubber babywear.

And there are lots of places an adult baby can visit including fully equipped nurseries with adult cots, highchairs, changing tables, all types of nappies & plastic pants, a large selection of adult babywear, and of course a Mummy to give them the full adult baby experience!

Story 20
MR BTK – Adult model based in the UK Dom/sub switch

This is one of my favourite ever experiences, let alone favourite BDSM experiences.

The date this happened was Valentine's Day 2016 and I had broken up with my girlfriend of 3 years the previous November. I had always been naturally dominant but had started to explore my submissive side with my ex-girlfriend and I wanted to explore some more.

I had made an Adult account and I was specifically looking for a Dominatrix in the Midlands area to try out a couple of my fantasies, but as I was browsing I noticed there was a popular porn star available in the Coventry area. I emailed her and asked what domination services she offered (at the time I was looking for foot worship, ass worship and watersports), she replied and I ended up booking a hotel room at the Days Inn at Corley Services.

I remember I was so nervous waiting in the hotel room for her to arrive, that I felt sick and started going dizzy. When she knocked on the door I was trembling and I was questioning whether I should have done this or not, but by the end of the night I was the happiest man in the world.

I had enjoyed myself over her on screen so many times before, but she really did look even more stunning in real life and I think I temporarily went into shock. She removed her coat and was wearing a tight black dress with stilettos. She looked amazing!

She ordered me to strip naked and put my hands behind my back, then she pulled her dress up and took her panties down and used them to tie my wrists together and then made me kneel in front of her. She explained that I was going to have 10 minutes to clean up the mess she makes on the floor, and if I manage to do it I will get rewarded by being allowed to rim her asshole. She then proceeded to empty a box of matches on to the hotel room floor around all sides of the bed before sitting on the sofa and starting the timer. The whole time I was scrambling around on my knees picking up matches with my lips off the dirty floor she was playing with herself and I was rock hard. I managed to drop the last match back into the box with a couple of minutes to spare and was ordered to crawl over to the sofa to eat her pussy and ass. I genuinely thought I was in heaven!

Next she stood up, untied my hands and led me into the bathroom. I lay on my back in the shower looking up at her in awe as she peed all over my cock, balls, stomach and chest. This was the first time I had tried watersports and I have been hooked ever since. I was told to take a quick shower and get dried then go back into the bedroom and lie on the bed.

She lay alongside me playing with my cock while I was sucking her toes and licking her soles until I felt I was close to cumming, then she sat on my face and ordered me to eat her asshole again. I was alternating between worshipping her feet and eating her ass while she brought me to the edge over and over again. Eventually she unwrapped a condom, put it on me and started riding me reverse cowgirl whilst telling me to not stop staring at her ass. It didn't take long for me to have one of the best orgasms I have ever had and I have now got vivid memories of how great my cock looked inside her pussy.

After I had come she made me go back into the bathroom and lie down in the shower so she could pee on me one more time before she left. This time it was over my face and in my mouth and I was hard again instantly.

When she was finished she got dressed (apart from her panties which she gave to me) and left me to wank several times over the next couple of hours before I left the hotel to go home and wank some more.

I have done much naughtier and kinkier things, but that night will stick with me forever and it definitely contributed towards making me enjoy being more submissive more often in a big, big way.

That night was a big positive for me because not only did I get to play with one of the most beautiful women on the planet, but it also made me want to try anything and everything to do with sex and submission that I had fantasised about. She also gave me a lot of confidence and I filmed my first porn clips a few months later with my friend PM and I filmed as a sub for the first time a few months after that with a now retired Dominatrix called Lady L.

Story 21
Mistress Ronelle Chambers

Kink has been a part of my life for over 30 years. I look at it as perverted therapy for my clients and a non-sexual relief for my own perverted kinks. I never plan what I am going to do in each session and it's always spur of the moment for me. My favourite kinky shenanigans are latex breath play. The soft, shiny latex against my olive skin, showing off all of my tempting curves pull me into the mindset of power where I feel sexy and controlling. The control over my victim's breath, while I'm watching him struggle as I press my latex covered body over him is such a delightful, erotic turn-on, his erection from inside the latex bag that captures his weak body and mind for my amusement. I have learned so much from BDSM in regards to people's wants and needs. There is really no right or wrong way when it comes to kink behaviour. Just enjoy it and have fun but always respect people's limits and how far they want to go. It's important as a female Dominatrix to respect your subs/slaves, as without subs you're not a dom. Always remember the sub is still a human like you and we all have our needs and wants and it's not always a sexual release, it can be a mental one, reliving past experiences can be a massive sexual turn-on and help greatly with mental health issues.

Kink helps with releasing these feelings that may have lay hidden unknown for years in the subconscious mind. My personal experiences of BDSM have been positive and I have always stayed grounded throughout. I think it's important to never get lost in your dom character and to not forget who you are and remember the real you. For me, I find it easier to look at it as we are two different people. There is me and then there is her "Mistress Ronelle," we are both strong characters, however I decide when each makes an appearance and when. This is what keeps me grounded, also never forgetting where I came from. You cannot force your views on society as that's for the individual to decide for themselves. We all see things differently and that's fine by me. I don't need anyone's permission to be who I am. I don't say in public, "oooh yeah, I'm a dom" as it is no one's business but my own. Plus there are all the questions… "So you have sex with men?"

No we do not as that's not what being a dom is. So I shy away from society and these stupid questions as it just makes my life easier and you cannot please everyone in life.

Be yourself and never compare yourself to others. Do what you're comfortable with at all times. If there is something you are unsure of doing , ask another dom for help or do your research before you try. Don't do anything you're unsure of or not clued up about just for money. Find a niche in the fetish industry that makes you stand out from the rest. Do not be scared to be your unique, wonderful self. Make time for oneself and enjoy your life.

Ronelle xx

Story 22
Lingerieboy 40 year old submissive sissy male

The first pair of knickers I sneakily wore was before I hit my teens. They were a white silk and lace blend from M&S and 'borrowed' from my sister's friend who was staying over at our house. Wearing them felt so erotic and naughty - not in the least because they weren't mine! That began my love affair with panties and satin. For some reason, I always felt drawn to satin and lingerie. This was compounded by shopping catalogues and any magazine that advertised lingerie. Occasionally, I'd tear a page out of the catalogue and put it under my pillow. I found it comforting lying on the bed with panties on under my PJ's.

I never thought it would lead to wanting to wear more than just panties but gradually, I fantasised about wearing stockings, basques, silky negligees and eventually, I bought a really sexy pink satin nighty, which I could wear under my PJ's. As I got older, I tried to repress all of this as it didn't fit in with my masculine persona but it was always there. This was difficult but necessary. I was terrified of asking a partner if I was allowed to wear her knickers and what would happen if she didn't approve and outed me. So, I cautiously built up my lingerie collection and developed a parallel sex life with some lovely escorts who embraced it and encouraged my feminine side. It was so erotic that I could finally be myself and we would have great sex as well as being friends. I loved the secrecy and intimacy of my fetish. It was so lovely to be encouraged, reassured and not treated as a weirdo. On the other side, I maintained my conventional, cotton wearing, macho identity. Eventually, in my 20's, I reached a point where I was fed up with not being able to share this with partners, so I decided to share my fetish with a dear girlfriend who ran a mile and told all her friends, which was humiliating and heartbreaking. After that, I decided it would be easier that never the twain should meet, so let's explore more! Having been encouraged by a dear friend to try pegging, I was hooked! At the beginning, although I felt pretty sore, it was empowering to be so feminine as a heterosexual guy being with beautiful women who became good friends and provided these lovely experiences.

Now picture this, I'm a 6 foot gym bunny who plays lots of sport and who hangs out with the lads in the pub, but occasionally I'll be glancing around thinking - wonder if anyone else here is like me! As I've got older, I've realised that my feminine side is to be embraced and not afraid of and it remains my private domain and is always such fun.

As I've become more confident, my extrovert side has become quite cheeky, so I deliberately do things to shock the general public, such as dropping a buzzing, pink, ten-inch-dildo on Kings Cross platform to see if anyone notices! Everyone seemed not to notice, apart from the gorgeous lady who picked it up and said, "I think you dropped this," and gave me a wink!

I also quite enjoy accidentally leaving the top button of my jeans undone on the tube to show a bit of pink satin. I occasionally get a wink from both sexes which is quite fun and it's made me realise that having fun kinks is so natural as a human being. Whatever sexual preference turns you on, my advice is to embrace it. It's been such a revelation to enjoy my naughty side.

From my extensive experience, anyone out there reading this who feels similarly, don't feel afraid! Rather than repress my fetish, it's now become a big part of me which I enjoy and have met some wonderful dommes and subs and fellow panty lovers. This has been incredibly rewarding and so different to the beginning of my nervous journey when I thought I was uniquely different.

Social media is so wonderful, interacting with like-minded people. I really enjoy being accepted for who I am and having such a great time.

Thank you

If you have enjoyed this book we command that you leave a five-star Amazon review and buy two copies each for your friends and family.

If you want to meet us in the flesh or buy
more of our content head over to:

Kaz B
Appointments via AdultWork:
https://www.adultwork.com/ViewProfile.asp?UserID=214509
LinkTree: https://linktr.ee/kazbxx

Lady Olivia Rampage
Appointments via AdultWork: https://www.adultwork.com/
ViewProfile.asp?UserID=7751495
Loyal Fans: https://www.loyalfans.com/ladyoliviarampage

Special thanks to our contributors who shared their stories and experiences with us to provide a deeper perspective into the world of BDSM, from not just dominants but from submissives and switches too.

Miss Kat - Anon
PDSF - anon
Krissy - anon
Steven - anon
Alexander G - anon

Spanks and kisses

Some of our favourite kink traders

Honour Clothing
https://www.honourclothing.com/
Address: 86 Lower Marsh, London SE1 7AB

Skin Two
Latex and rubber
https://www.skintwo.com/

Intimate Torment of Swindon
Club wear, Lingerie, Adult toys, Gifts and Novelties.
https://www.intimatetorment.co.uk/
Unit 49a BSS House
Cheney Manor Ind. Estate
Swindon, Wiltshire, SN2 2PJ
01793 430097

More about the author Kaz B

When I'm not obliterating bottoms, I indulge in my passion for writing and write blogs for my two websites and have published various books which include, Sordid Secrets, Dreaming in the Dark, The Promise, Time Heals, Confessions of a dominatrix: My Secret BDSM Life; and Death, The Illusion, so this collaboration with the fabulous Lady R and the community will be my 8th publication.

I'm a total film buff and love acting in films too, and have starred in various horror movies, my most recent film role being 'She's a Bitch' for Eileen Daly where I play an actress who becomes possessed by a demonic entity – well, I just played myself first thing in the morning before a coffee really! It wasn't too much of a stretch to imagine being denied a mug of the holy beverage from The Goddess Caffeine.

I run a kink education channel over on rumble with my friend Podopheleus - Pod means feet in Greek, so if you haven't guessed it, he has a foot fetish but we cover all areas of the industry issues along with kink safety. You can find us on Rumble at KazBPodCast and while you are at it do have a little peaky-week at my blog www.uk-fetish.co.uk where you can find out more about me and what I do.

Free time is somewhat a luxury but if I do have some time off from playing the villain, I can't get enough of travelling to cities, the countryside and seaside towns and indulging my senses at spas and losing myself in nature.

My other huge love is cats and I can see why the ancient Egyptians worshipped them. They were aware of cats' healing abilities and how soothing they are to the soul. I have a particular affinity with Tabby cats and often seem to be followed by them as if there is a mysterious thread between us.

Finally, if you were wondering, my favourite tipples are Gin and Champagne, so feel free to spoil me with a bottle or visit my wish tender list, which you will find in the back of this book.

I hope you enjoyed reading this book, please do let us know and don't forget to give us a glowing review...or I may just leave you in the stocks for a few days!

How the authors met

It seems bizarre to think we met only a few years ago over a love of BDSM, books and late night movies and sushi. After being introduced by a mutual sub, Alan, with a penchant for having his nipples punished, the two of us met for lunch at a tapas bar in Reading and found out we had many common interests. Shortly afterwards, we were meeting on a monthly basis to join forces, dominate slaves and whip mens bottoms. Afterwards, we'd slip into our PJ's and watch pop videos or settle in for a Netflix session with a bottle of Pinot Noir or a nice herbal tea. Over those many hours, we discovered our mutual fascination with the psychology of BDSM and our passion for writing. We shared our stories, our history. We giggled, we roared with laughter, sometimes we cried and sipped wine, and danced, and ate pizza…always with extra pineapple and jalapenos on! Swapping anecdotes and tips we were struck by a thought - what if we wrote a joint book about our experiences and asked some of our subs to write a passage too?

We decided to create a ruthless, warts and all guide to BDSM through a kink positive lens, not only from our perspective, but also with accounts from real-life submissive men and real life sessions. This book is an explosive leap into the arts of femdom, which also considers the human element. We looked at topics such as, why is kink so popular and what inspires people to indulge in power exchange and what is the driving force behind these desires? Do dommes ever get domme drop or feel dissatisfied? How can dommes and subs safeguard their mental health? The subs featured in this book also have some incredible insights about the many facets of kink.

First of all, we looked at the importance of consent and safety, before looking at individual kinks. Along the way we shared many anecdotes. We hope you enjoyed reading about them as much as we enjoyed partaking in them! And don't forget to leave us an Amazon review!

Thinking of becoming a Dom

When I started out dommes mostly advertised on forums such as Collarme but these are defunct now with the advent of social media. Many sex work providers use social media as well as specialist Mistress directories. AdultWork is a great site to utilise for drumming up new clients. Adapt your advertising for each, for example, if you are not out as a domme you may wish to set up profiles that do not show your face or location. Discretion is key.

Get friendly with other dommes and subs and support one another. Share each other's posts and think about how you can share accommodation costs and expenses on tour. Advertise your tour dates and let your audience know when you will be available. Creating a schedule can be tricky, but consistency is key.

Domme work can be quite a lonely experience so if you can build a network of good people around you, it will help you to stay motivated. From a network comes a community and you get out what you put in. Don't be shy about getting your brand name out there.

READ Kaz B's other book

Confessions of a Dominatrix: My Secret BDSM Life by Kaz B

"Reading the stories about Latex Trooper the gimp,
I almost choked on a samosa."
– Shaun Attwood, true crime author/YouTuber

As a shy little bookworm whose hair obscured her face, Kaz never imagined that she would enter the adult industry and travel worldwide, partying at pool-side villas with porn stars and participating in kinky photoshoots on the beach.

But the dark energy of the adult industry and abusive relationships damaged her mental health. From rock bottom, she emerged with an epiphany: to become a dominatrix and train men to serve women.

Accompany Kaz as she cracks the whip, clamps nipples, crushes balls and electroshocks genitals, while issuing commands to her whimpering sissies, servants, slaves and subs, including the legendary Latex Trooper.

From drugs, porn parties, scandal and domestic violence to an empowered dominatrix who had to heal herself before helping others – join Kaz on a rollercoaster journey through her life!

Printed in Great Britain
by Amazon

55991080R00165